Images of America
Andrews

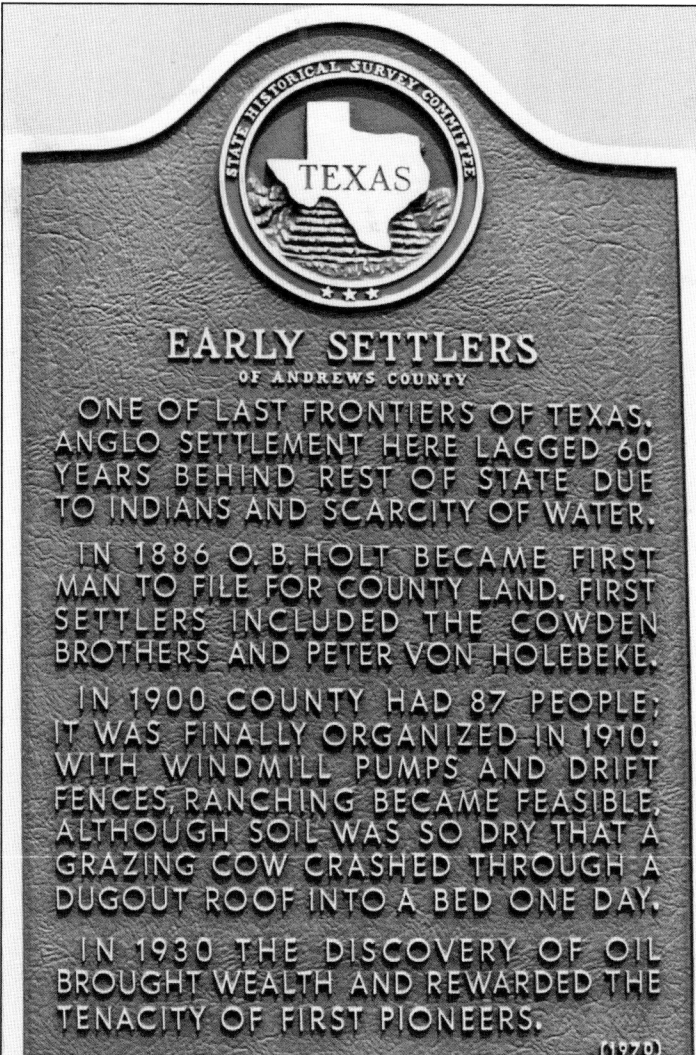

A plaque in far western Andrews County on the Eunice Highway (State Highway 176) offers some insight into the early settlers that first arrived in the county. Andrews lagged behind other areas of the state in being settled due to several factors, including Native Americans, who inhabited the area into the late 1880s. The lack of water and the distant proximity to building materials, foodstuffs, and other supplies also played a major role. One of the first settlers to brave the elements was O. B. Holt who, according to deed records in Austin, was one of the first people to file on land in Andrews County in 1886. (Courtesy *Andrews County News*.)

ON THE COVER: Perhaps no other event in the 100-year history of Andrews County was as significant as the discovery of crude oil in the southwestern region. After exploration by the Deep Rock Drilling Company, a well was opened on December 5, 1929. It was named the C. E. Ogden No. 1 after the landowner who allowed the well to be drilled. Standing in the forefront of the picture is Ogden, the proud landowner who had moved to Andrews to farm. Finding crude oil had a major impact on Andrews County, which today nears its three billionth barrel of production. (Courtesy Martha Page.)

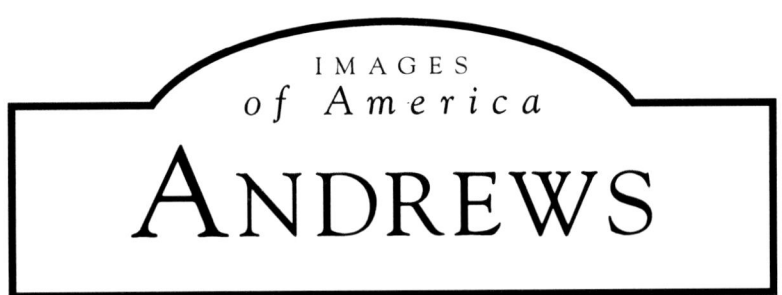

Don Ingram and Linda Drake

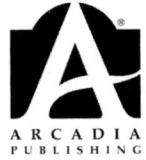

Copyright © 2011 by Don Ingram and Linda Drake
ISBN 978-0-7385-7980-1

Published by Arcadia Publishing
Charleston, South Carolina

Printed in the United States of America

Library of Congress Control Number: 2010936555

For all general information, please contact Arcadia Publishing:
Telephone 843-853-2070
Fax 843-853-0044
E-mail sales@arcadiapublishing.com
For customer service and orders:
Toll-Free 1-888-313-2665

Visit us on the Internet at www.arcadiapublishing.com

To all those who contributed and shared their pictures and memories of Andrews County, and to the community of Andrews for its support and encouragement, we gratefully dedicate this book to you. Thank you.

Contents

Acknowledgments		6
Introduction		7
1.	The Early Years	9
2.	Boom and Bust	43
3.	A Grand Jubilee	85
4.	Our Community	105

Acknowledgments

Getting together a brief photographic history of Andrews County was like pouring all the sand hills in the county into a mason jar. There are far too many pictures, facts, and recollections to squeeze into one book about so many people who have achieved so much in 100 years. Without a museum, the chore fell to the authors, who were faced with the daunting task of finding, collecting, and choosing what went into this pictorial history of Andrews County. Unless otherwise noted, all photographs appear courtesy of the *Andrews County News*. Images used in this book came from Martha Page, Mark Hooper, the Andrews County Library, the *Andrews County News*, and many other contributors who generously donated their photographs to the newspaper for use in this volume. All Golden Jubilee photographs were provided by photographer Sam Hollis.

It would take multiple editions to fully depict all that has happened in this small part of the West Texas and the Permian Basin. Be that as it may, we greatly appreciate and thank all the contributors who submitted pictures and/or helped with identifying them, since so many of the true old-timers have passed on. We hope that we managed, in some small way, to tell in pictorial sequence how Andrews County came to pass, how the determined role and efforts of ranchers, farmers, settlers, and others played such a pivotal role in taming a land that was thought to be unsuitable for anyone but the Native Americans who had lived there for generations and anything but wild horses and the West Texas wind. Those settlers and the others that followed were, in our humble opinion, true pioneers of the West—heroic in nature, steady in deed, and containing no small sampling of true grit.

Introduction

Newcomers, passersby, and others may think Andrews looks like other West Texas oil field towns, but through its early beginnings with ranchers, settlers, and oilfield wildcatters clawing out an existence in wide open spaces, Andrews was born and bred from the frontier's pioneering spirit. The county is only 100 years old—a relative teenager as counties in Texas go—but it has packed a lot of action in a short span of years.

In the beginning, Native Americans claimed this land. The Comanches were so feared that settlers heading west to California either avoided the area or sought troops for protection. First arrivals encountered frigid winters and blazing summers that produced little rainfall, and a seemingly relentless wind—a regional trademark—that was cursed by new arrivals and ignored by natives.

Though created by the Texas Legislature in 1876, and politically controlled by other nearby counties until its own political organization in 1910, the population of Andrews County remained as sparse as trees with only 24 residents noted in 1890. By 1910, the population had reached 975 with two main communities—Shafter Lake and Andrews. Shafter Lake was larger and would eventually have a bank, hotel, and several stores. An election, however, between Shafter Lake and Andrews, both seeking to be the county seat, would prove pivotal for one, disastrous for the other. To woo qualified voters, Shafter Lake offered free lots to people, enabling them to vote for Shafter as the governing community. Yet a refusal to extend the deadline for registering in Shafter Lake resulted in one individual, R. M. Means, returning to Andrews and buying land and giving it to cowboys and others for their vote in making Andrews the county seat. The result was that Andrews won the election using Shafter Lake's idea. Such was the dramatic and tumultuous beginning of Andrews.

Soon after, Andrews County was duly separated from Midland County on May 11, 1910, through a petition signed by 150 voters of Andrews County. On July 22, 1910, the records were transferred from Midland and the Andrews Commissioners' Court held its first meeting on that date.

Andrews would become the hub of a vast ranching operation during this early period. Outside investors and operators provided innovative techniques to cope with the scarcity of surface water and weather. As a result, barbed wire and windmills were pioneered in this corner of Texas. Yet the fortunes of many would be forever changed when oil was discovered in 1929, several miles west of town with the C. E. Ogden No. 1 well. At the time, however, a barrel of oil only sold for 10¢; it was hardly worth having it shipped out of the county.

World War II, however, and its huge demand for oil resulted in the first boom conditions. At one time in the 1940s, more than 100 drilling rigs were operating in the county, zooming from 1,120 in 1940 to 13,000 by the end of the 1950s. During the war years and for a time afterwards, Andrews County led the entire nation in percentage of population growth.

By the time the drilling turned to more mundane production, more than 7,200 wells had been drilled in the county and one-thirtieth of the proven oil reserves of the nation had been found beneath the 1,500 square miles of the surface of the county. Most of the development of the oil reserves was done by major national and international companies, and because of the extensive formations, those companies often times sent their best and brightest personnel to Andrews County. The newcomers helped with the development of the oil industry and played a major role in the community, along with others who wanted Andrews to be more than just another little oilfield town. Over the years, it proved to be anything but ordinary.

Today the physical plant of the Andrews Independent School District is valued at more than $183 million, and its flagship, Andrews High School, built in 1961, included carpeted classrooms and was the first in the nation to explore a central dome to reduce costly corridors and halls. Following public meetings known as ASAP—Andrews Strategic Answer Plan—that were conducted in response to population loss and the shuttering of businesses, a $31 million bond issue was passed by voters in 2000 to totally enhance existing schools and build new ones.

The county pioneered the use of a truck route around the city as a means of obtaining the paving of 98 percent of all city streets and aided in the city's developing of a water field that could supply the needs of a town of 30,000 for 90 years.

The local 18-hole golf course is a veritable oasis because of the use of 110 million gallons of water reclaimed from the city sewer system each year, while the local airport, first made operational in the early 1940s, features one of the longest runways serving a non-metro area in the state.

Later additions included the James Roberts Civic Center, the Andrews County Library, the chamber of commerce, a new middle school, new elementary schools, and a stunning new performance center with a 3,000-seat basketball arena, indoor pools, and a performing arts auditorium signifying the community's commitment to excellence in education and extracurricular activities. The creation of a hospital district helped revitalize the local medical community, resulting in new physicians, a new first-class nursing home, and a senior living campus.

During the 1970s, in an effort to stabilize a boom and bust oil economy, the community began seriously exploring diversification and eventually landed Scott & Fetzer Company of Cleveland, Ohio, to make Kirby vacuum cleaners. Kirby West continues to turn out the latest in Kirby designs and has proved to be a significant employer. Still eyeing more diversification, the city fathers capitalized on changing the county's liabilities—little water, sparse rainfall, and population—into assets in regards to luring non-oil related industry to the county.

In the 1990s, a low-level radioactive waste company, Waste Control Specialists, was courted by the Andrews Industrial Foundation to take advantage of near-perfect geology—dry land and a deep ridge of red clay—in the far western segment of the county. Approval by the Texas Legislature helped establish the Texas Compact for the proper disposal of low-level waste from medical institutions, universities and other companies. WCS and an unrelated uranium-enrichment company, LES, nearby in New Mexico, have stirred much growth in Andrews and the area. In 2008, and again in 2009, the U.S. Census Bureau named Andrews the fastest-growing micropolitan or small city in the United States.

Today, Andrews still embodies that pioneering, robust spirit that pitted settlers against Native Americans and the elements and resulted in a wild election with cowboys and farmers wanting cheap land to build their dreams upon. *Andrew County News* publisher the late James Roberts said it best in his Drifting Sands column in 1976, during the U.S. Bicentennial celebration: "In between the beginning and now, came a lot of people who were seeking more fortune than fame. Many passed this way and a few remained to watch, work, and wonder at the marvel of creating a modern day city, county, hospital and school district from scratch."

One

THE EARLY YEARS

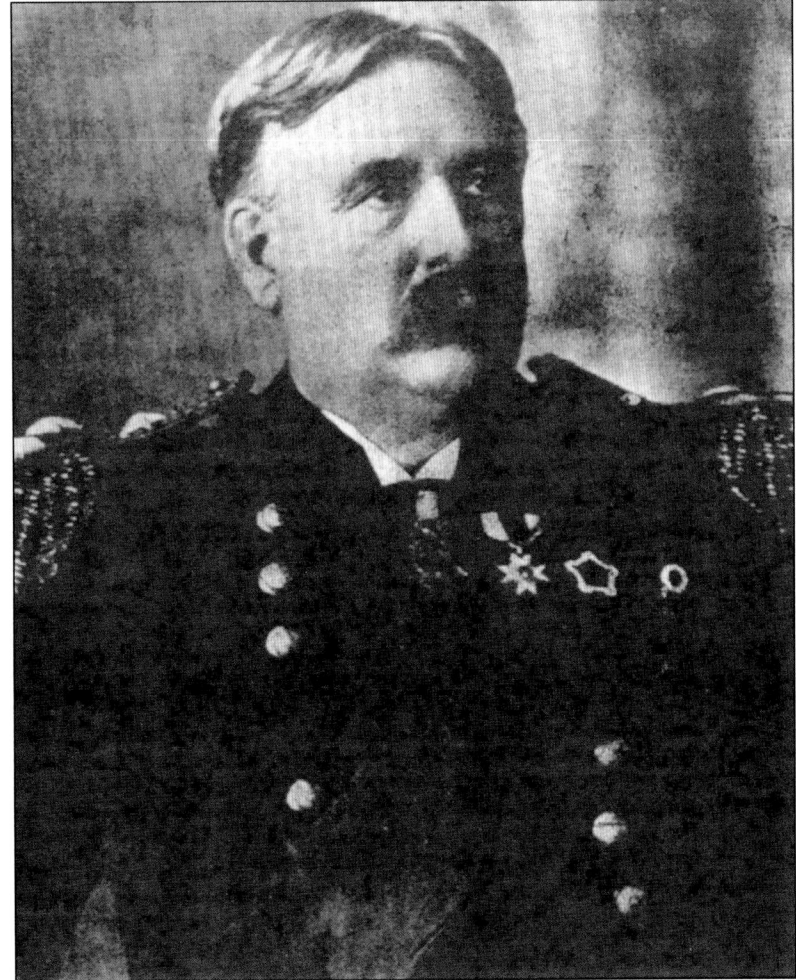

In October 1875, U.S. cavalry colonel William Shafter is credited with conducting the most thorough exploration of much of West Texas and Andrews County, where his expedition stumbled onto Shafter Lake. He described the dry lake bed as a "deep depression of the prairie with hard ground all around it with grass excellent and very luxuriant." He noted teepee poles that were left behind by Native Americans, who apparently left in a hurry. (Courtesy Andrews County Library.)

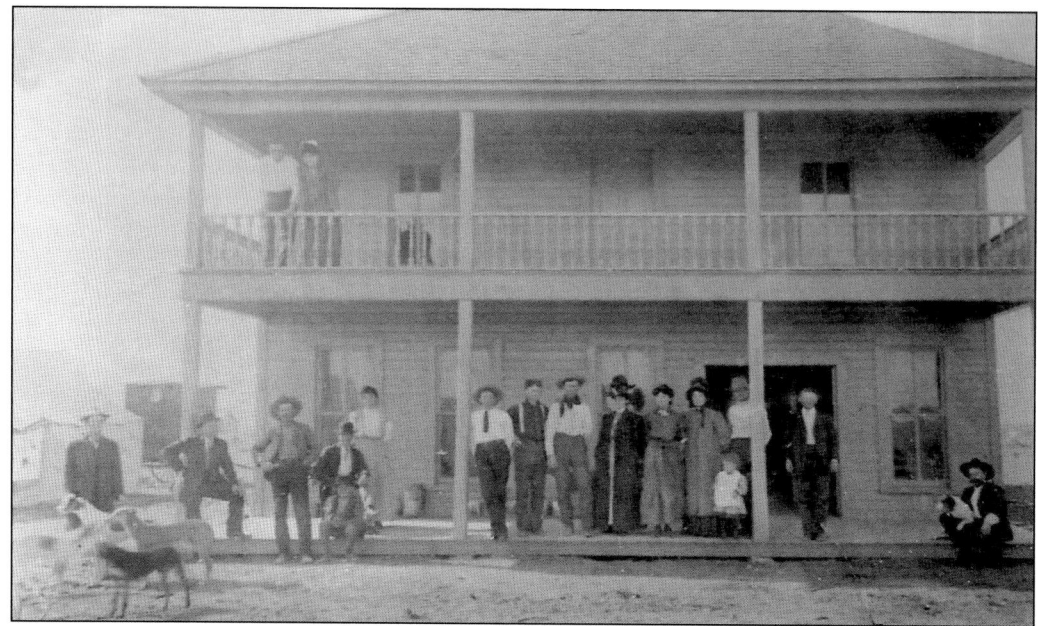

The first organized community in Andrews County was Shafter Lake, which came into existence around 1906. In its heyday, Shafter Lake had several businesses including a grocery store, the Cowboy State Bank, a school, a newspaper, and the Shafter Hotel. Shown here is the hotel, owned by the Elam family, who are pictured in the photograph along with Lee Haywood, Annie Williamson, and T. J. Cumbley, the editor of the *Shafter Lake Herald*. (Courtesy Martha Page.)

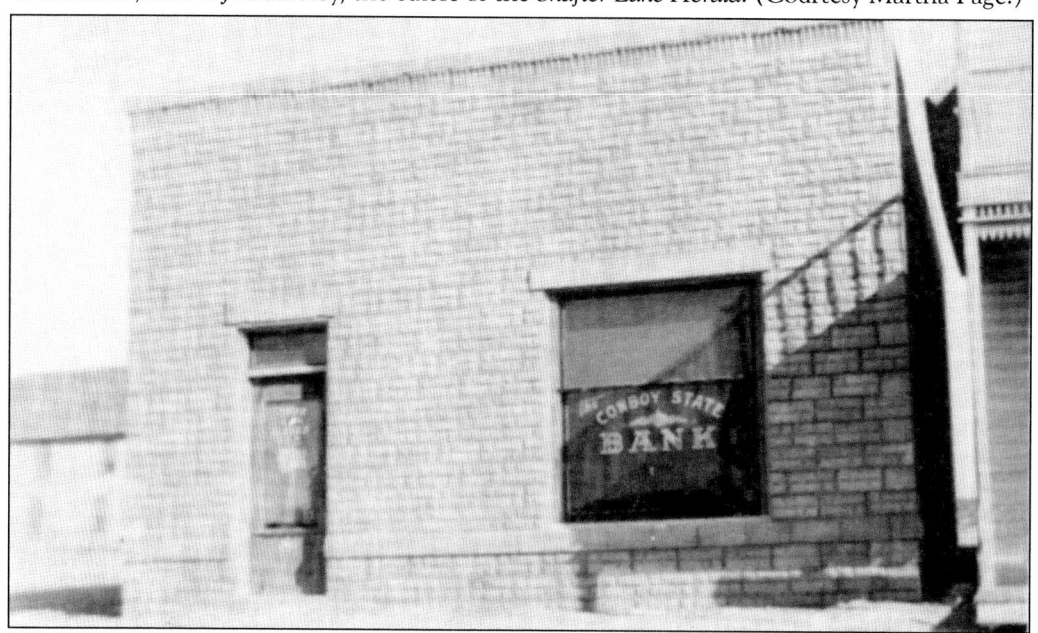

In 1909, the Cowboy State Bank was among the businesses at Shafter Lake when the town was bustling with enthusiasm that it would be the county seat of Andrews County. The bank folded when voters approved Andrews as the county seat in a hotly contested election. Among the shareholders for the Cowboy State Bank were B. M. Irwin, W. W. McQuatters, T. J. Pierce, J. M. Speed, K. H. Irwin, D. M. Pinnell, W. Howard, and Arlen B. Davis. (Courtesy Martha Page.)

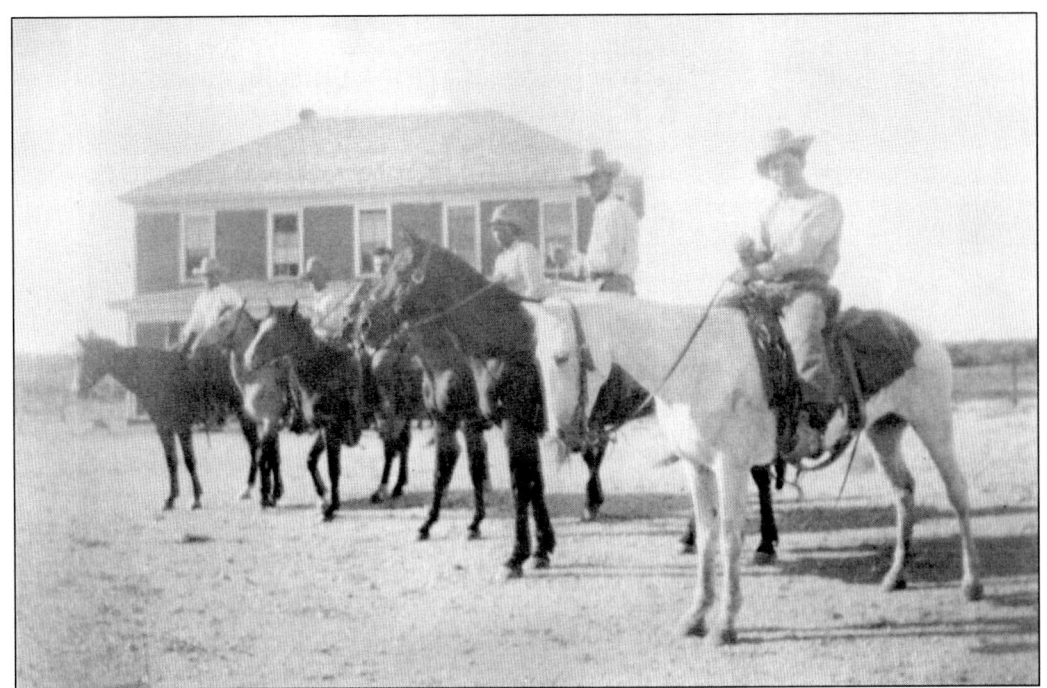

The C-Ranch in southeastern Andrews County was the largest ranch in the county. Nelson Morris, a wealthy Chicago meat packing plant operator, purchased the land in 1883 and the headquarters was located near Baird Lake, named after an army officer killed there in 1862 by Native Americans. C-Ranch cowboys shown in the picture include, from left to right, Wren Wrinkle, unidentified, Henry Carnes, Floyd Goodgame, Sam Nix, and Johnny Abers. (Courtesy Martha Page.)

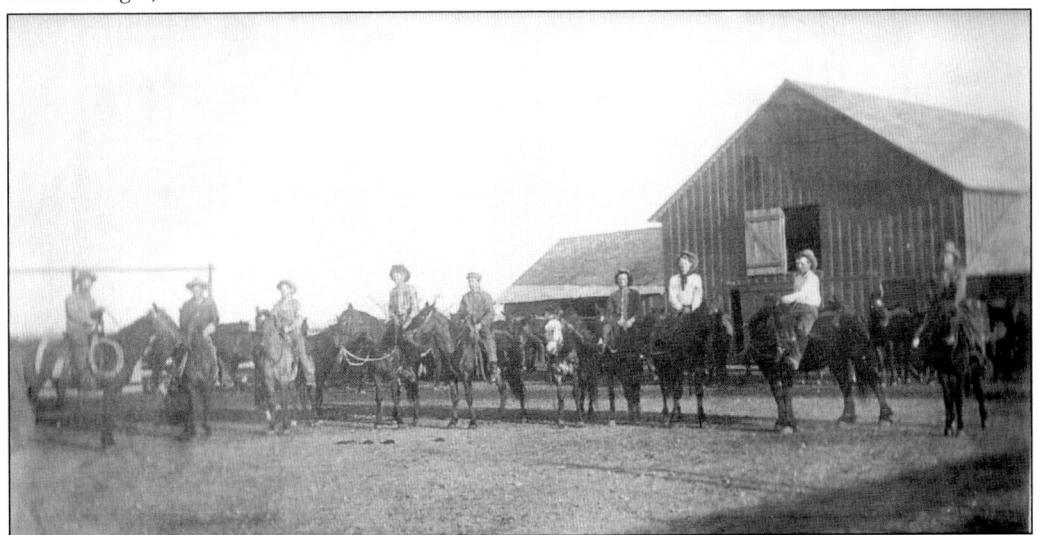

Early ranches like the C-Ranch in southeastern Andrews County, established in 1883, depended on cowhands to work the cattle, tend to the range, and perform other chores. While windmills and barbed-wire fences were relatively new tools of the trade, the main bulk of the work was up to the cowboy and his ability to handle his horse, livestock, weather, and other elements of ranching, which remains much the same today. (Courtesy Martha Page.)

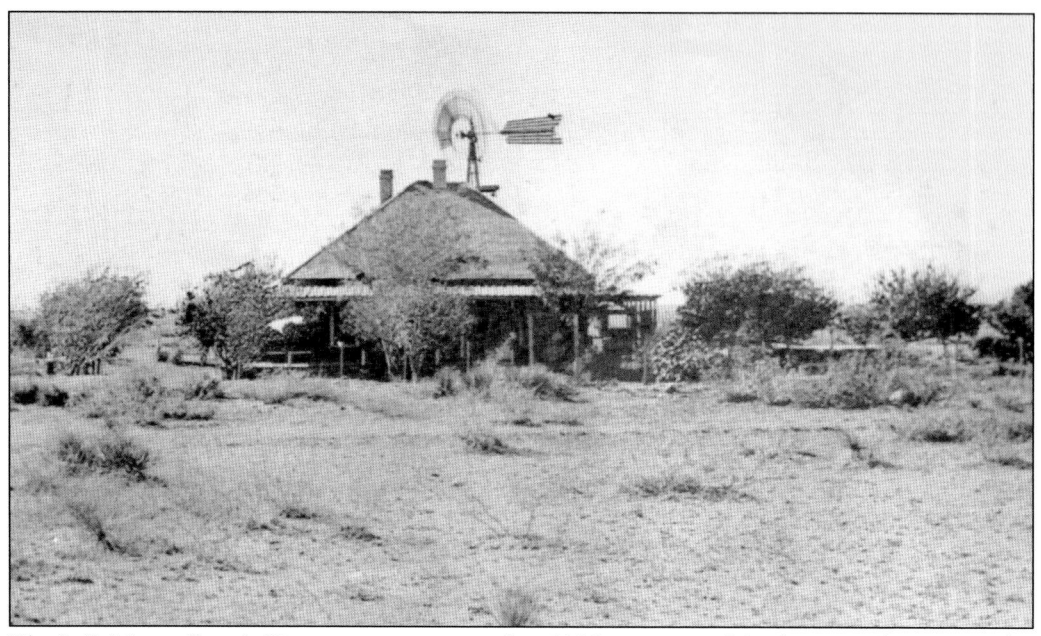

The J. S. Means Ranch House was constructed in 1900, just east of Andrews, and is among the oldest surviving houses in the area. Means established a successful working ranch, which carried on later with the Ellison Tom family. Means's son, R. M. "Bob" Means, played a pivotal role in Andrews being the county seat after persuading cowboys on the C-Ranch and others to vote for Andrews instead of Shafter Lake.

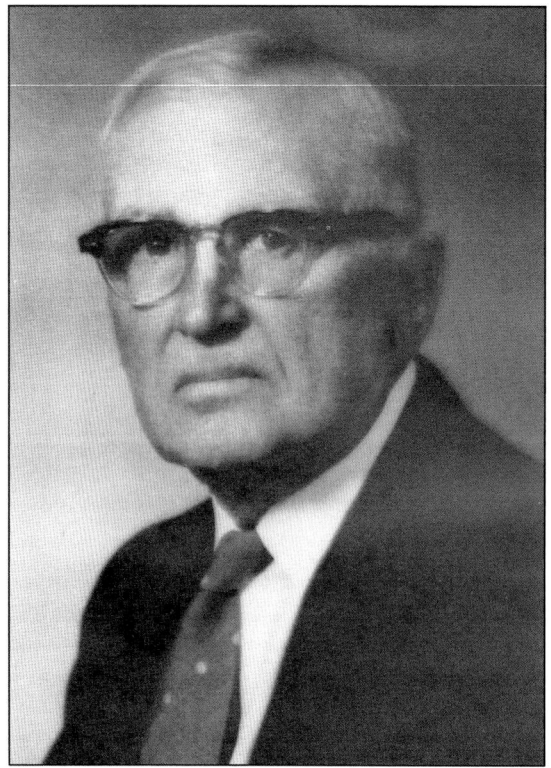

R. M. "Bob" Means was instrumental in Andrews being named the county seat instead of Shafter Lake following an election in 1910. Means is believed to have given free lots to cowboys to vote for Andrews. He formed Andrews Abstract Company in 1909, the oldest surviving business in town. He was also the first Democratic party chairman, donated land for the first courthouse, and served as county clerk from 1919 to 1922.

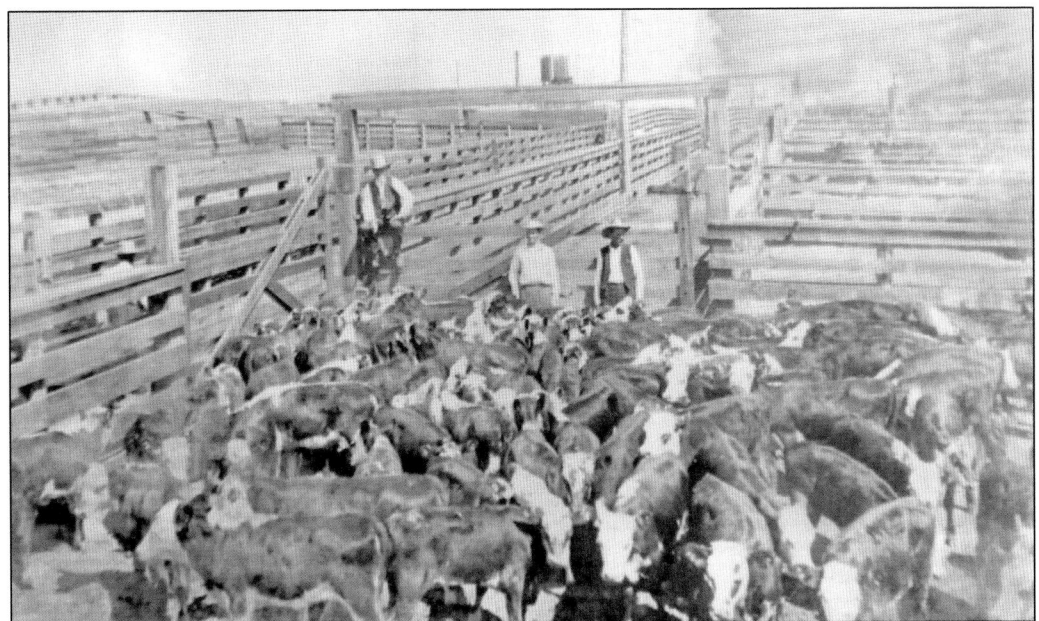

Early Andrews rancher J. S. Means is shown atop a fence in 1918 in the Fort Worth stockyards with cattle that was herded there from Andrews. Besides ranching, Means helped establish the first school and opened the first bank, serving as its president. Later he retired from ranching and moved to Fort Worth, and the ranch eventually was leased to George Tom and managed later by son Ellison Tom Sr. and Ellison "Sonny" Tom Jr.

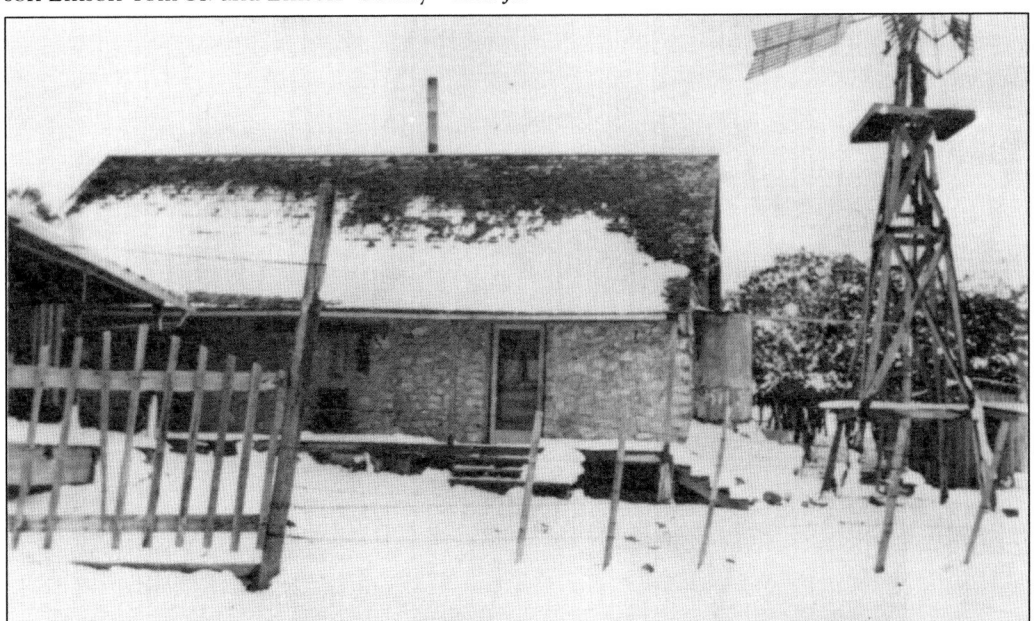

The 5 Wells Ranch in northeastern Andrews County was established at the turn of the century by Col. C. W. Wells. Wells sold the ranch to John Scharbauer in 1894, who started the Scharbauer Cattle Company. The Bill Kelton family moved to 5 Wells in 1910, where he managed the ranch while his wife, Daisy, cooked for the ranch hands and people who stopped there traveling to and from Midland and Seminole.

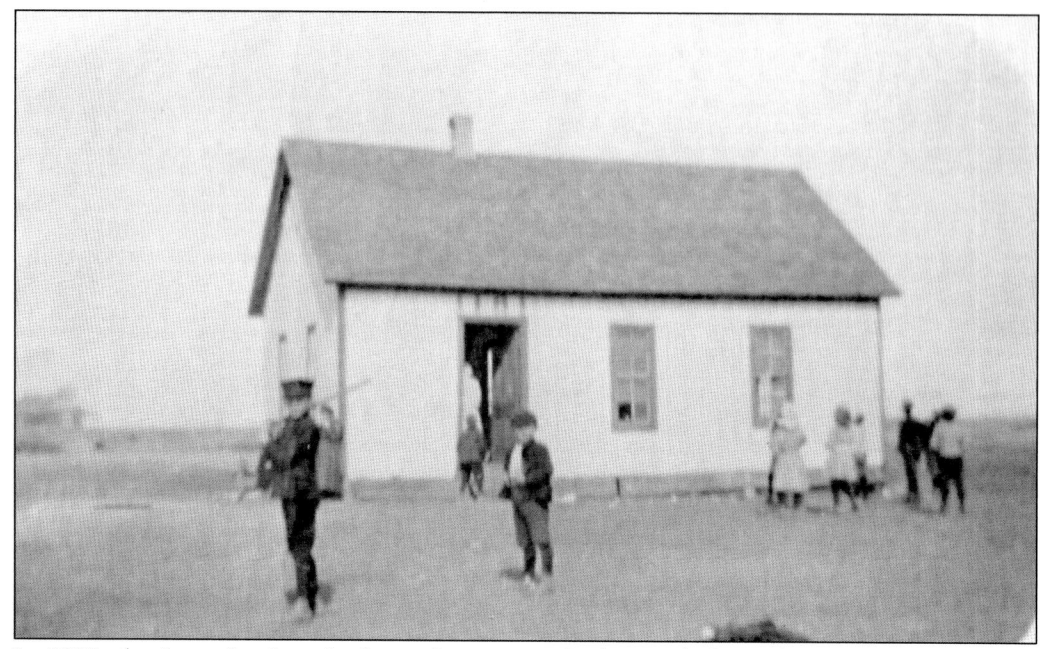

In 1907, the first school in Andrews County was built at Whalen Lake, a small salt lake 16 miles west of Andrews. Lumber for the building was hauled 60 miles from Midland by wagons furnished by Will Gates, an early settler. The school was in existence until 1910. The first teacher, Gracie Stanford, was paid $25 a month and was given free room and board. She had 10 students. (Courtesy Mark Hooper.)

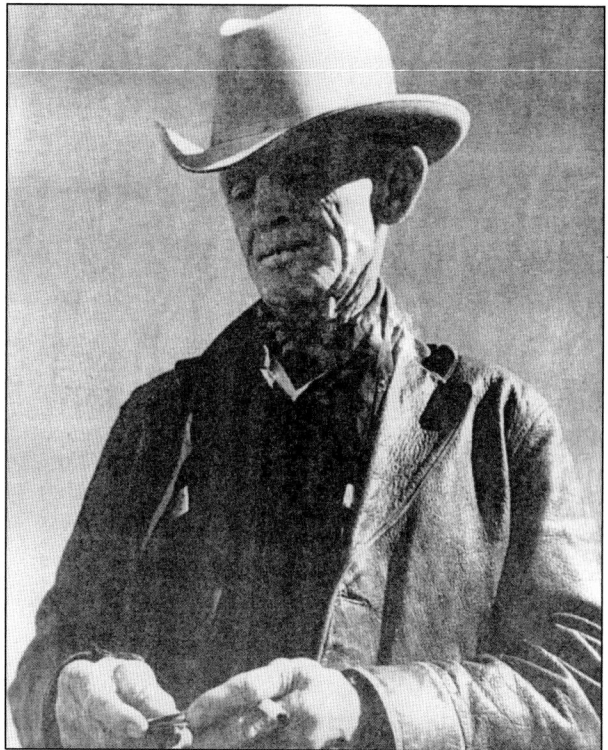

In 1913, Jim and Bessie Ola Parker purchased 800 acres from A. A. Horne and it became the basis for their Adobe Ranch located southwest of Andrews. They eventually acquired title to 27 sections in this area and at one time operated on about 40 sections. Parker operated the ranch until 1945, when it was leased to various people. Parker, shown in this photograph, died in 1954 and was buried in Andrews.

A. H. Hall moved his family to Andrews from Odessa in 1909 after purchasing the Tom White place. At the time, Andrews had a mercantile store, barbershop, drugstore, small hotel, blacksmith shop, a wagon, and post office. Hall was the first tax assessor. Included in this 1916 photograph are, from left to right, (first row) Edna, Edith, A. H. Hall, and unidentified; (second row) Nan, Sarah, and Mary.

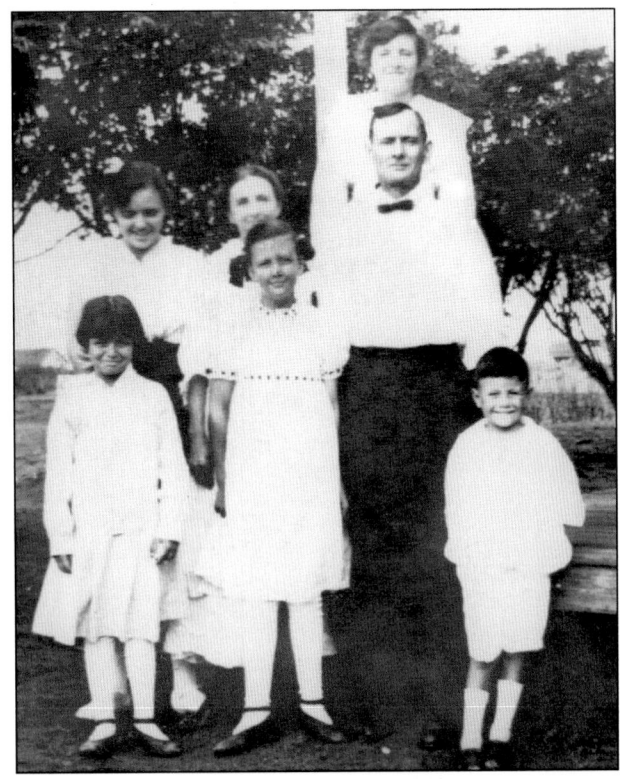

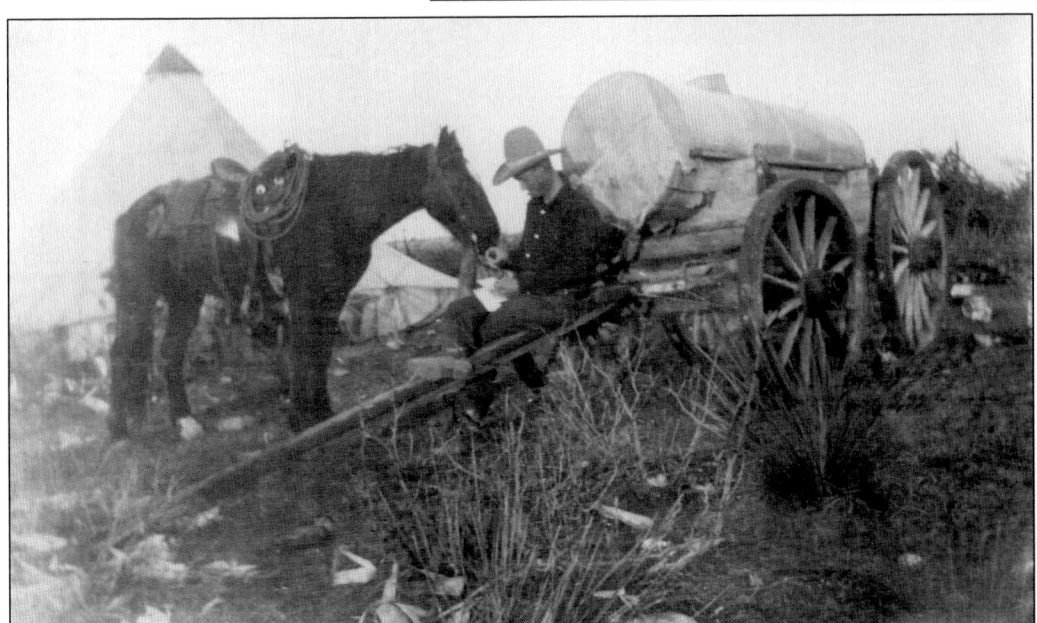

In 1908, early settlers in Andrews County were faced with many hardships, including the scarcity of good water for themselves and their livestock. Farmers and ranchers had to use ingenuity to provide water for their animals, some resorting to homemade water wagons, as shown above with Marvin M. Fisher Sr., an early rancher in northwestern Andrews. Sometimes water was hauled for miles from the nearest windmill or watering hole.

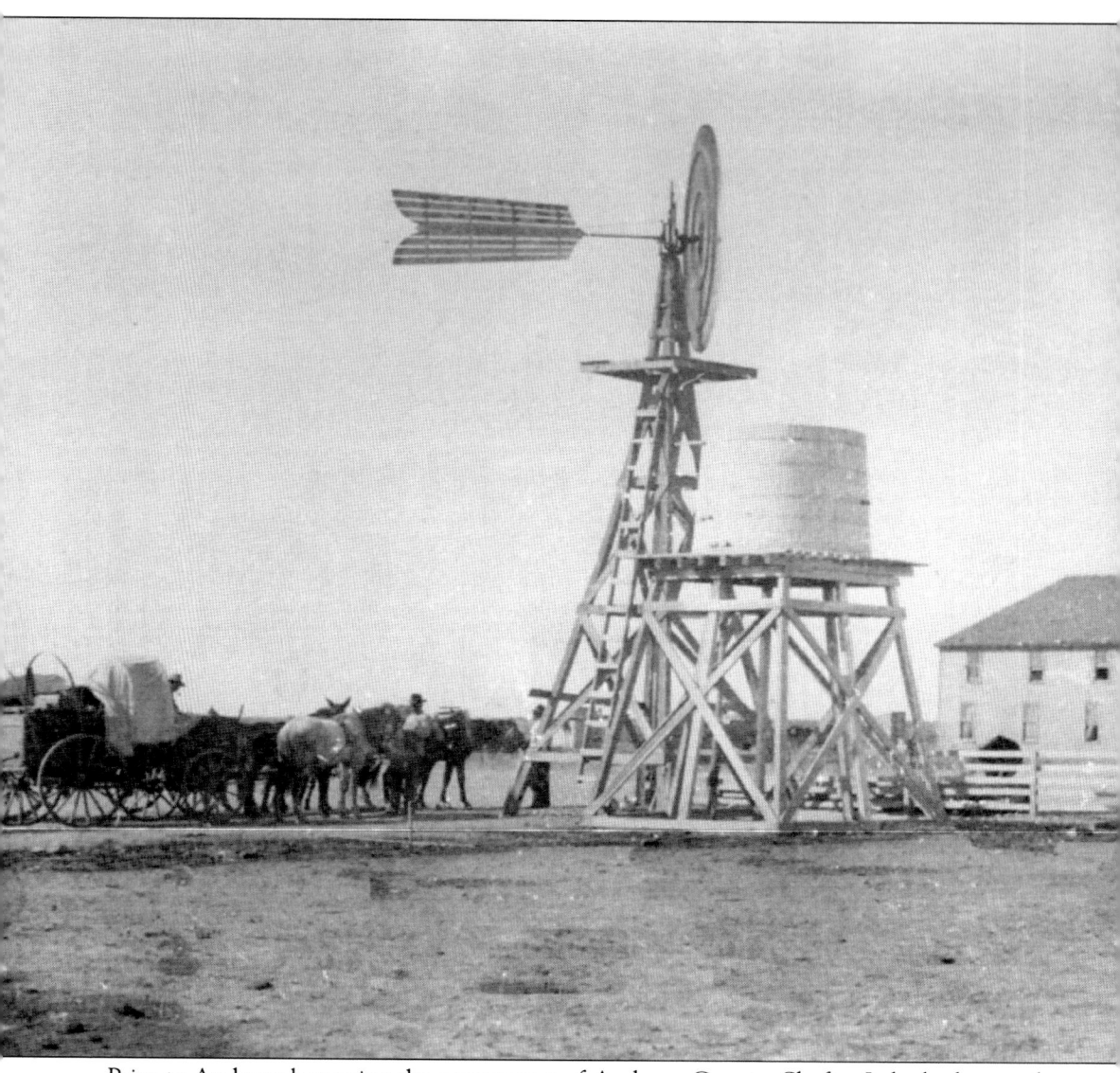
Prior to Andrews becoming the county seat of Andrews County, Shafter Lake had more than 500 residents after being established in 1906. Shafter Lake had a two-story hotel, bank, café, and other establishments. The promise of cheap land sent out across the country resulted in much interest, with some residents actually moving or just coming to see Shafter Lake. Colorful brochures were mailed out all over the nation that featured a carefully laid out town,

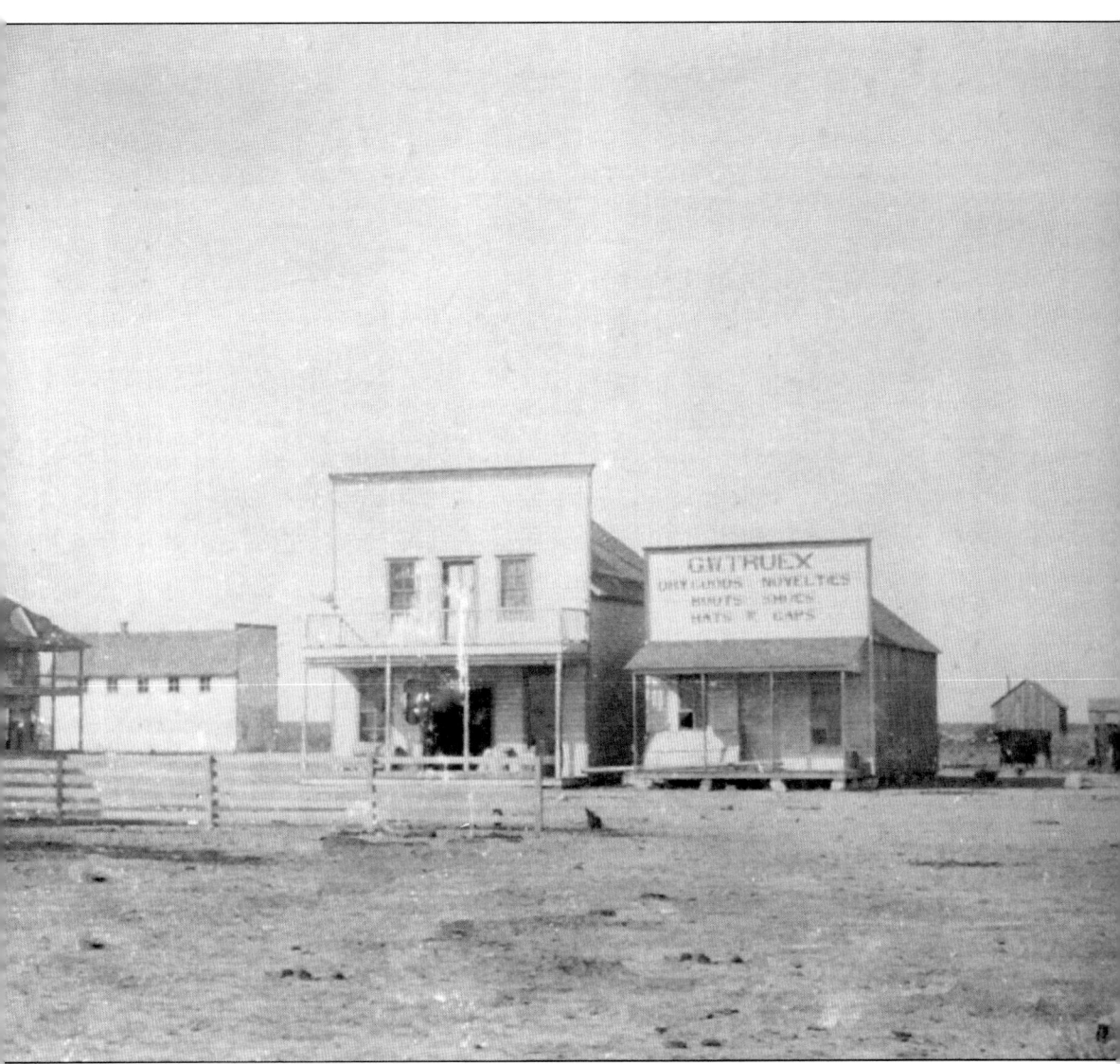

a courthouse square, a University of Shafer Lake, and massive marshalling yards for railroad trains. The advertisement campaign, containing much fabrication, resulted in many people buying lots via the mail. It was billed as the "City of a Thousand Wonders," but by 1910, following an election making Andrews the county seat, the downhill progression had started.

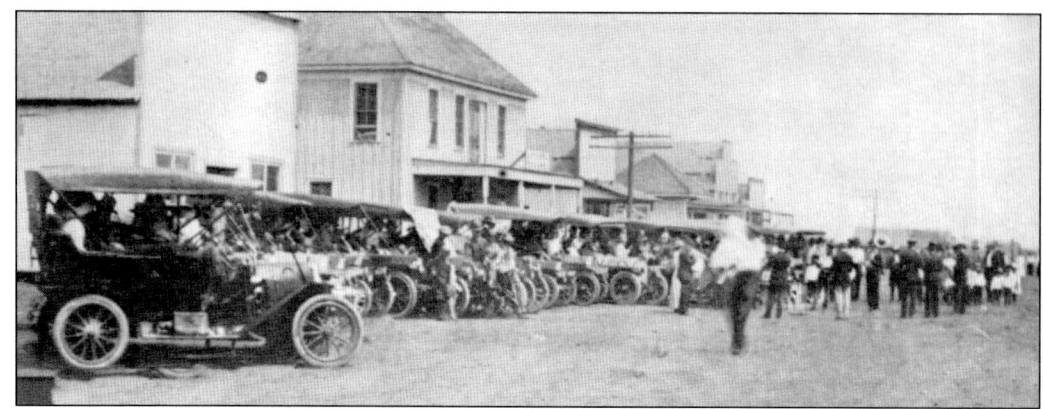

Numerous cars were arranged on the street in Andrews in 1908, evidently for a special event, while a band played nearby. From left to right, the buildings in the picture are the Dollarhide Building, the Josephine House (Dunn Hotel), Umberson Land Office, Logsdon Millinery Shop, a grocery store, and the Thomason Barber Shop. Today the National Bank of Andrews' drive-through facility and the Andrews County Library occupy the same sites. (Courtesy Mark Hooper.)

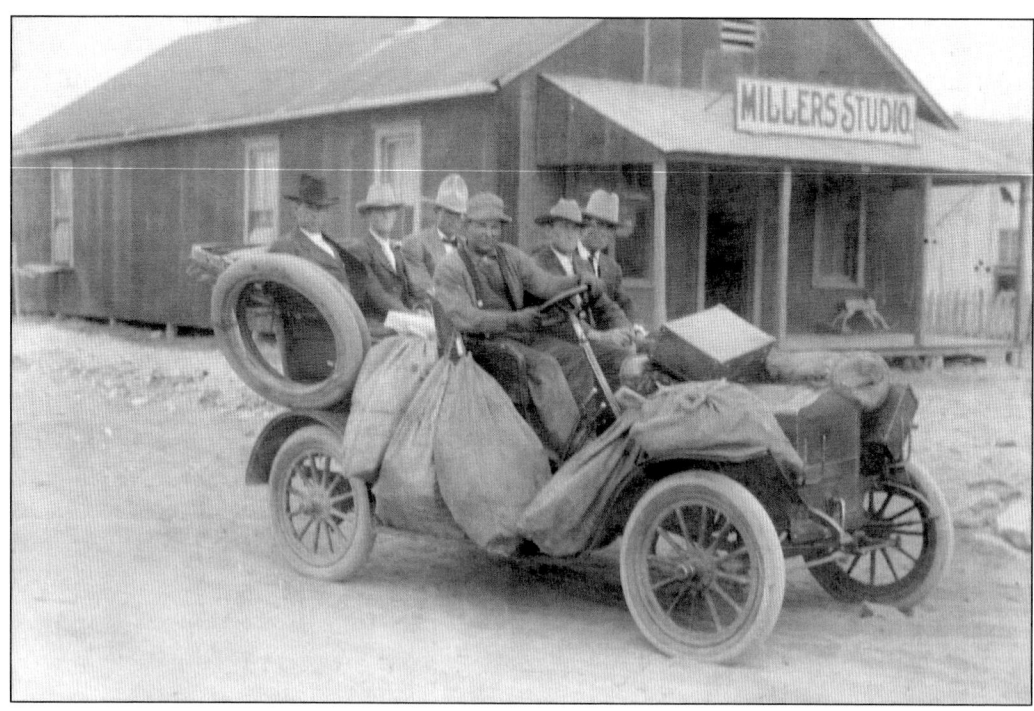

In 1909, the mail run between Andrews and Midland was the only link with the outside world, and it not only brought mail, but freight, groceries, and passengers to Andrews and Shafter Lake. Shown in the photograph, from left to right, are (back seat) Tom White, one of the original founders of Andrews, Roy Wright, and Lewis Begers; (front seat) Shorty Dixon, Bob Means, and Dan Cobb. (Courtesy Andrews County Library.)

The first U.S. postmaster in Andrews was T. C. Wilder, shown here in 1908, prior to Andrews being officially organized and named the county seat. Wilder's daughter, Annie Atwood Wilder, married R. M. "Bob" Means, another noted county pioneer and considered by many to be the "father" of Andrews. Once Andrews was named the county seat, T. C. Wilder was elected justice of the peace, precinct No. 1.

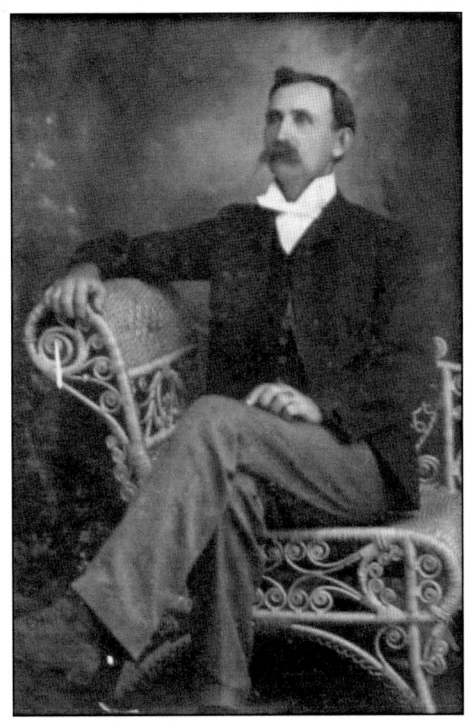

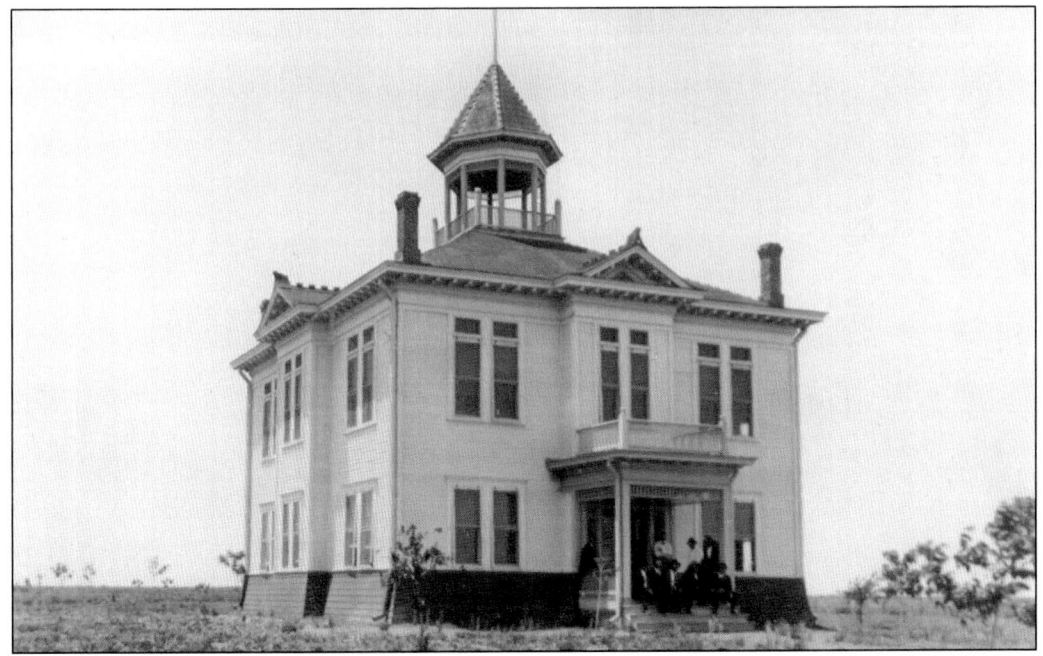

In 1911, the first courthouse in Andrews was constructed after 66 residents voted for and 44 against spending $8,000 for its construction. This occurred following a contentious election the year before over where the county seat should be located and voters approved Andrews over Shafter Lake. The county was not duly recognized until 1910, when Midland County transferred the county's legal records and documents to Andrews on July 22, 1910. (Courtesy Mark Hooper.)

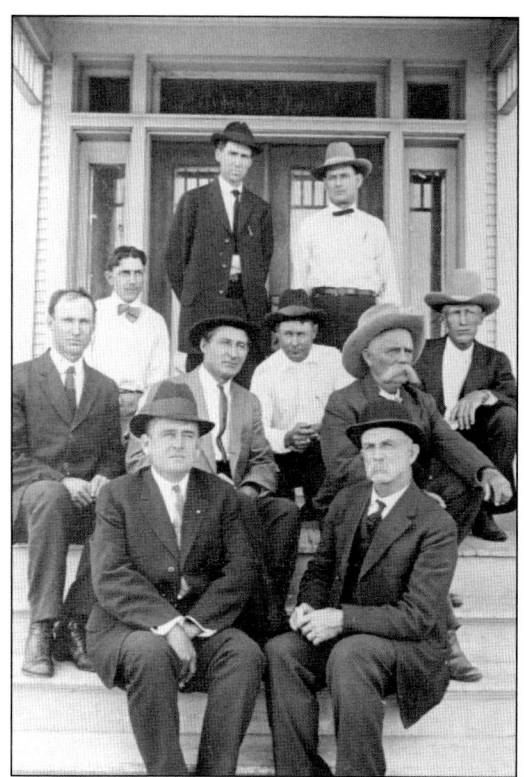

Included in the photograph of gentlemen sitting on the steps of the first Andrews County Courthouse in 1911 are, in no particular order, N. P. Ross, judge; Tom Smith, county clerk; S. E. Umberson, treasurer; G. Allen, official stenographer; Boyd Douglas, surveyor; A. J. Hall, tax assessor; T. W. Craddock, sheriff; Sen. H. M. Hill, commissioner of precinct No. 3; Andrew Kind, attorney; and M. A. Thornberry, commissioner of precinct No. 4. (Courtesy Mark Hooper.)

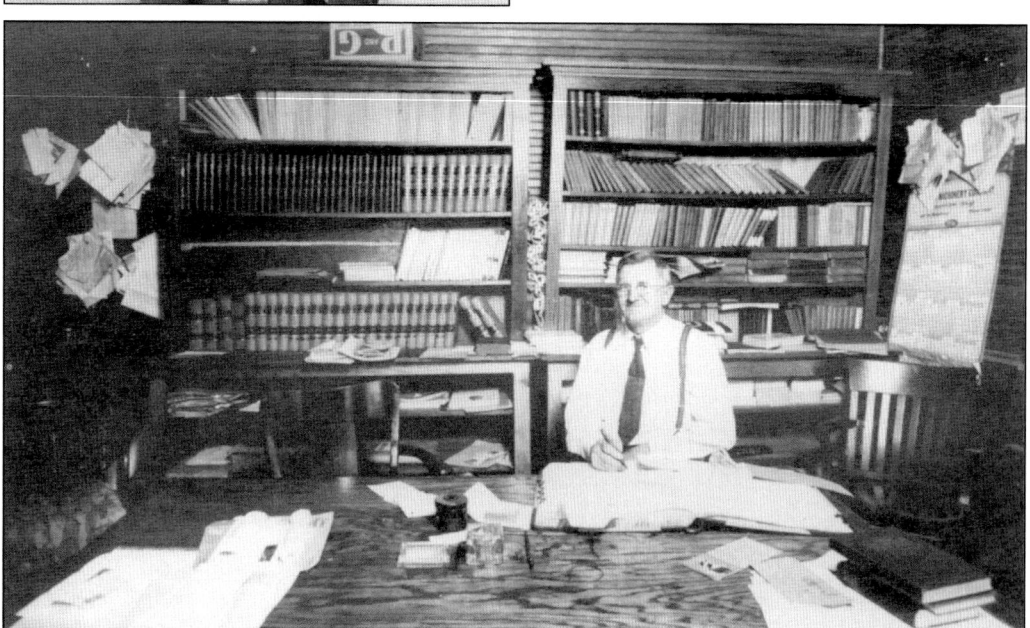

One of the last judges to serve in the first Andrews County Courthouse was W. J. Underwood, who served from 1935 until 1938. Underwood was an Andrews pioneer, moving near Shafter Lake to farm in 1905. His family moved to Andrews in 1926, when he was elected county commissioner. Besides county judge, he also served as sheriff, tax assessor-collector, and treasurer. He died in March 1964.

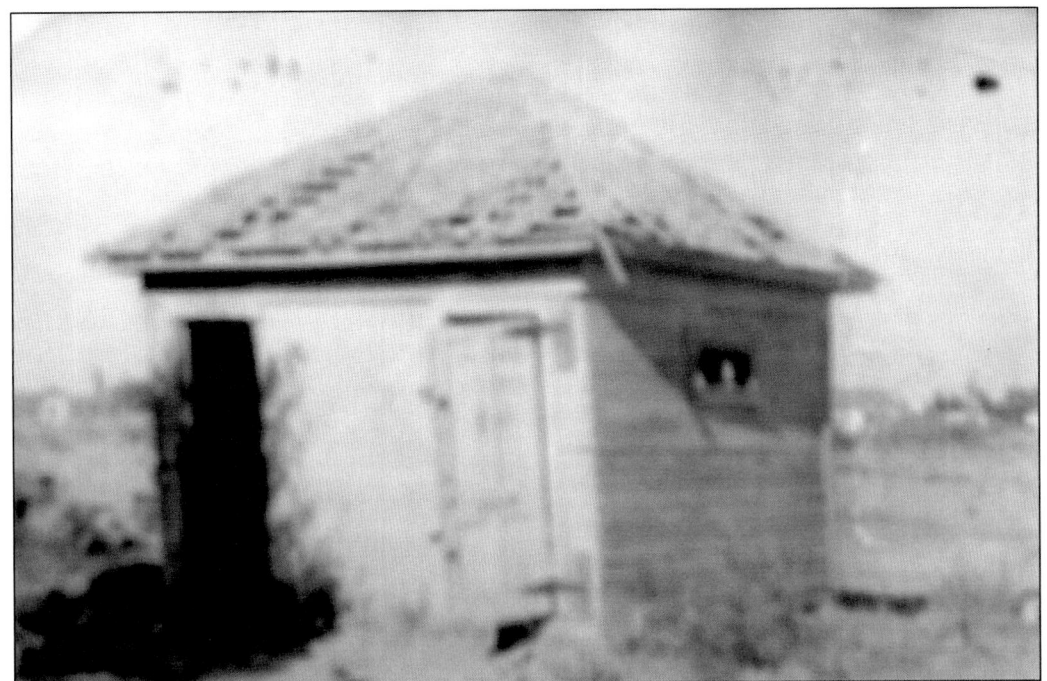

The very first jail in Andrews was often described by those who lived in the community at the time as a "storage shed with bars." The small facility was used when needed, and depending on the severity of the crime, lawbreakers were allowed to leave the jail to answer the call of nature. Old-timers said most offenders did not violate the honor system.

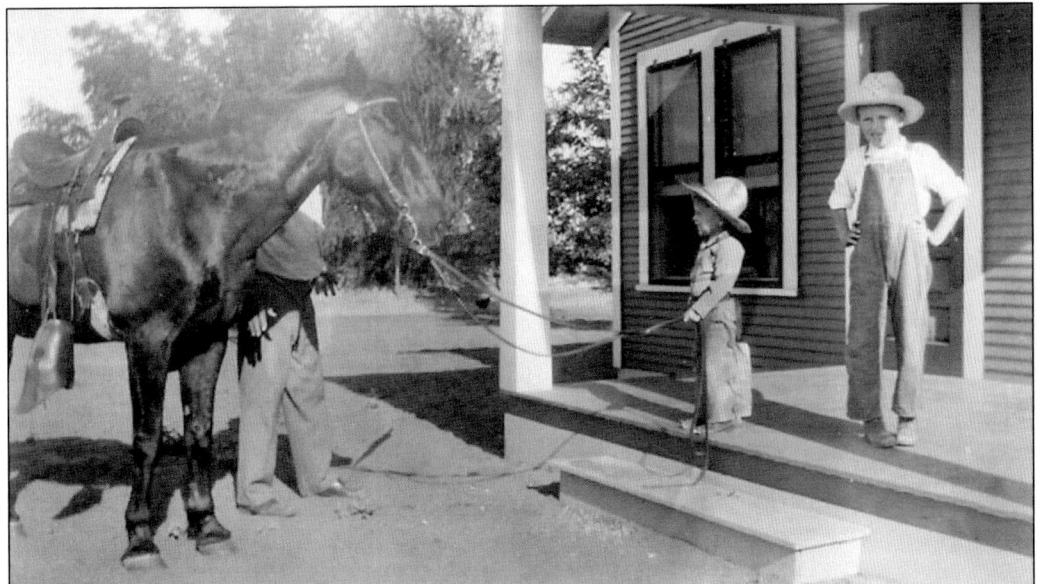

A young Marvin M. Fisher Jr. helps steady his father's horse at the Fisher Ranch in northwestern Andrews County as cousin Wesley Paddock stands nearby. The Fisher Ranch was started in 1908 by the senior Fisher. Marvin Jr. married Earlene Jeffreys in 1947, daughter of Tom and Ina Jeffreys of Andrews, other longtime residents. Earlene and Marvin Jr. had two children, Dan and Jan. Dan manages the ranch today.

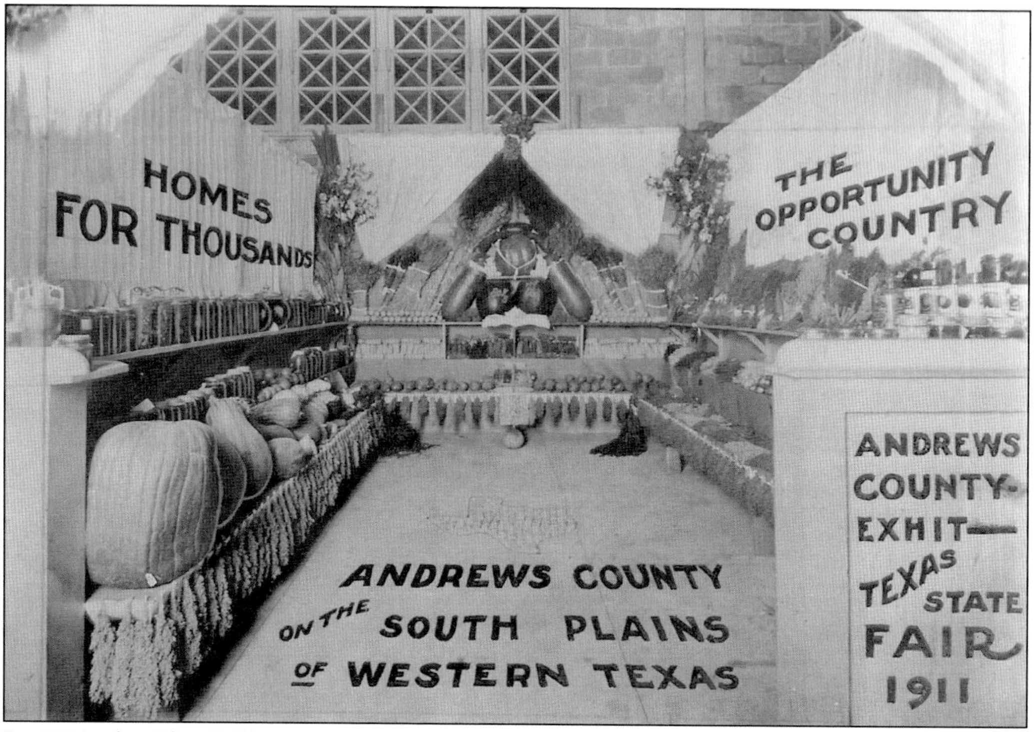

In 1911, the Blue Ribbon Farm in Andrews County won a blue ribbon at the state fair in Dallas for growing the best all-around farm products. The farm was on the J. F. Bustin Ranch in northwest Andrews and had an ample supply of water due to the use of windmills. The W. W. McQuatters family purchased the Blue Ribbon Ranch later and continued raising crops and large watermelons. (Courtesy Martha Page.)

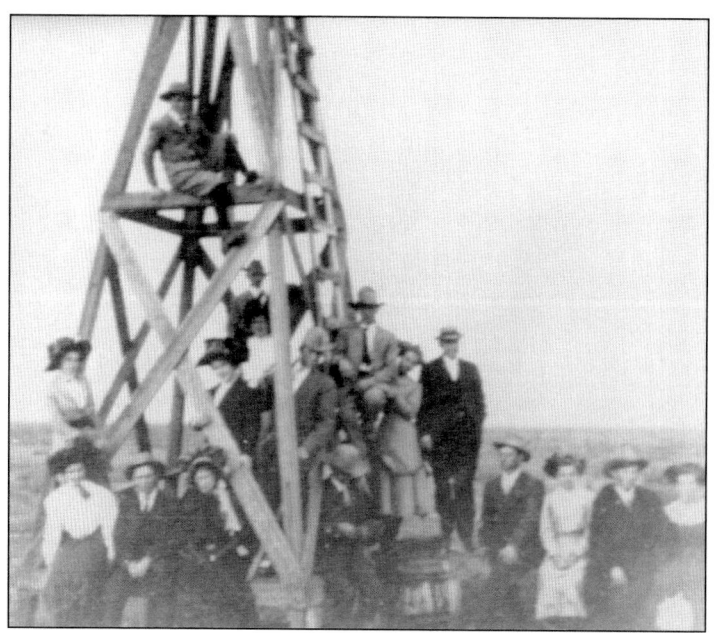

Windmills were crucial to ranching in West Texas, including in Andrews County, where they provided water for families and livestock amid the often dry environment of the semiarid desert. This photograph, taken in 1910, included residents Roland Dunn, Earl Dunn, Edna Collins, Guthrie Allen, Ed Haag, Lurline Wilder, Harvie Rhodes, Lillie Mae Knight, Mae Alexander, Frank Haag, Carrie Mae Rhodes, Alliene Routh, T. C. Nunn, and Mae Dunn. (Courtesy Martha Page.)

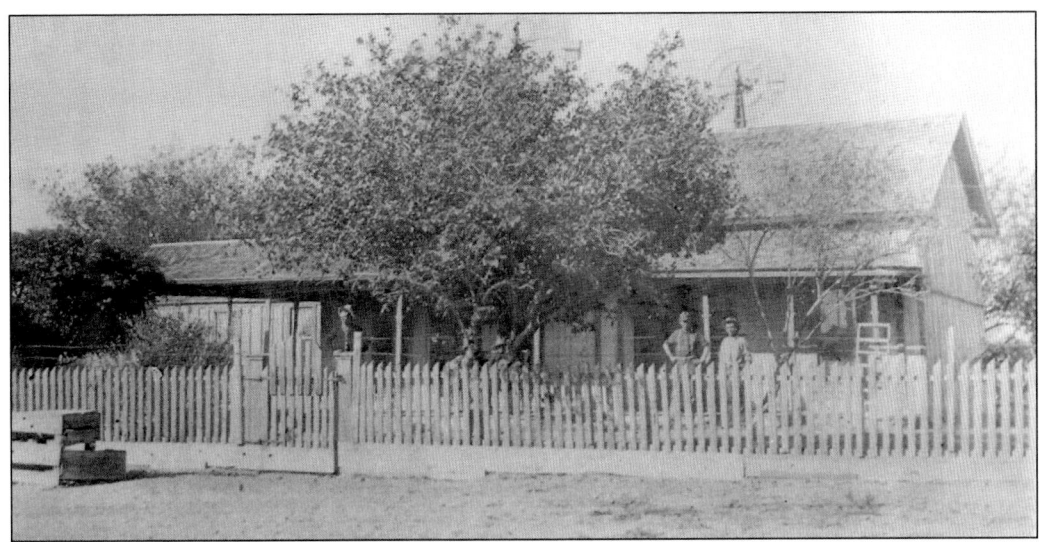

The C-Ranch in southeastern Andrews County became one of the first privately owned properties in the county in 1883 when Nelson Morris, a Chicago meat packer, purchased 228,000 acres. He brought new ranching techniques to Texas in response to droughts and blizzards, including barbed-wire fences and windmills. The net effect of windmills and fences made it possible to continue grazing large areas during extreme periods. (Courtesy Martha Page.)

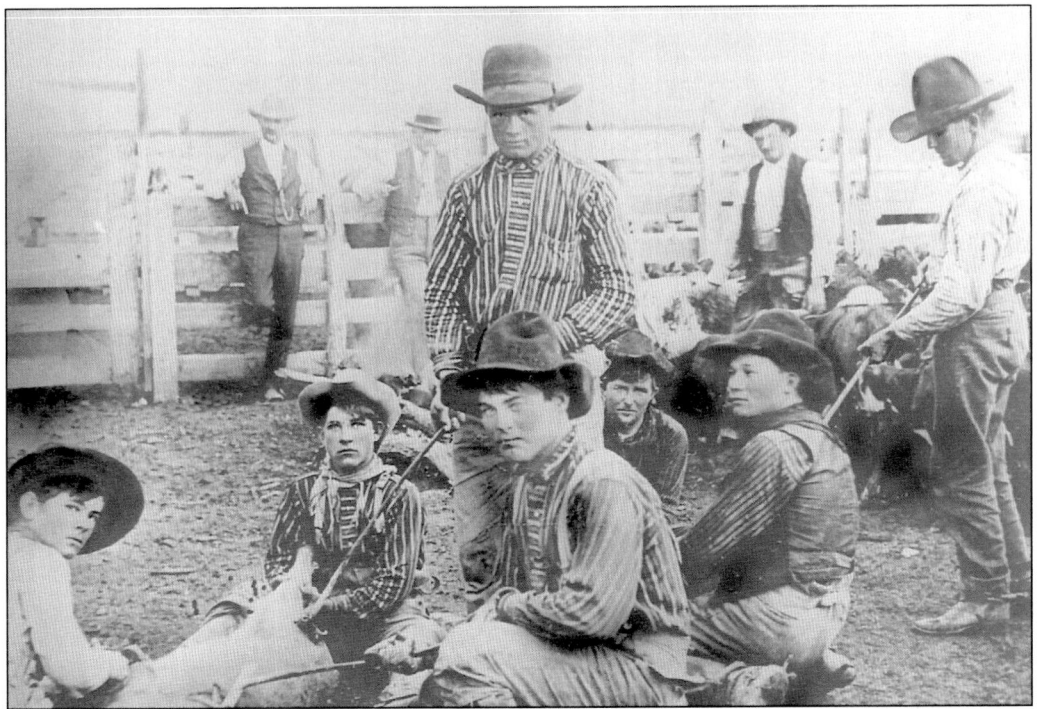

Cowboys were kept busy during the early times branding cattle in order to distinguish them from other ranches' livestock on the open prairie. The Crews Ranch was established in 1902 by Rush Crews, who continuously acquired more land as neighbors became discouraged and decided to sell out. In the photograph, believed to have been taken in 1915, Rush Crews, center, is shown standing amid a group of other cowboys. (Courtesy Martha Page.)

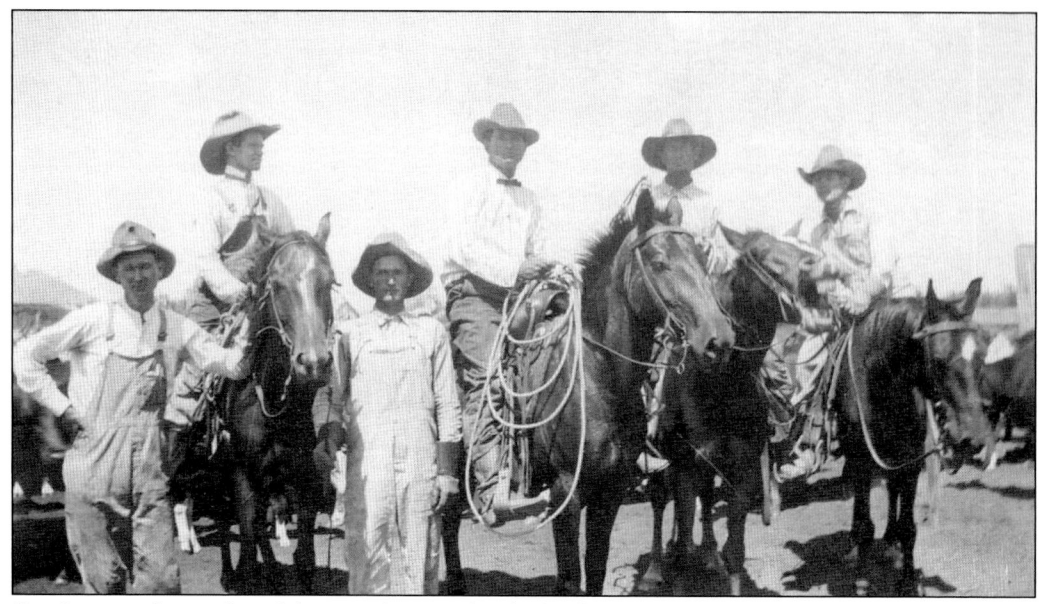

Cowboys made up a lot of the population of early Andrews County as ranches were the mainstay of the economy during the late 1800s and early 1900s until oil was discovered in 1929. Cowboys' pay was low, depending on age and experience, but normally getting on with an outfit meant room and board and a steady job for those considered a "good hand."

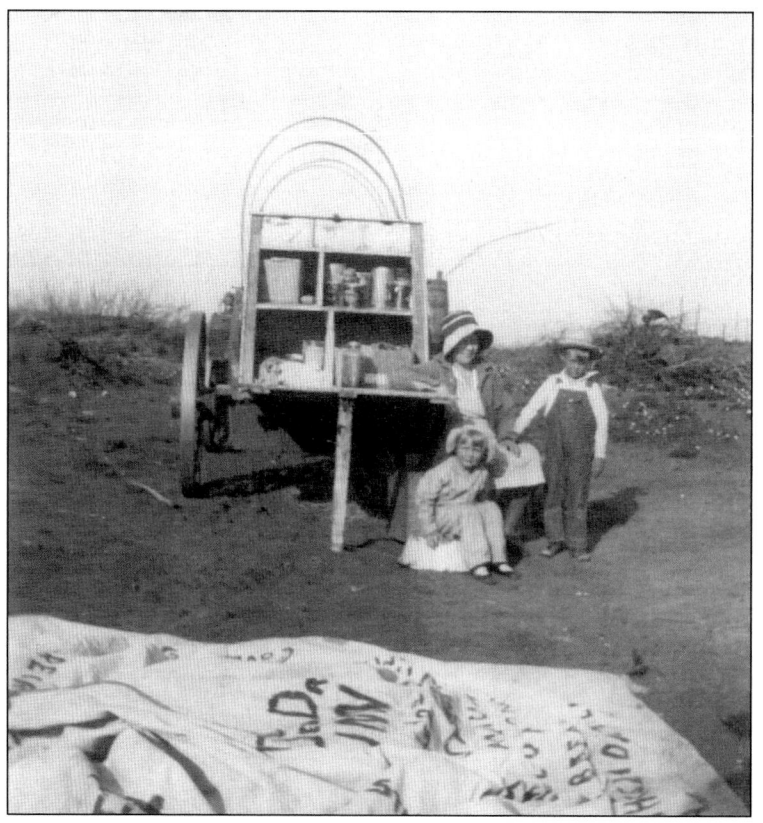

The chuckwagon proved crucial in the lives of ranch hands during the early days of pioneering West Texas and Andrews County. Cowboys on the range and on cattle drives were usually a hungry bunch by the end of a long, dusty day. Shown in this photograph is pioneer ranch owner Mattie Tom tending to the chuck wagon, while seeing to son Ellison "Sonny" Jr. and daughter Rosenelle.

Early inhabitants of Andrews County spent much of their time tending to herds of livestock or toiling over crops, but they also had their duds for church, dances, and of course, special events like having their pictures taken. Shown here are pioneer rancher M. M. Fisher Sr., center, and two unidentified companions, obviously friends, taking time to be photographed.

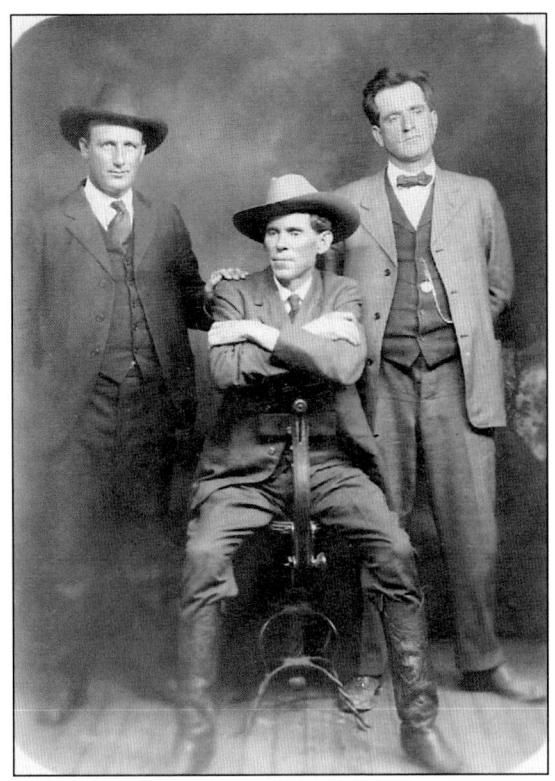

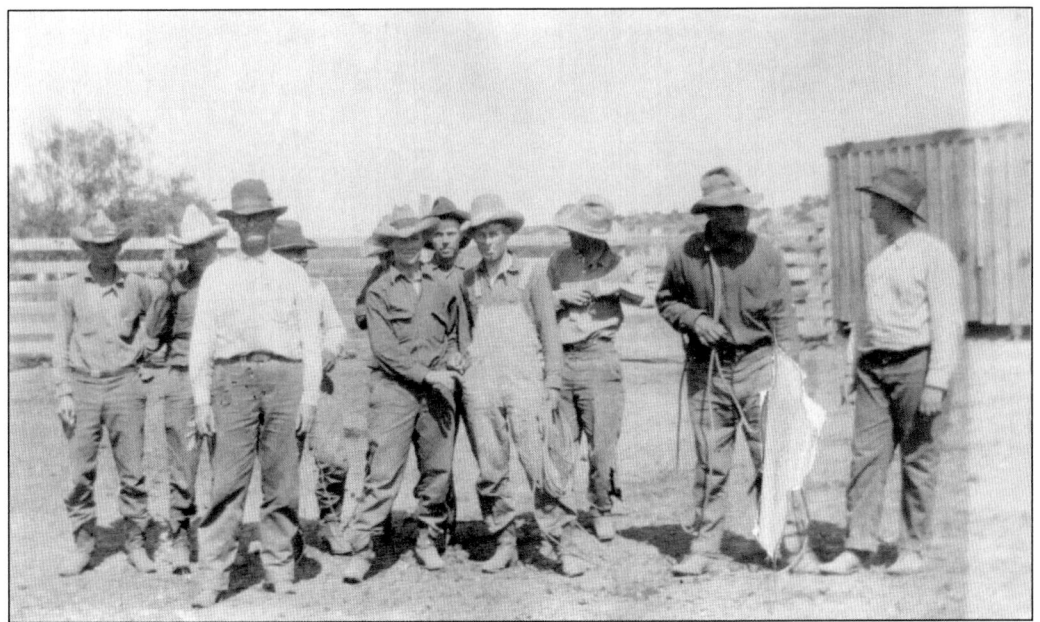

Ellison Tom Sr. and his new bride, Mattie, arrived in Andrews in 1924 to manage the newly acquired J. S. Means Ranch. In 1950, Ellison Tom Jr. returned to Andrews with his wife, Billie, to become the third generation of Toms to ranch in Andrews. In this group picture, taken sometime in the 1930s, Ellison Tom Sr., appears to be dumping ashes into a cowhand's pocket in a lighthearted gesture.

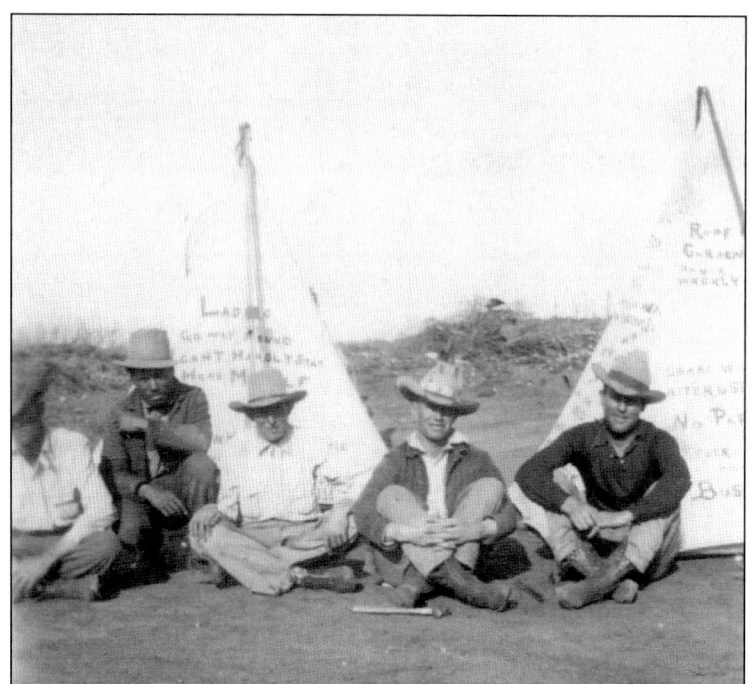

Ellison Tom Sr. began ranching in Andrews County in 1924 on land that was formerly the Means Ranch northeast of Andrews, established in 1899. The ranch was operated by Ellison Tom Sr. and Ellison "Sonny" Tom Jr. and, thereafter, by Sonny's son, the late Bill Tom. This picture shows Ellison Tom Sr., third from left, seated with ranch hands in front of teepees out on the range.

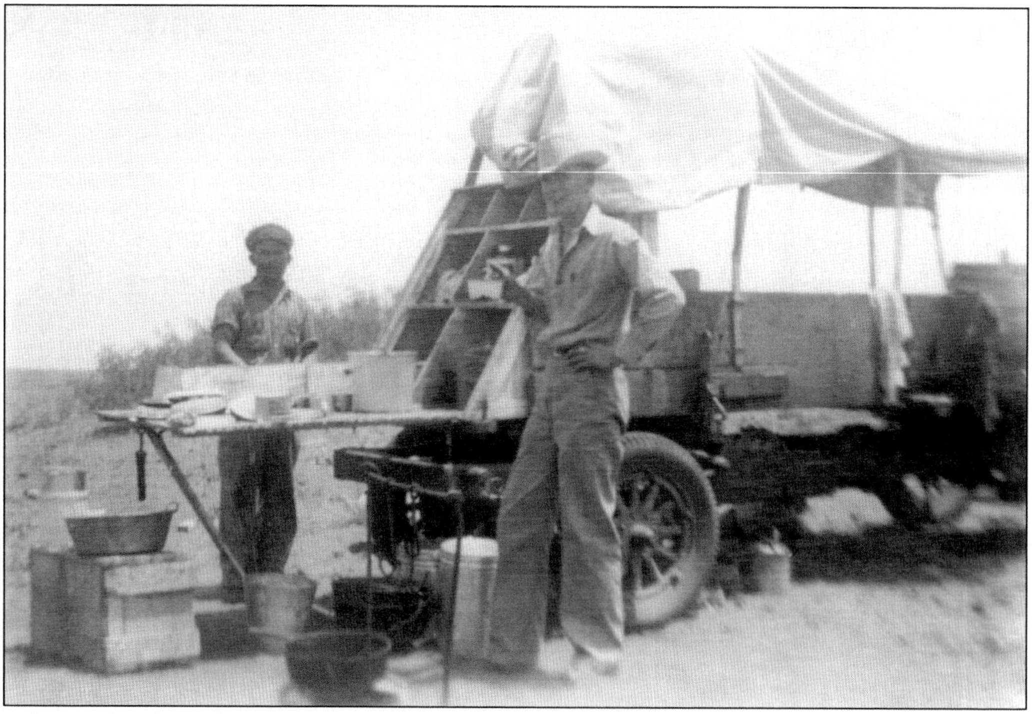

Taking a break at the chuck wagon is Ellison Tom Sr. with cook Joe Munoz on a trail drive to Seagraves. During their time on the ranch, the elder Toms recalled bad sandstorms that sometimes blew down telephone lines. Since repairmen were few, the lines were often repaired by ranchers, who strung them along barbed-wire fences until telephone repairmen arrived to fix the problem.

Shown in this photograph with Bill Tom, top left, and his father, Ellison "Sonny" Tom Jr., far right, is another longtime Andrews rancher, Bill Wyche Jr. The Wyches ranched in the southwestern area of the county for many years. Bill Wyche Sr. initially came to the county in 1914 working for W. F. Cowden.

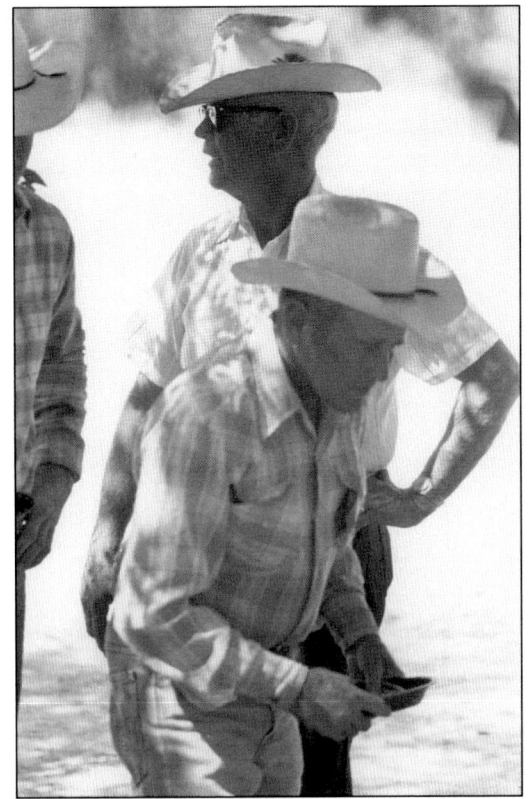

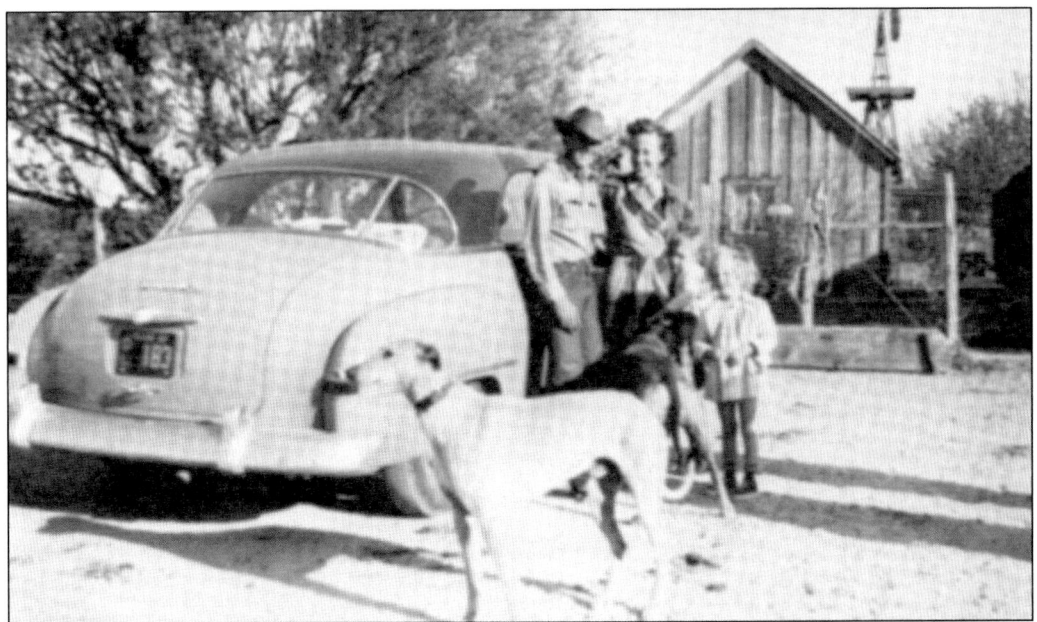

Bill Wyche Jr. and his wife, Ruth, moved to the Wyche Ranch, located 22 miles southwest of town, in 1946 to work for Bill's dad, Bill Wyche Sr. Bill Wyche Jr. had served in the military during World War II. He and Ruth raised three daughters on the ranch, Nancy, Cindy, and Sara. Bill, who was considered an expert in rangeland grasses and conservation, died in 1999.

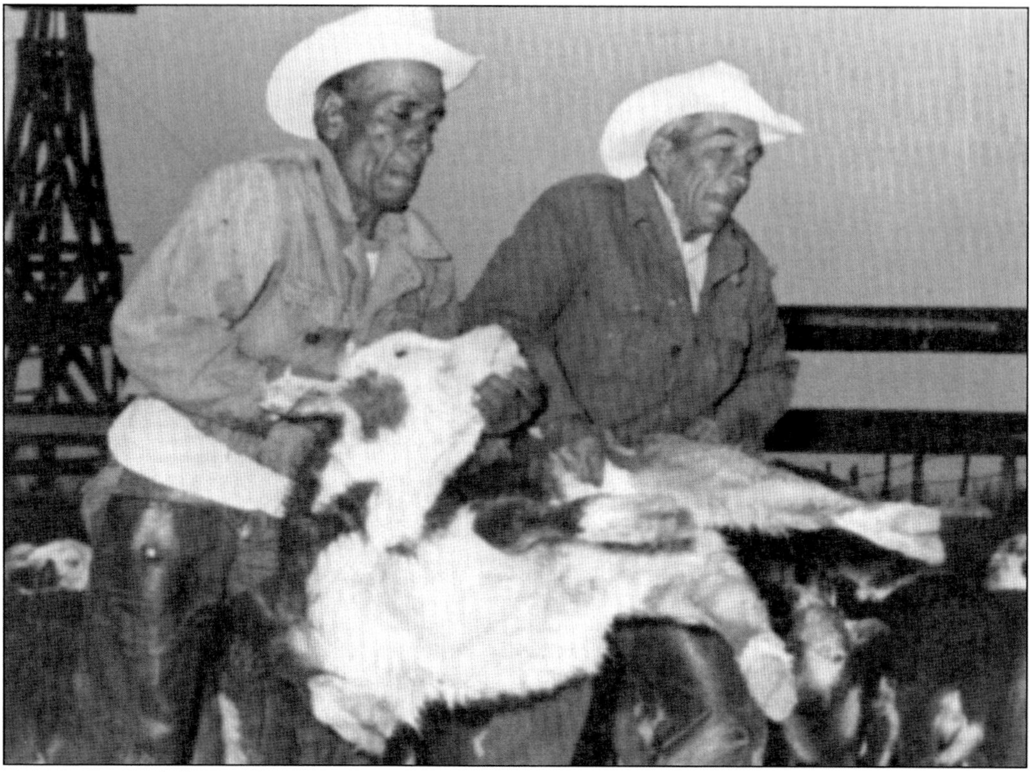

Longtime ranch hands for the Tom family were Alfredo Cordova, left, and Jose Zamora, right, shown here flanking calves. Zamora was born in Mexico and in 1964 was sponsored by Ellison "Sonny" Tom Jr. on an immigrant visa. Zamora's family joined him later in 1966; he raised eight children in Andrews.

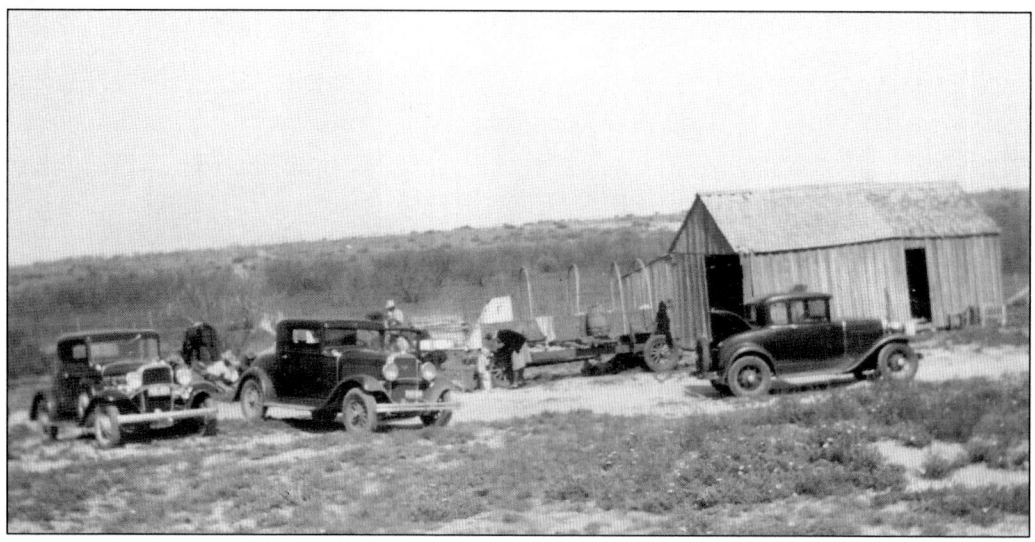

As times progressed, so did ranchers in Andrews County, as shown above with the early model vehicles used to get to a cattle camp on Mustang Draw in northern Andrews County. Of course, once at the camp, the cowboys saddled up their horses, which were used the rest of the day. This particular camp was on the Tom Ranch in the early 1930s.

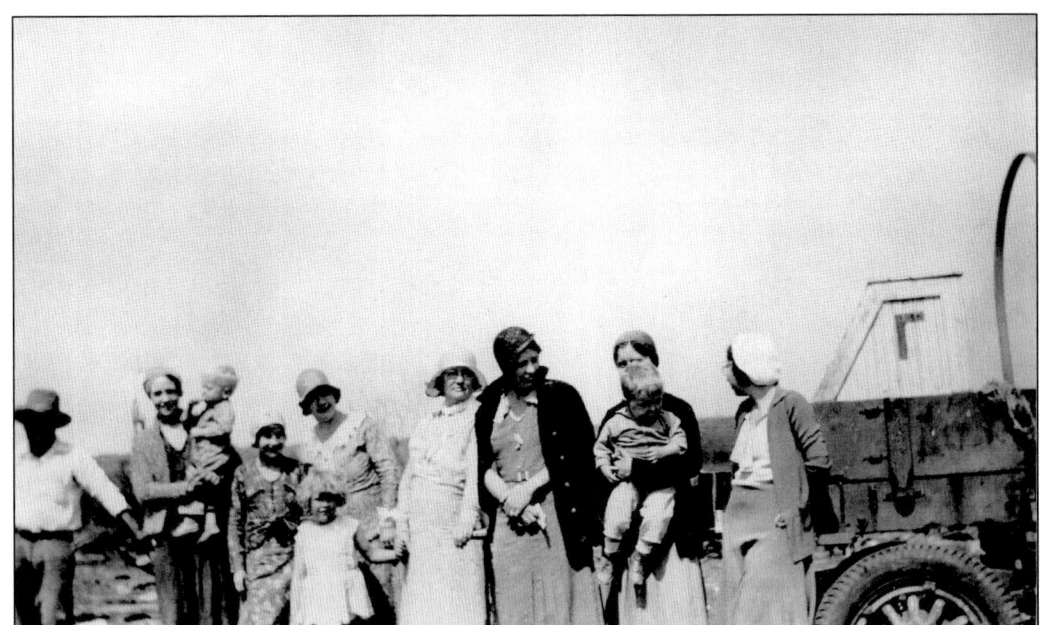

Not every day on the Tom Ranch was a work day; often friends and guests from town would arrive for a barbecue at the ranch hosted by the Toms. This picture was taken in the 1920s as the women and children visit a campsite and inspect the chuck wagon. The chuck wagon shows the Tom's brand, the reverse seven, on the side.

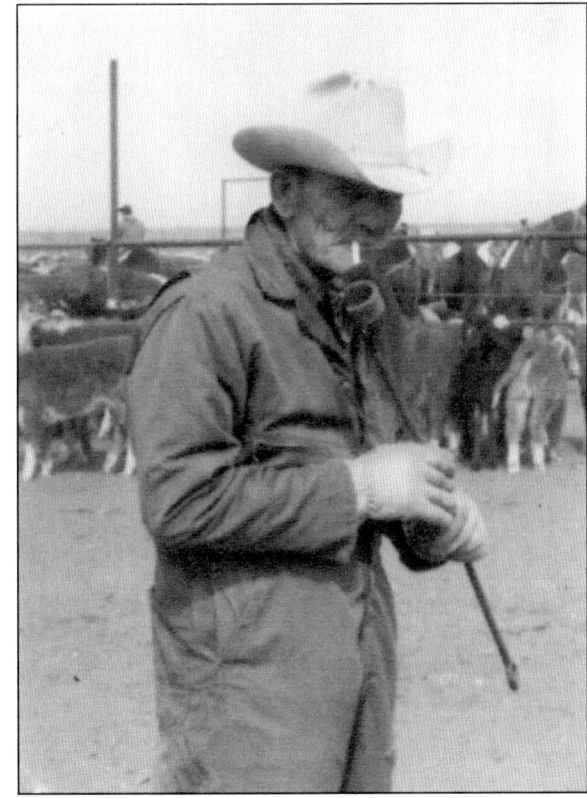

Lighting a cigarette with a branding iron in the 1960s is Bill Price, who worked most of his life ranching in Andrews County. Price was born in Andrews on April 12, 1926, to Charles W. Price and Hazel Price. Besides working on ranches, he also drilled water wells. He and his wife, Hedy, had four children, Charles Winston "Little Bill" Jr., Karla Marie, Stephanie Kay, and Hermann Claude.

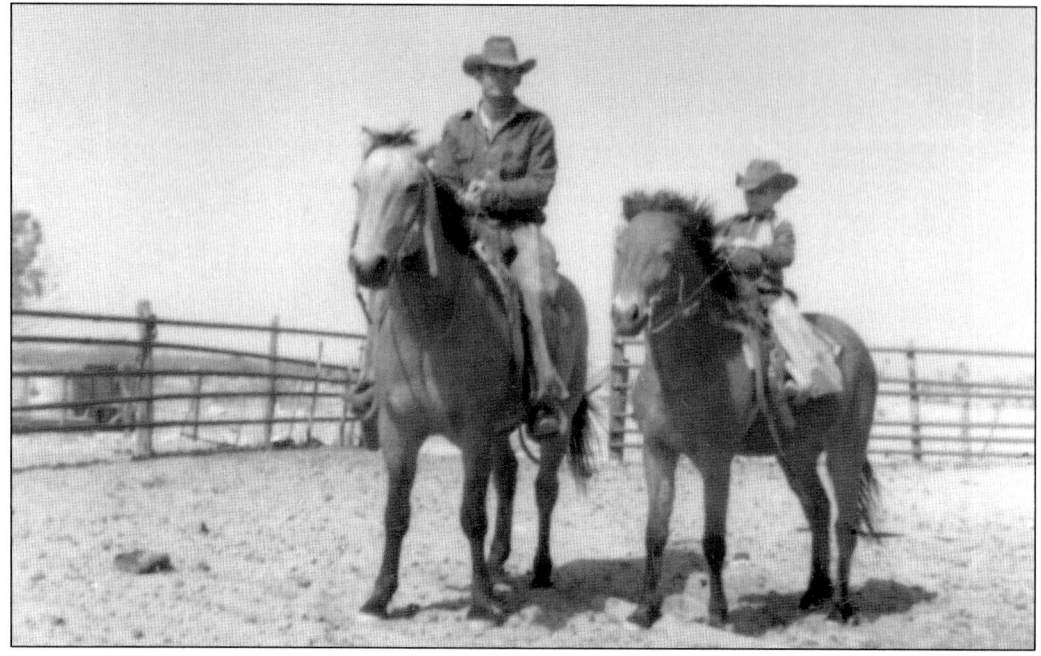

The Bill Price family was involved in ranching for more than 50 years. Bill Sr. worked on various ranches early on in his career as a cowhand and rancher. Following a stint in the army during World War II, he returned home to continue cowboying and working at his own ranch. Pictured above, Bill Sr. and a very young Bill Jr. handle cattle at the ranch.

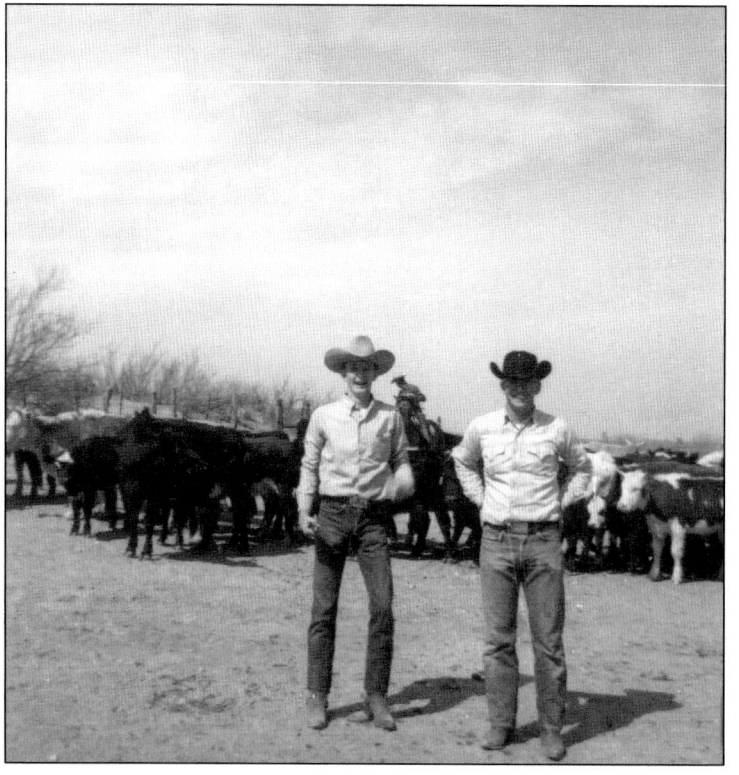

Andrews native Doug Irwin, left, was born in Andrews County to Gene and Virginia Irwin, a longtime ranching family. Doug's grandfather, Hunter Irwin, was a pioneer rancher in the county, moving to Andrews in 1911. He bought land at Shafter Lake and the home and ranch has remained in the Irwin family ever since. Doug carried on the ranching tradition for the Irwins following the death of his father.

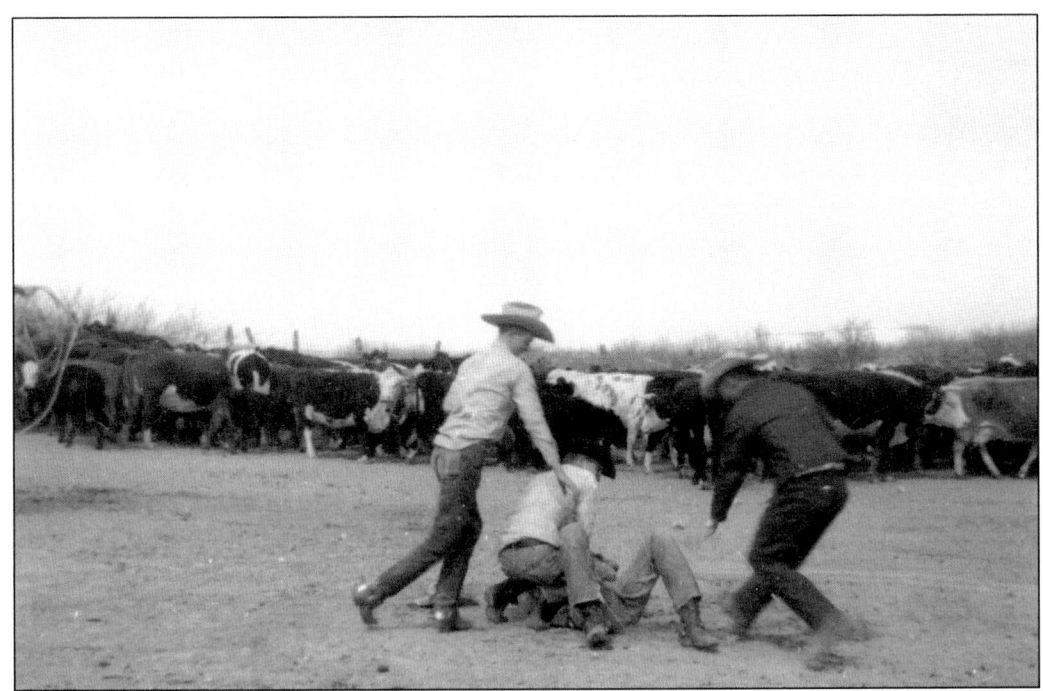

Andrews native Doug Irwin has worked on his family's ranch at Shafter Lake since adolescence, growing up watching his father, Gene Irwin, and grandfather, pioneer rancher Hunter Irwin, work the family spread. Doug graduated from Andrews High School in 1969, and following college at Sul Ross University in Alpine, returned to help run the ranch. Pictured here, Doug participates in a little roughhousing with other cowboys at Price Ranch.

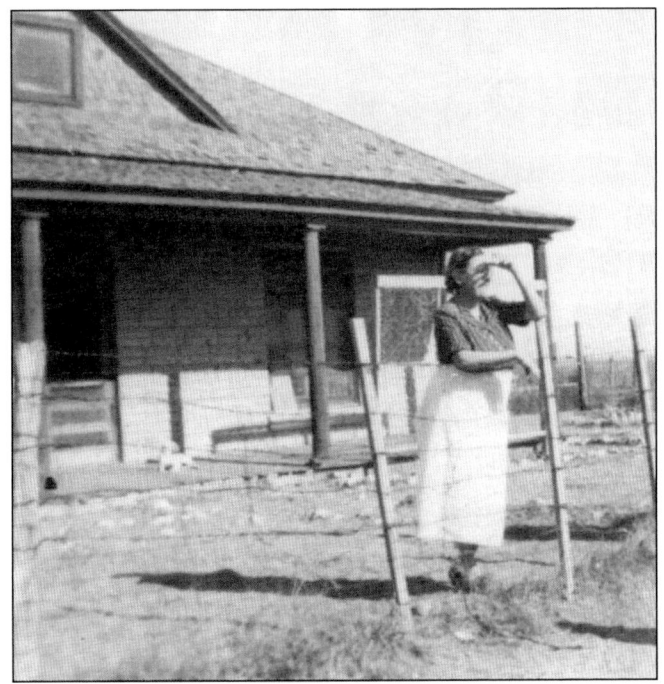

Hunter and Lee Irwin were pioneer residents of Andrews County and lived at Shafter Lake until their deaths in the 1960s. Hunter served as postmaster of Shafter Lake and later as county commissioner of Andrews County precinct No. 2 for 12 years. Lee served on the school board at Shafter Lake until the school district consolidated with the Andrews school system. Their son, Gene, eventually ran the family ranch.

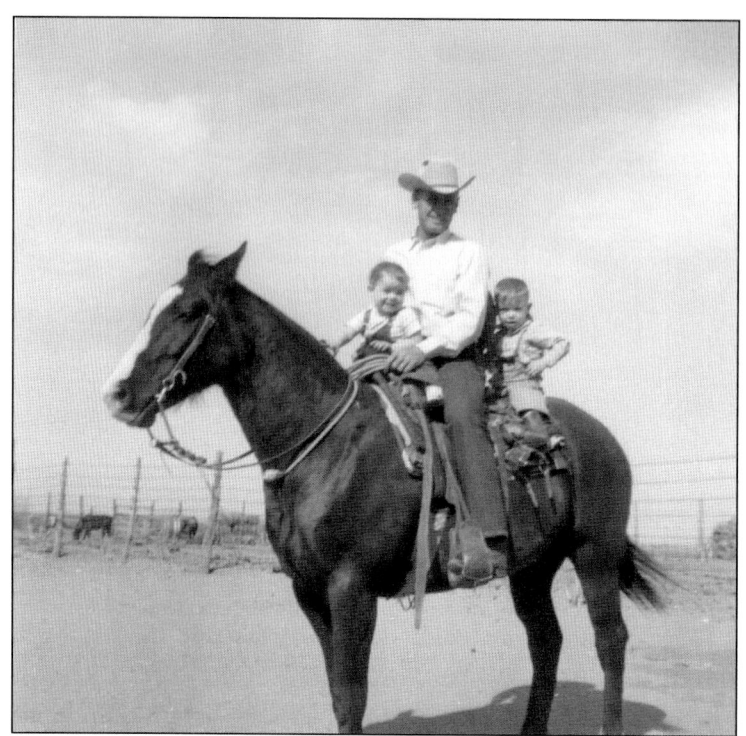

Marvin Fisher Jr. and his wife, Earlene, raised two children, Dan and Jan, on the Fisher Ranch in northern Andrews County. Marvin Jr. took the reins of the ranch from his father, M. M. Fisher Sr., who was a longtime Andrews rancher. Shown on the horse with Marvin Jr. are Jan in front and Dan at the rear. Dan, who graduated from Andrews High School in 1969, now manages the ranch.

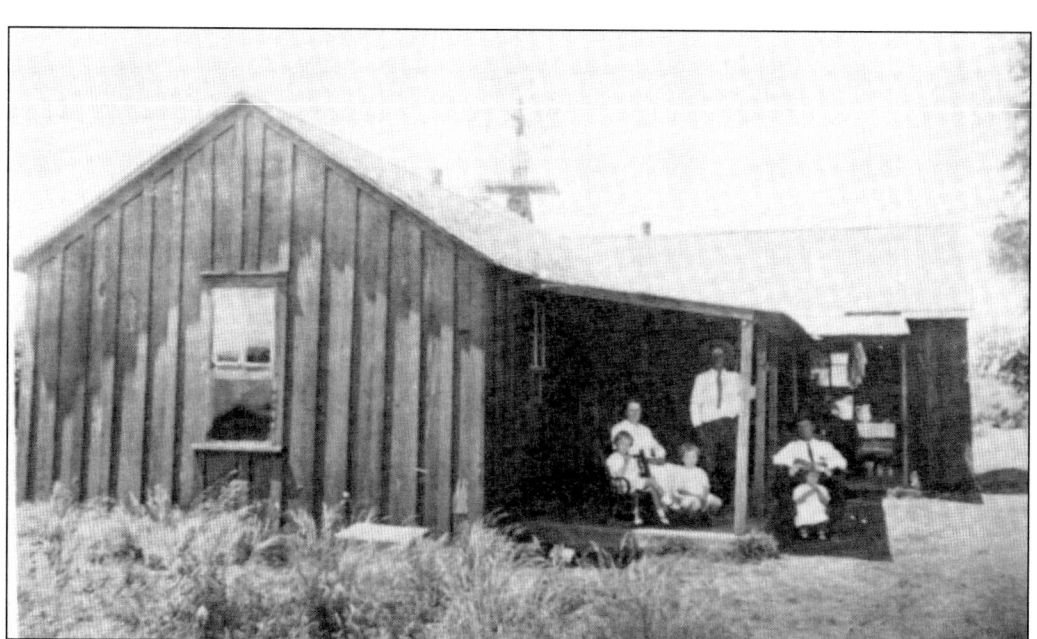

The –F Ranch, known later as the Ratliff and Bedford Ranch, in southwest Andrews, Winkler, and Ector counties had its beginnings when George Ratliff homesteaded in those counties in 1904. He married Annie Bedford in 1906, and she joined him on the ranch. For a number of years, children from the Wyche and Cowden ranches rode horseback to the –F Ranch to attend school taught by a daughter of the Ratliffs', Frances Blevins.

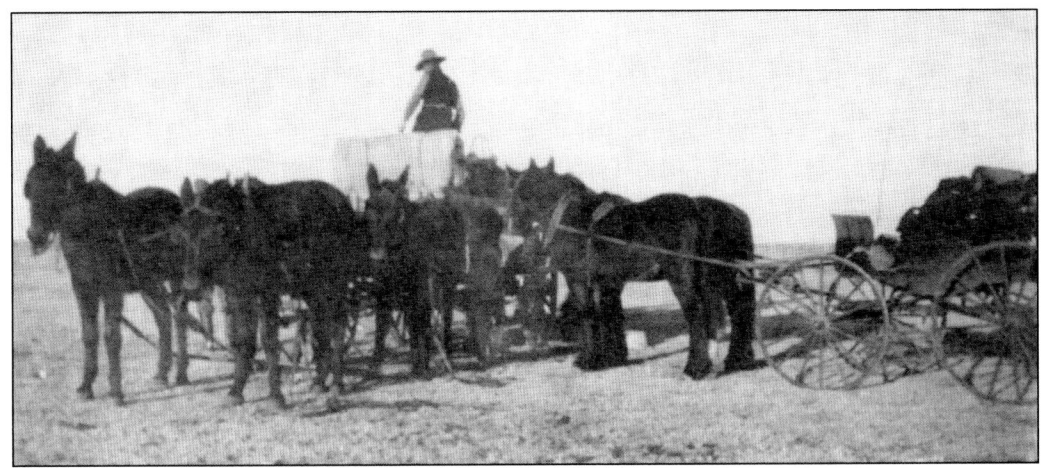

Because of the remoteness of Andrews County, freight had to be hauled in by wagons from Midland and Odessa. This was not easy because of the sandy terrain, which made a round-trip take a week. Freighters traveled in pairs or more in case one got stuck in the sand; they could unhitch one set of mules or horses and use them to pull the team out of the sand.

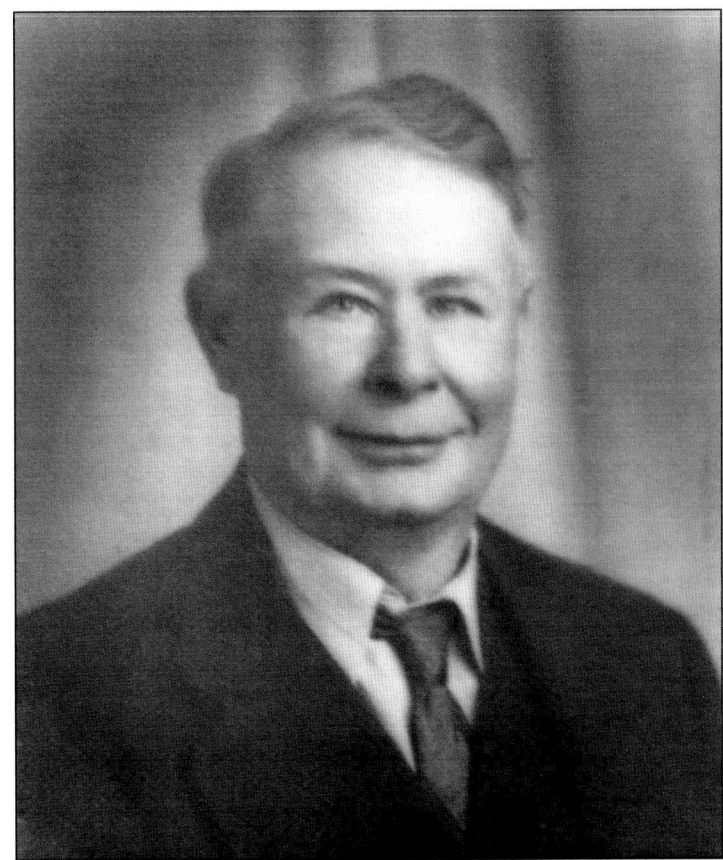

T. W. Craddock was one of the original organizers of Andrews, moving to the county in 1902 with his wife, Daisy. He was elected the first sheriff in 1910 when the county was organized and Andrews was named the county seat. He also served as tax collector, along with being sheriff, and served many years as a school trustee. Daisy helped organize the First Methodist Church. (Courtesy Mark Hooper.)

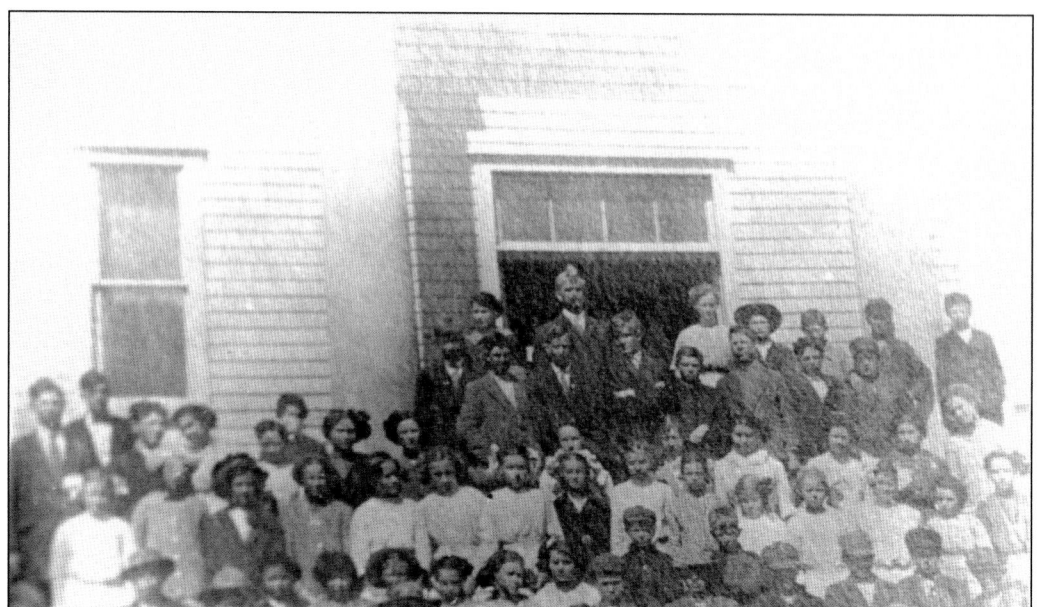

This photograph from around 1913 shows a large group of students as Andrews began to attract more students after being selected the county seat. The first school was in the Methodist church, which is believed to be the structure pictured here. Over time, more of the smaller school districts began to close as the population of Andrews grew and more businesses opened.

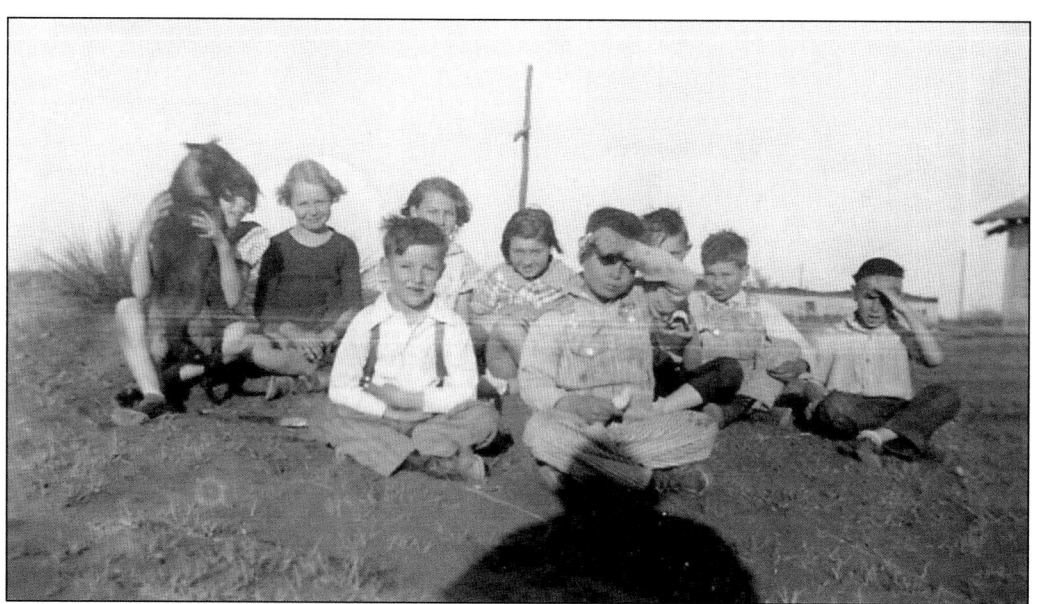

This picture shows a group of students posing for a photograph in the late afternoon. Note the first student holding onto a dog while other students shield their eyes from the glaring sun. The lateness of the day is also reflected in the long shadow of the photographer. (Courtesy Mark Hooper.)

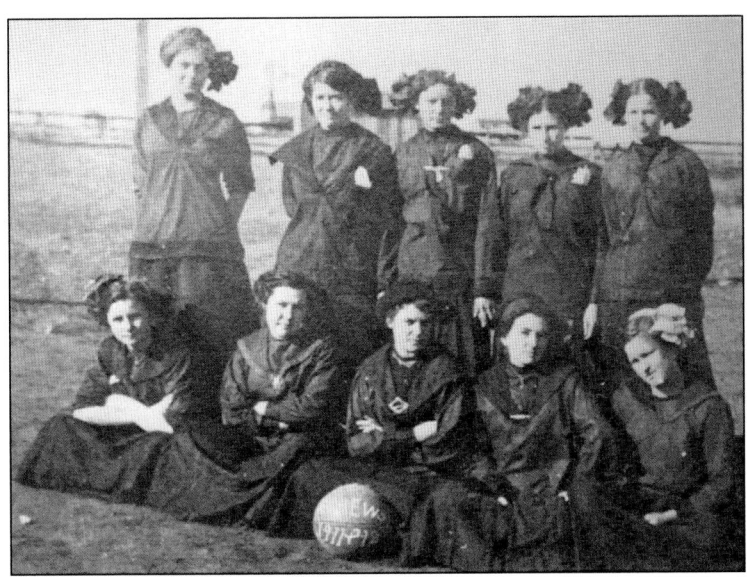

This photograph shows the dress attire of young women participating in sporting events during the early days of schooling in Andrews. Pictured are, in no particular order, (first row) Fern Mathis, Edna Collins Hague, unidentified, Lurlene Wilder Sealy, and unidentified; (second row) unidentified, Jenny Carr, Carrie Mae Rhodes Holloway, Rebecca Thornberry, and Lillie Mae Knight Dunn.

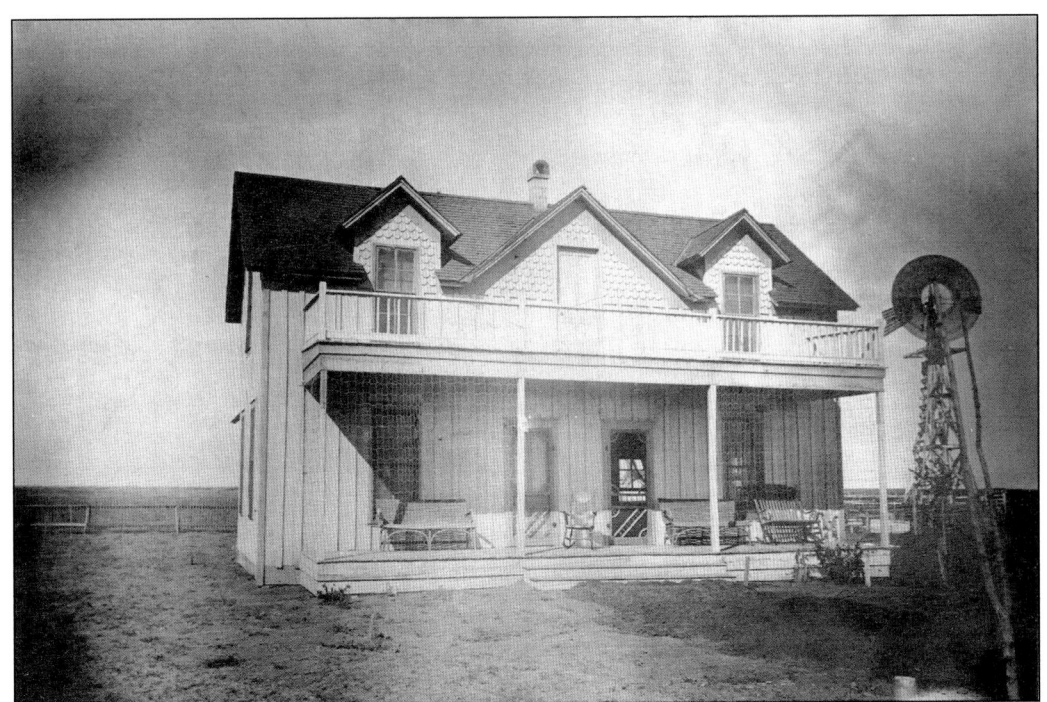

Smith E. and Delma Horn Umberson's home in Andrews was located at North Main and Northeast Avenue G. The Umbersons moved to Andrews in 1907 and farmed before Smith was elected as county treasurer, tax assessor, and county judge. His other previous occupations included hauling freight by wagon from Midland to Andrews and Florey and real estate. (Courtesy Mark Hooper.)

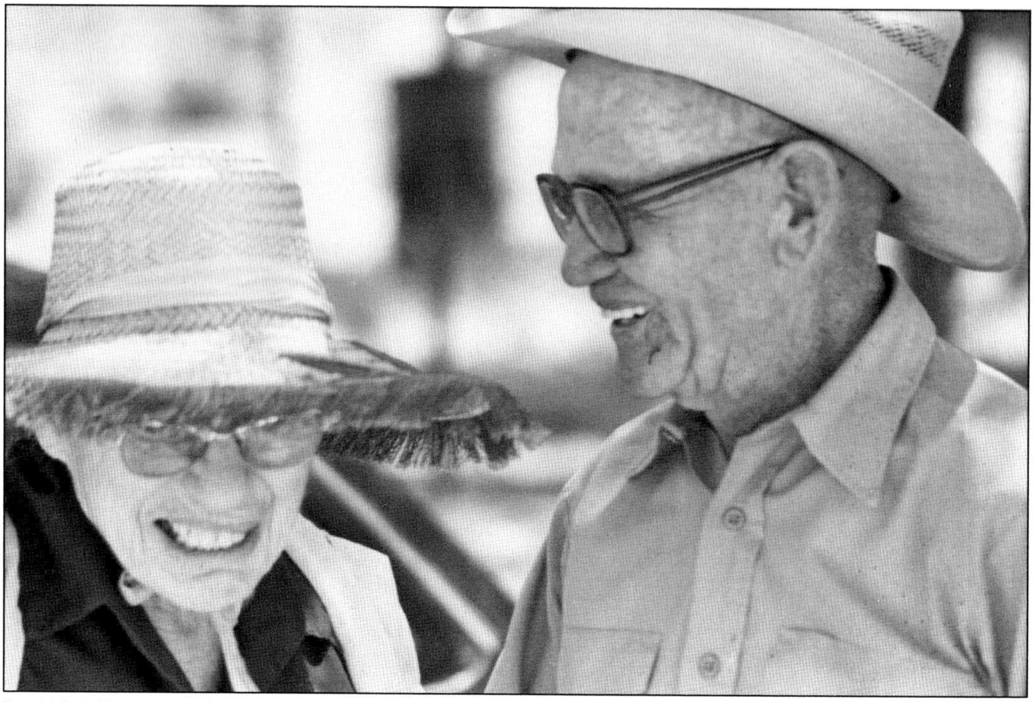

In 1936, Emma and Conner Sutphen moved to Andrews from Mitchell County to work for the Ellison Tom Ranch where Conner did mostly fence work but also helped as a chuck wagon cook. Emma, pictured left, visits with Ellison Tom Sr. She cooked at the first hospital in Andrews for a while and afterwards cooked for the school district, where she remained for 20 years.

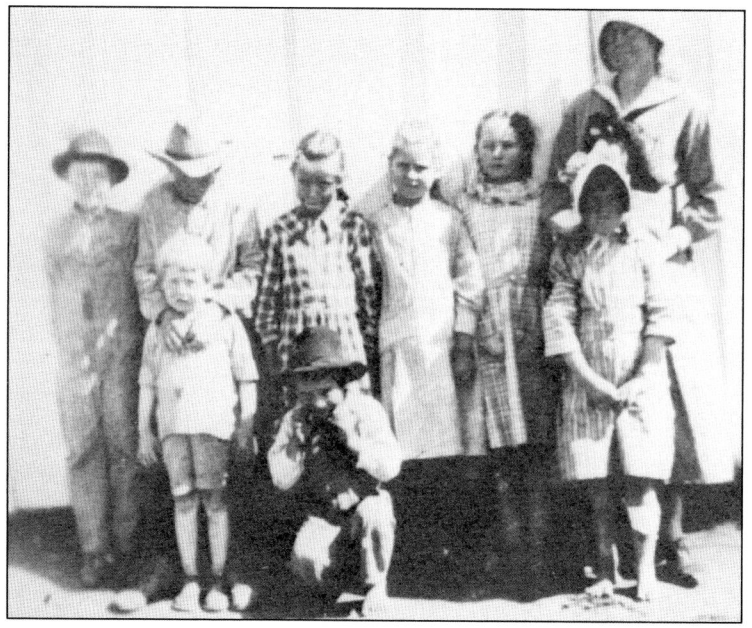

Located on the northeast Andrews County line, Florey was first settled around 1903. A school was started there in 1908 when A. J. Florey and his wife arrived. Mrs. Florey was a teacher. After collecting donations, the men in the community built the school, which was also used as a church. Included in the picture are Ben Kelton, Bill Howell, Truman Howell, Lucille and Avis Johnson, Ben Florey, and Carrie Florey.

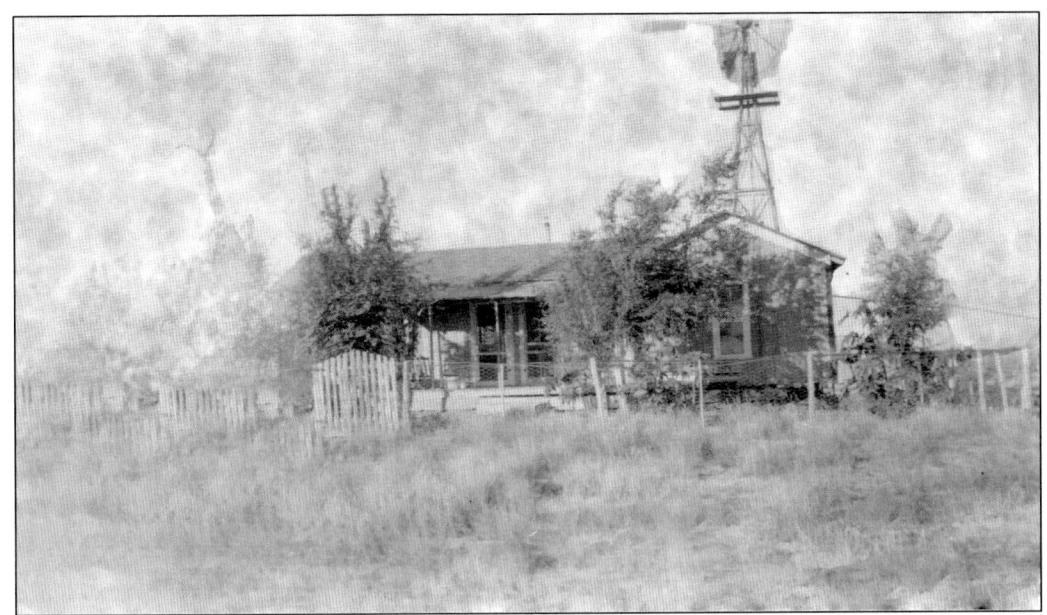

An early ranch in far western Andrews County belonged to the C. W. Post family. Post married Lou Edd Eriksen in 1914; her family had owned the ranch since 1908. The Posts had three children, Zonelle, Charles W. Jr., and John Edward, the latter of which began managing the ranch in 1954. He married Hazel Ruth Schneider that same year.

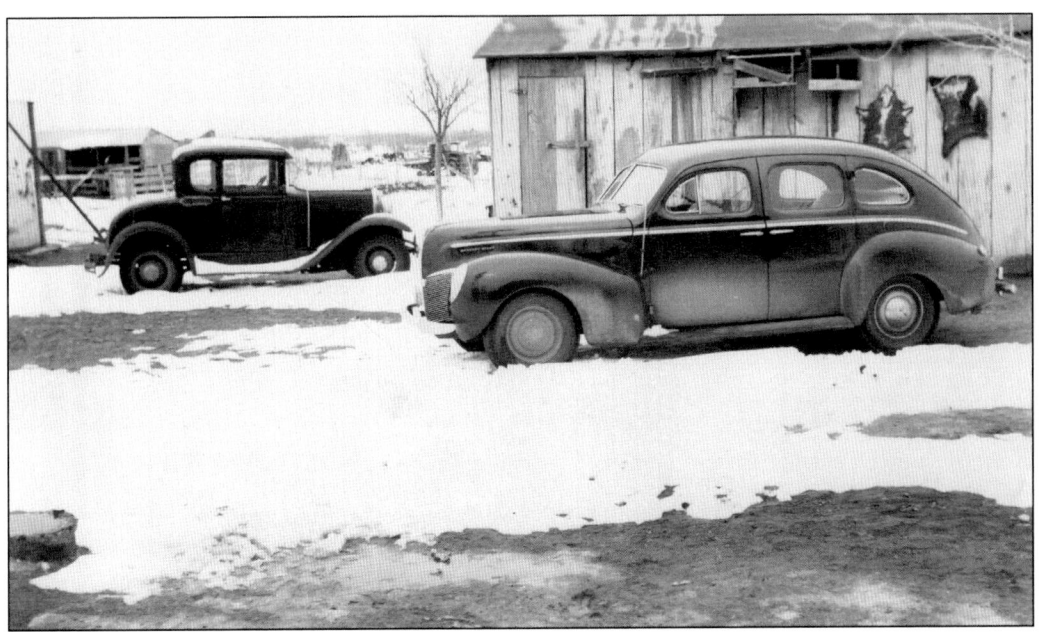

The Post Ranch in 1940 was located 25 miles west of Andrews near the New Mexico state line. Because of its proximity, the Post children attended school in Jal, New Mexico. John and Hazel Post operated the ranch after acquiring it from John's father, C. W. Post. They also acquired the C. D. Woolworth Heirs' Ranch in Lea County, New Mexico. John and Hazel had two children, John Edward Jr. and David Allen.

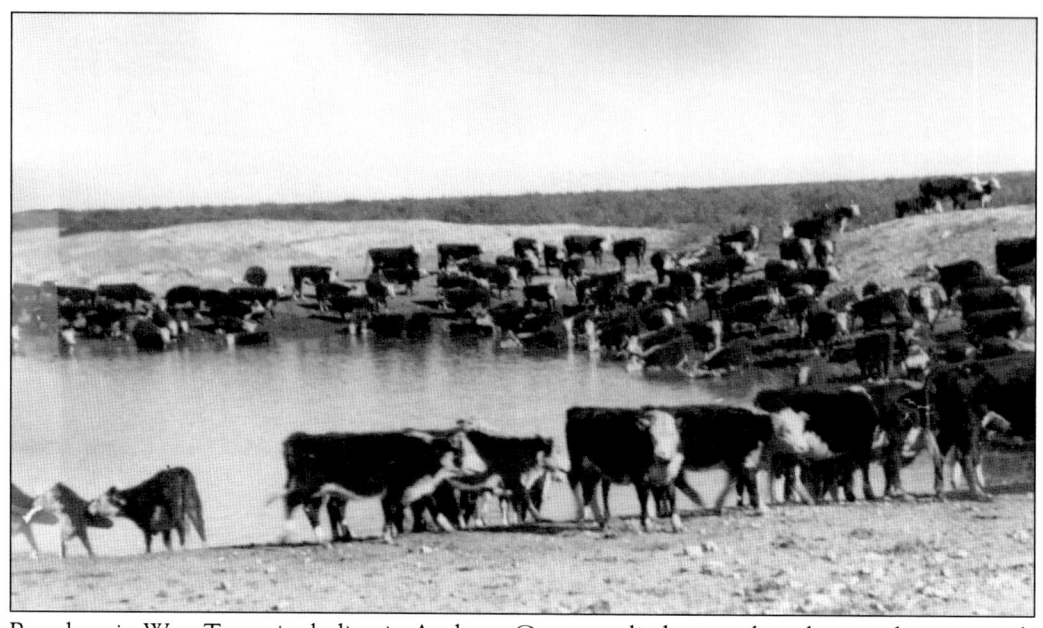

Ranchers in West Texas, including in Andrews County, relied on stock tanks or gathering ponds for supplying water to their livestock. The annual rainfall in West Texas and Andrews County is around 14 inches, which makes providing feed and water challenging. Pictured above is a stock tank on the Post Ranch in western Andrews County. The Post family has operated the ranch since the early 1930s.

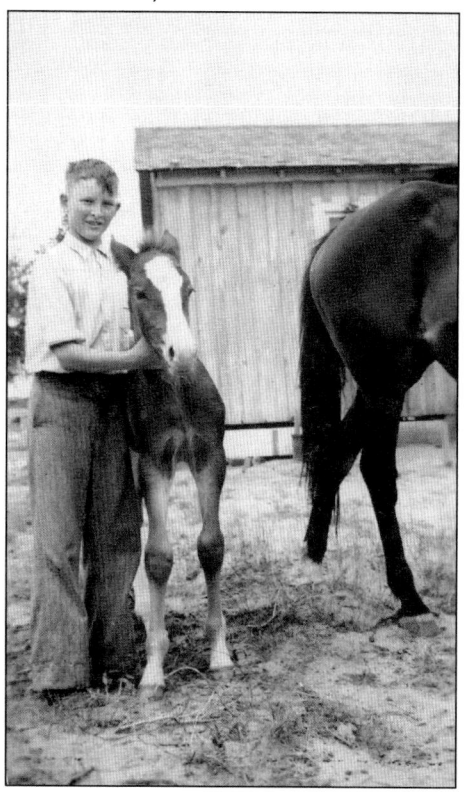

John Post began his ranching days in the 1930s, after his father and mother acquired the ranch from Lou Edd Post's family, the Eriksons, who had purchased the ranch in 1908. Because of the lengthy distance to Andrews, John and his brother, C. W. Jr., attended school in Jal, New Mexico. Here a young John shows off a colt.

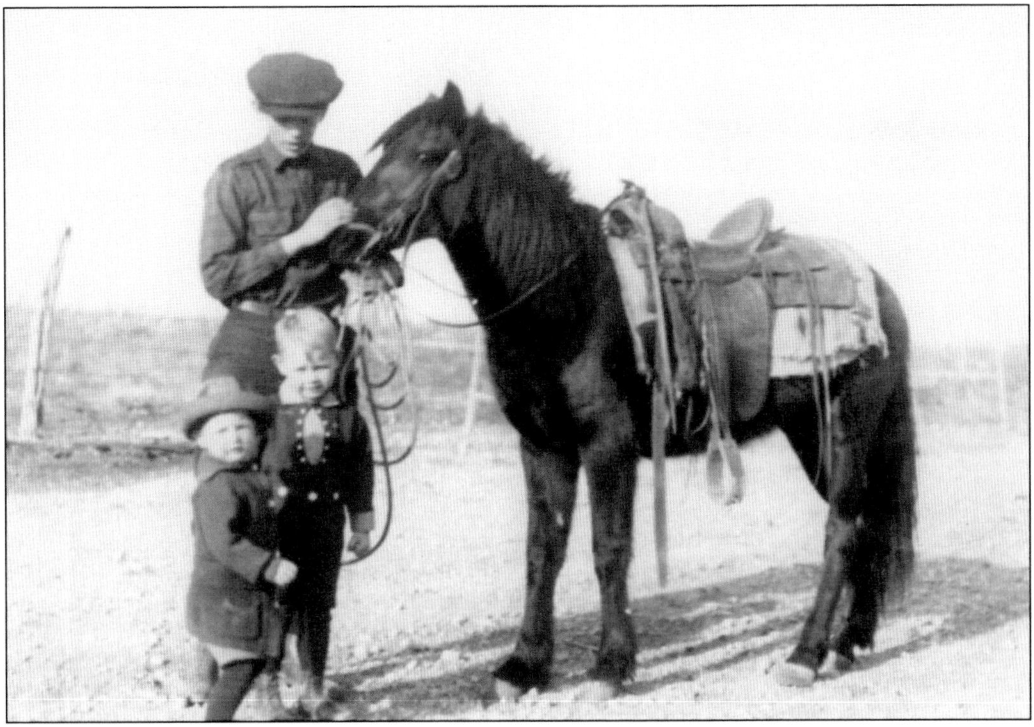

Pictured above is Jackson Parker with John E. and Charles Post Jr. seeing to Topaz, a half Shetland pony that had been given to them by the Post children's grandparents, Edward A. and Mary A. Erikson. The picture was taken on a farm south of Midland.

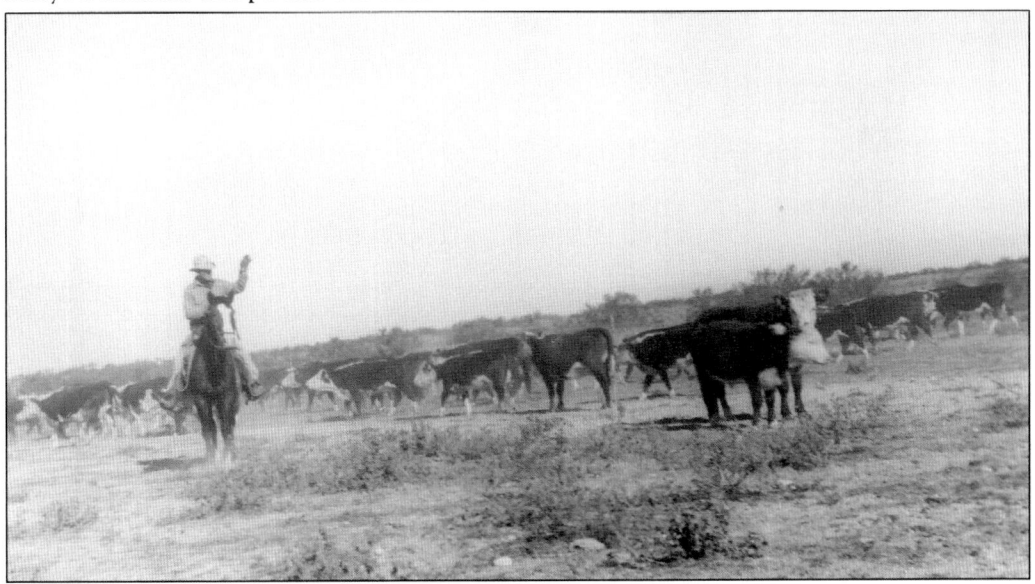

Taken in 1944, this photograph of Jack Mounts, a cowboy for the Post Ranch, works cattle at the Adobe Ranch where C. W. Post had leased the rangeland to graze his cattle. Mounts was considered an "old-style" cowboy who rode his horse everywhere, including into Andrews, and as far away as Midland. He worked his entire life as a cowboy and never had a driver's license or owned a car.

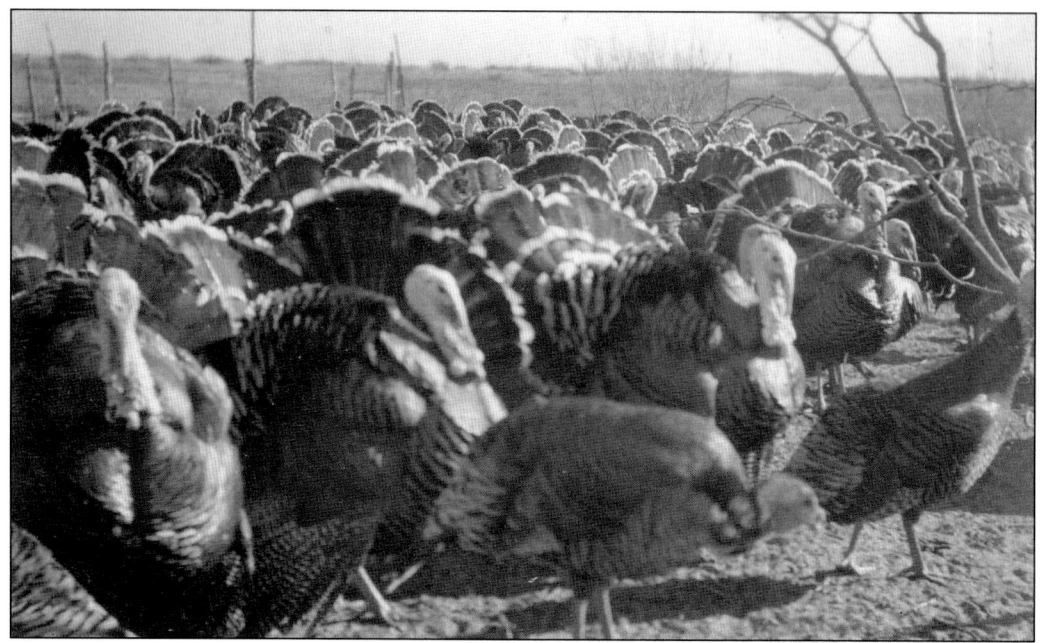

While cattle and horses were the main elements of livestock raised on ranches in West Texas, the Post Ranch in far western Andrews County had a large gathering of turkeys in 1941. Lou Edd Post raised more than 600 turkeys, which, besides vegetation, also feasted on acorns from shinnery oaks and grasshoppers. This large flock of turkeys was herded on horseback and followed acorns dropped by the riders.

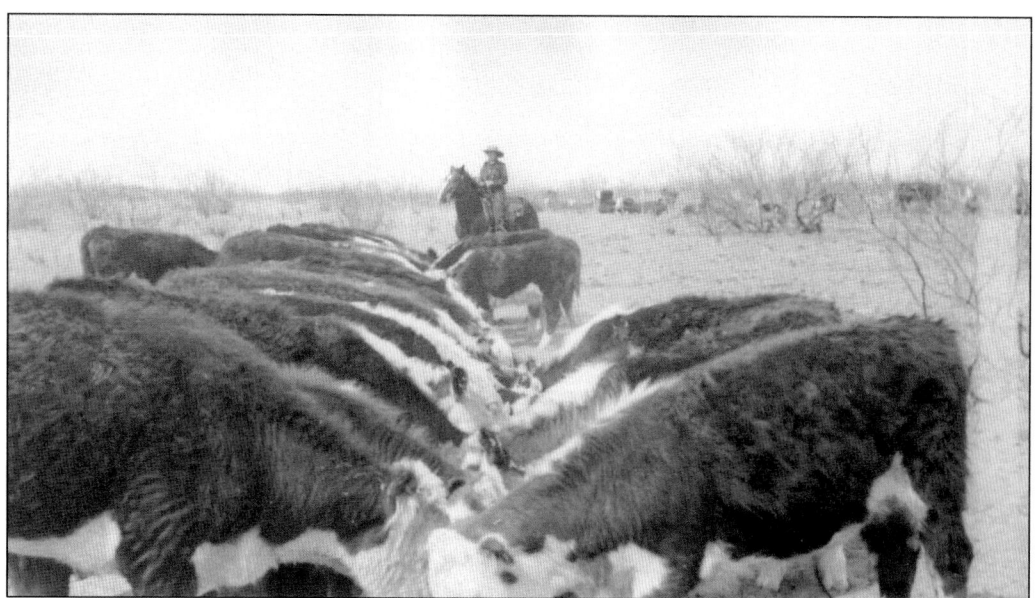

Everyone did their part on the Post Ranch in western Andrews County. With a large ranch and plenty to do, sometimes Lou Edd Post helped round up cattle at feeding time. Ranching is known for being a rigorous, outdoors occupation with most ranch families involving everyone in the family in one manner or another.

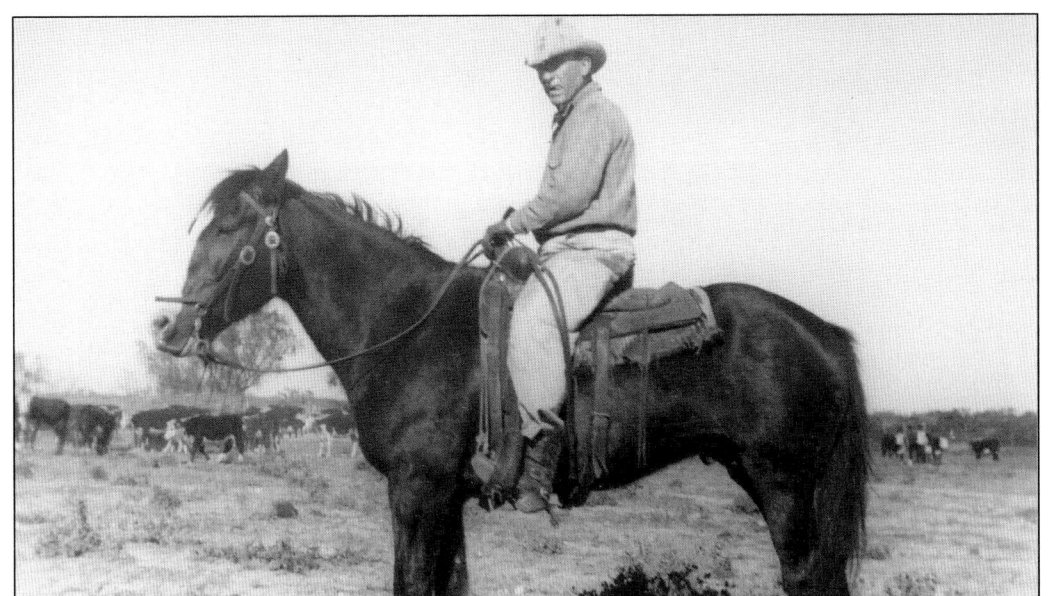

Jack Mounts was a lifelong cowboy who worked on the Post Ranch in western Andrews County. Mounts's means of transportation everywhere was his horse, which he rode to town sometimes on his days off. The ride to Andrews was 25 miles, 50 miles to Midland, but Jal or Eunice, New Mexico, were nearer.

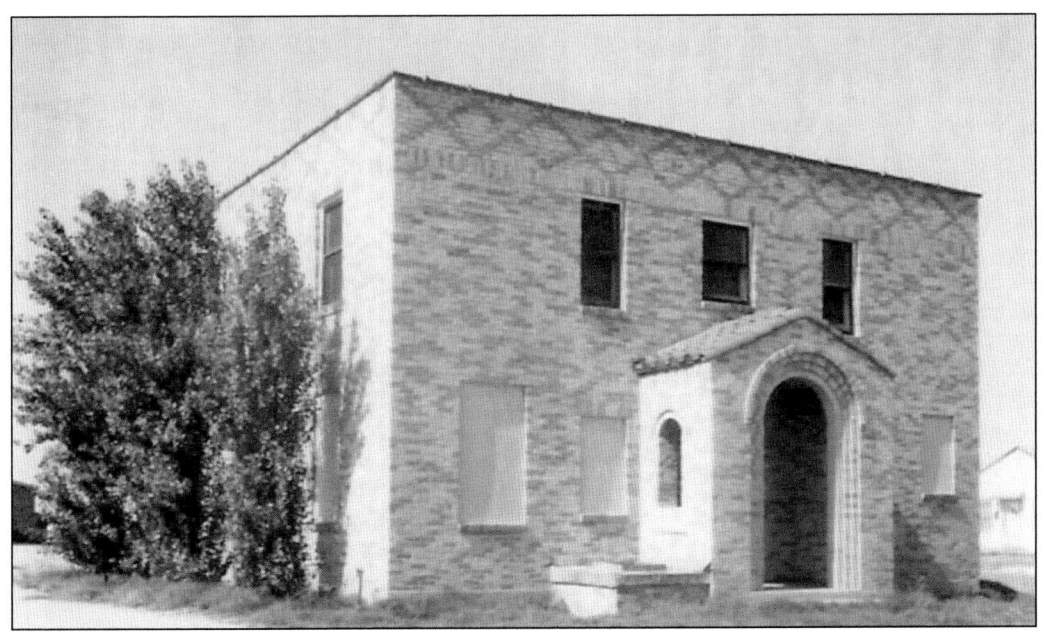

In 1930, Andrews County constructed a permanent jail and records room near the first courthouse located today behind the Andrews Chamber of Commerce. The facility was used until the second courthouse was constructed in 1940 on North Main Street. The old jail was eventually shuttered but remains one of the oldest buildings in town.

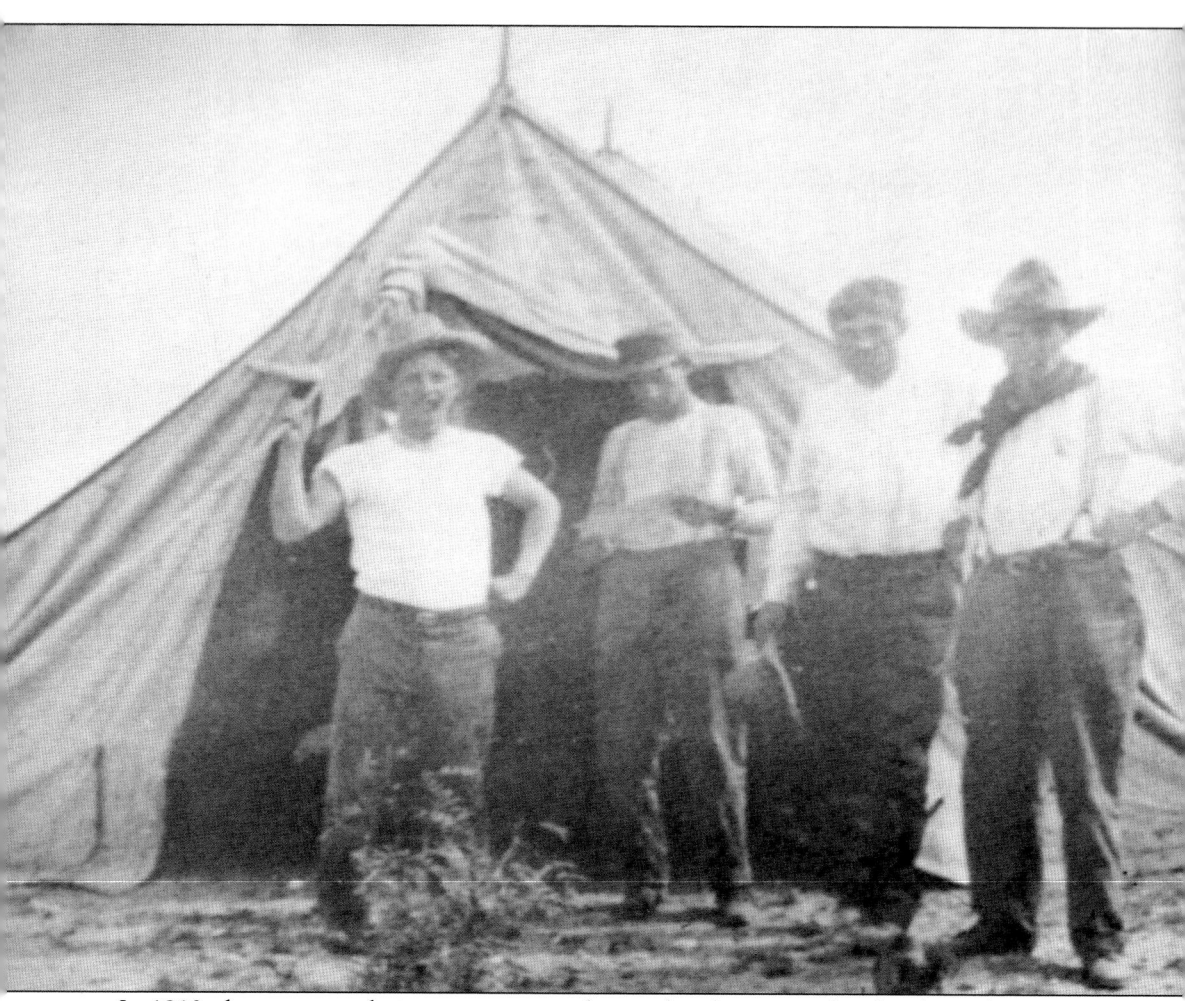

In 1910, the accommodations were sparse during the election to decide where the county seat would be located. A tent on the C-Ranch provided one of the official polling places for residents in eastern Andrews County, which included many cowboys on the C-Ranch and other people on farms. The election was held on July 12, 1910, and Andrews narrowly won the election that resulted in the county seat being closer to Midland and Martin counties, where most residents obtained many of their supplies, including building materials. It is believed that R. M. "Bob" Means and the Andrews Township Company had a major role in Andrews winning the election by giving away lots in town. This resulted after Means was turned away from Shafter Lake after missing a deadline to register for the election after his wagon broke down. He promptly went back to Andrews and began campaigning in earnest for that community. Pictured are election officers, including Johnny Abers, Jack Childress, H. W. Cross, and J. W. Yeakle.

Two

BOOM AND BUST

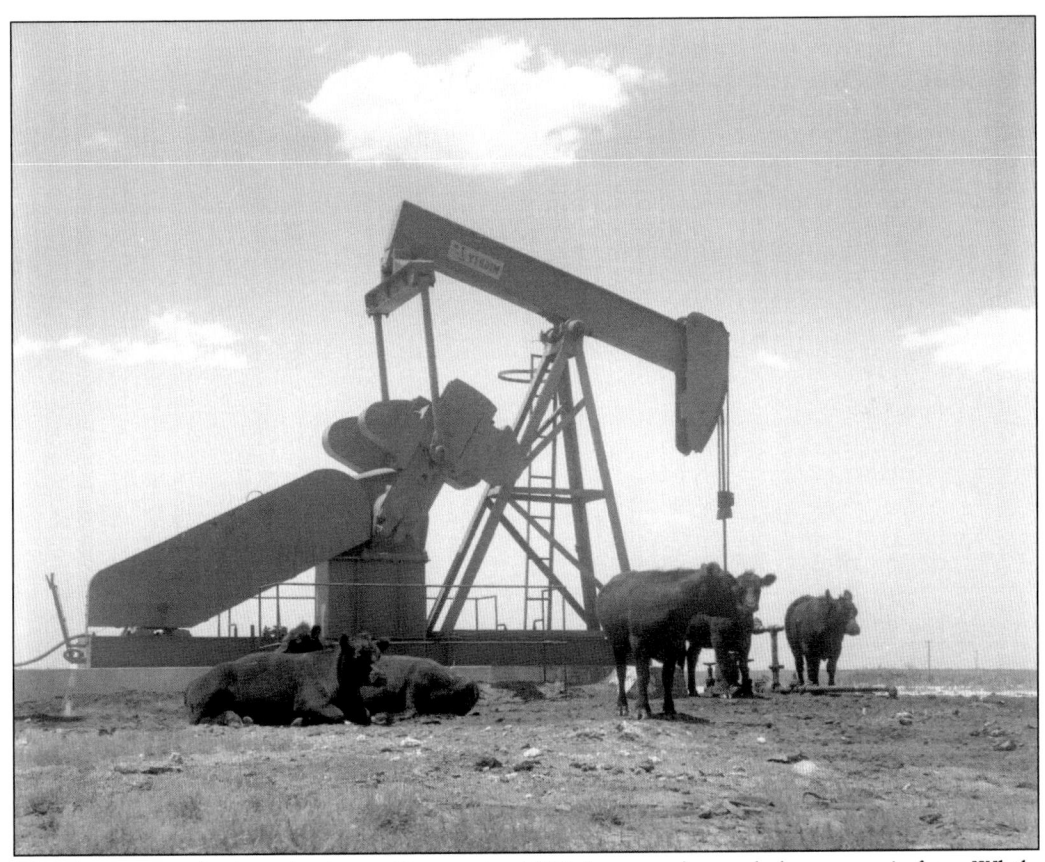

The discovery of oil in Andrews County in 1929 forever changed the county's fate. While ranching and farming continued to play a role in the development of the county, the exploration of oil, its production, and numerous other services—not to mention the hundreds, if not thousands, of employees associated with mining the mineral—meant steady jobs for county residents for more than 80 years.

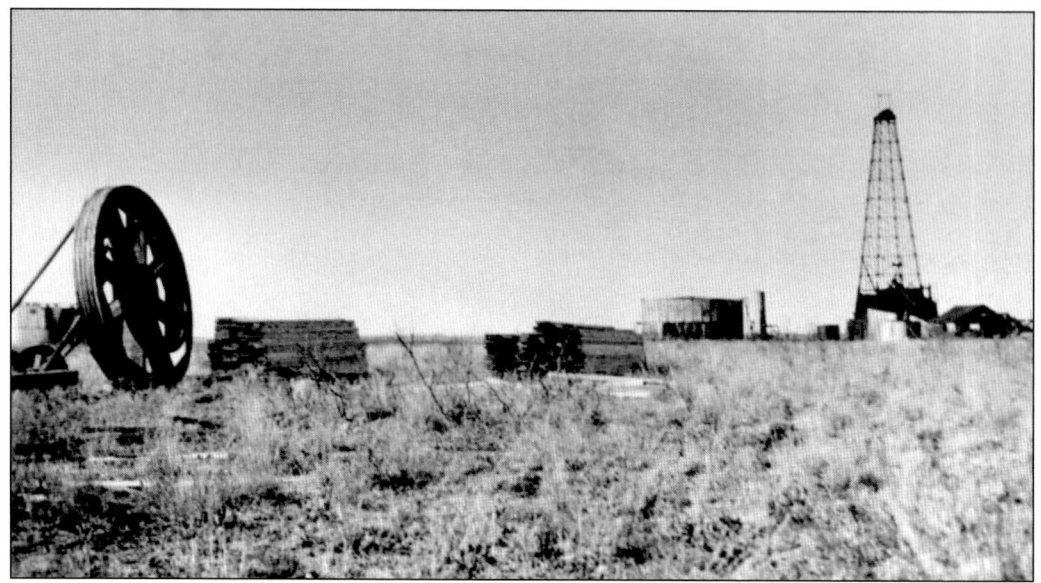

Hundreds of oil company scouts descended on the site just southwest of Andrews in December 1929 when the Deep Rock Oil Company's C. E. Ogden No. 1 Well opened, pumping 200 barrels a day. It continued pumping oil for more than 50 years. Today, Exxon-Mobil, the predecessor of Humble Oil, still has production in Andrews County, along with many other companies. The county has produced more than two billion barrels of oil. (Courtesy Martha Page.)

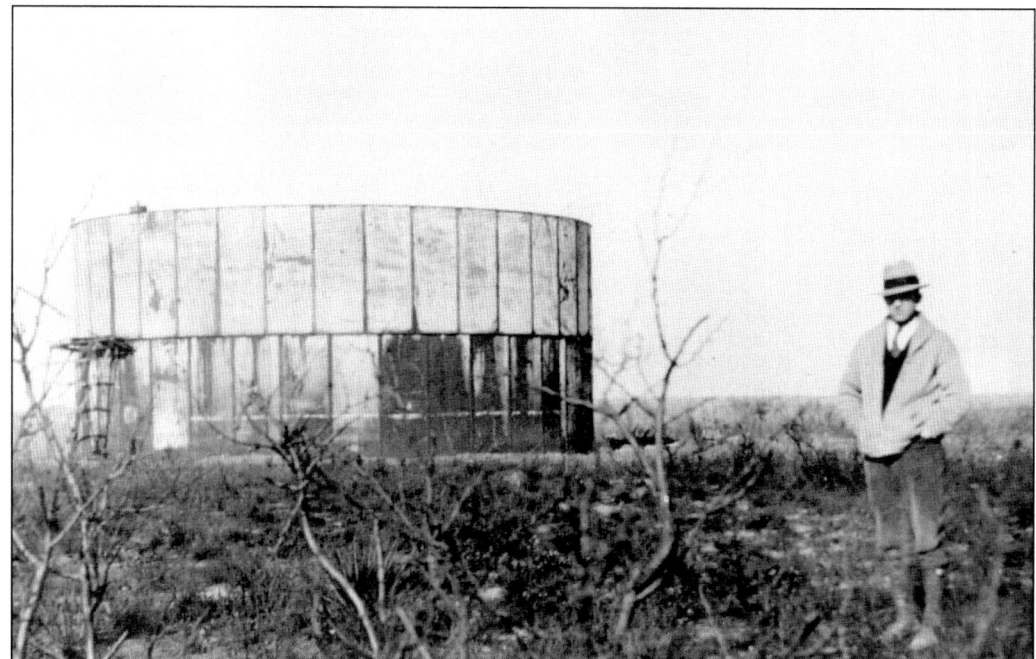

When the Deep Rock Oil Company's C. E. Ogden No. 1 gusher began operating, oil was eventually piped to a large storage tank shown in the photograph with an unknown individual standing in front. Because of low prices, the company had trouble finding buyers and J. W. Tripplehorn of Fort Worth purchased the lease for only $7,000. It was the beginning of a long relationship between Tripplehorn and Andrews County. (Courtesy Martha Page.)

Despite slow beginnings, perhaps due largely to the Great Depression, the C. E. Ogden well was considered a milestone in Andrews County and West Texas. It brought statewide and national interest as well. Humble Oil, the precursor to Exxon-Mobil, extended a pipeline to Andrews County from nearby Ector County in 1934, and once development occurred, it took oil from Andrews County to the larger markets and refineries. (Courtesy Martha Page.)

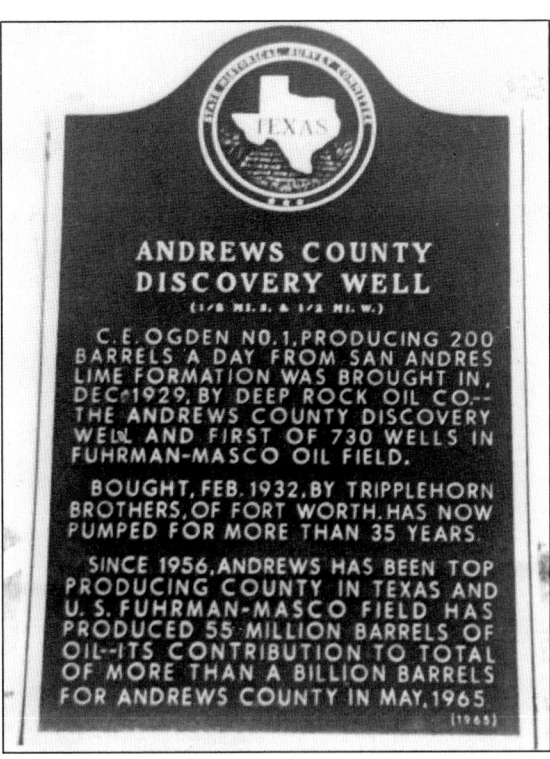

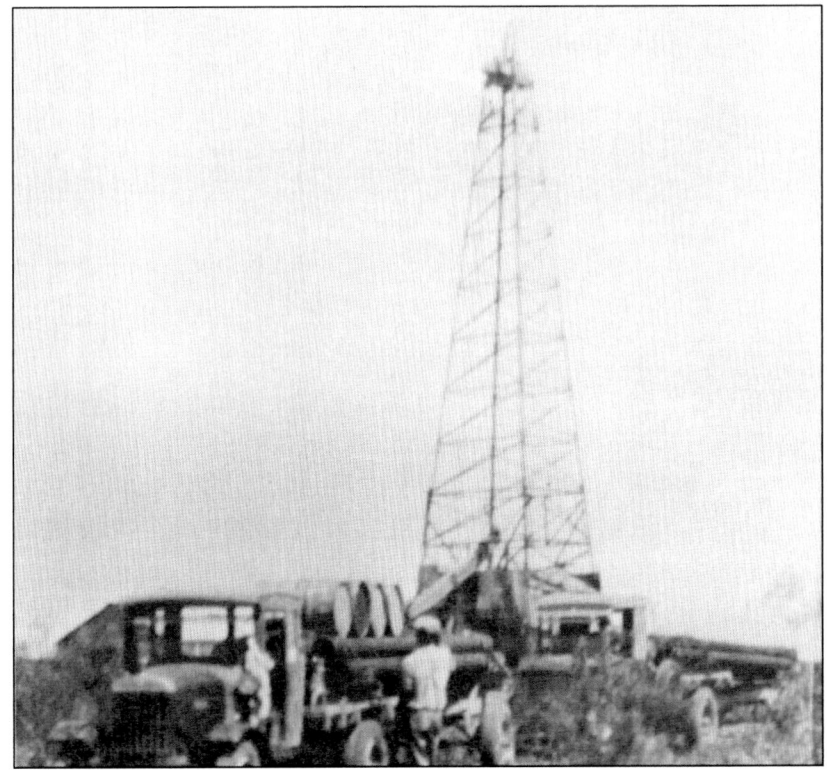

The discovery of oil started a flurry of activity in Andrews County, as the oil had to be stored in wooden barrels and hauled away by trucks until a buyer could be found. Scouts for oil companies from across the country began eyeing property in the county for future exploration. Unfortunately it would be a few years before oil was worth the trouble to be shipped outside the county.

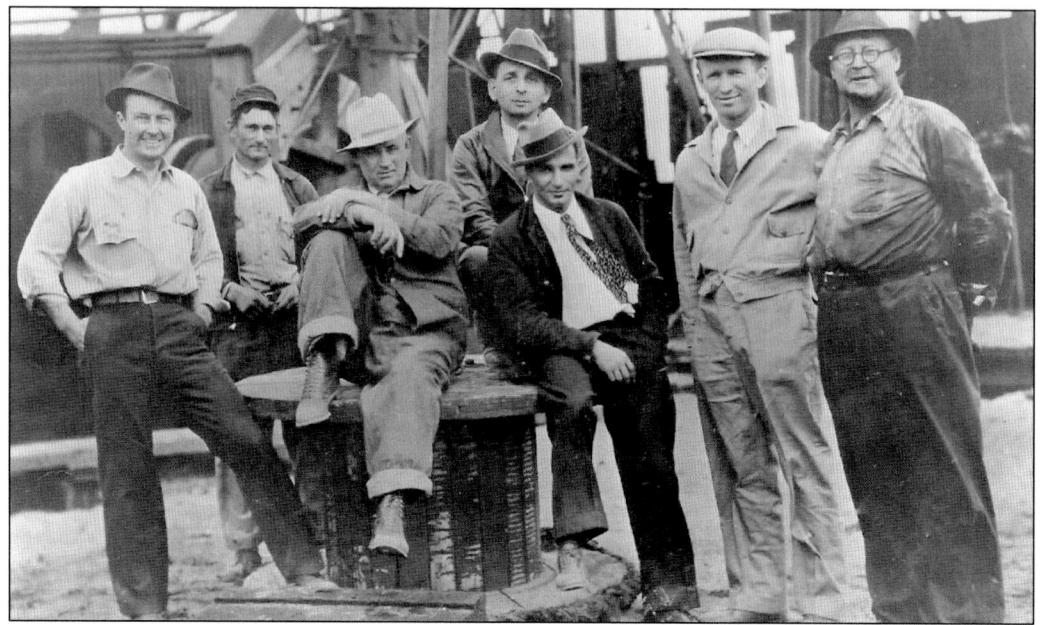

Fred Fuhrman of Midland kicked off his fortunes in Andrews County with the discovery of the Ford No. 1 oil well, completed on November 21, 1930. It was the second major find in the county and confirmed what many thought about the county having significant underground reservoirs of crude oil. Shown in the photograph are, from left to right, unidentified, Alvin Williams, Ed Lucas, Fred Fuhrman, two unidentified, and Sam Kneppley. (Courtesy Martha Page.)

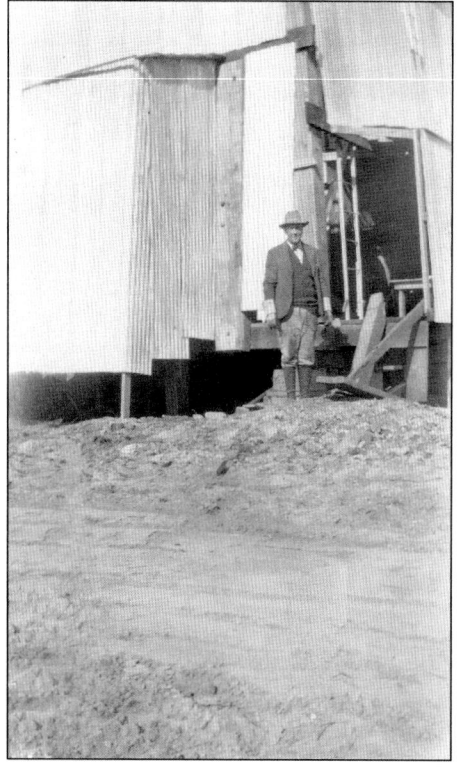

Joining Fred Fuhrman on some of his oil ventures was oilman Fred Mascho, another wildcatter or oilman speculating on drilling oil wells with hopes of bringing in productive oil wells. The Furhman-Mascho leases were in southwest Andrews County and many proved to be very worthwhile oil producers. Here Mascho stands beside one of their early oil well projects.

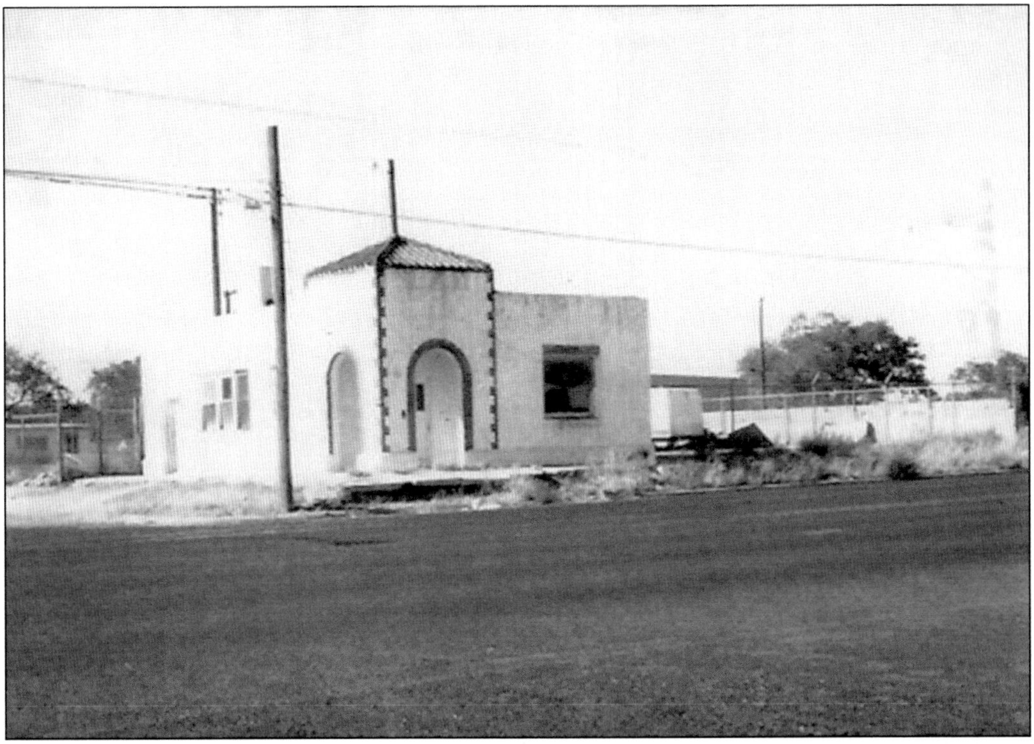

A landmark of the old days is the Andrews State Bank on West Broadway Avenue. The bank was started in 1929 by J. S. Means, its first president. When the bank moved to Midland due to the economy, the ownership of a small insurance company associated with the bank was transferred to the assistant cashier, O. G. Weatherby, on September 25, 1934. The company continues today with the Weatherby-Eisenrich Agency.

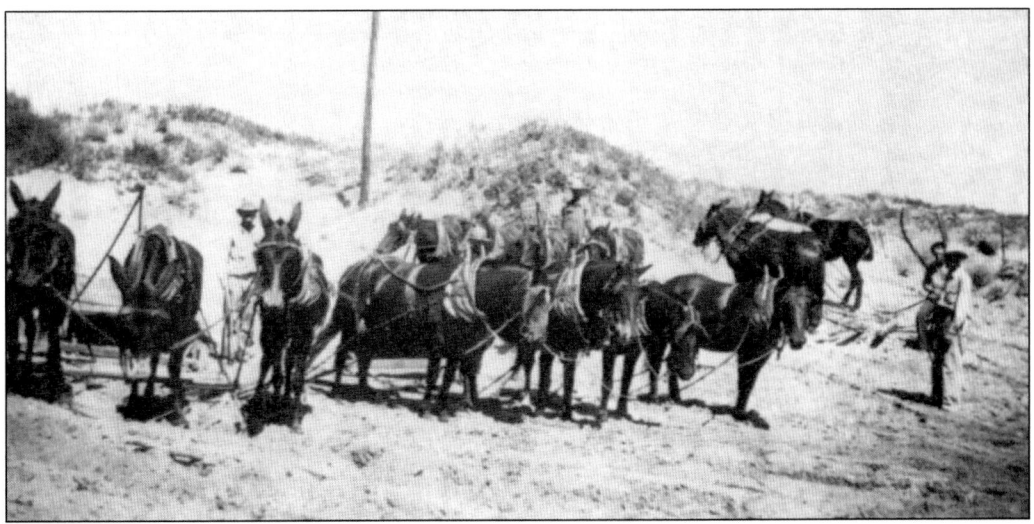

Early pipelines were constructed with teams of mules. The process was laborious and took days to complete only a short distance. The teams of mules were also used in clearing locations for drilling rigs. Shown above in 1935 are Herman Turnbow, Willard Price, and Bart Allison.

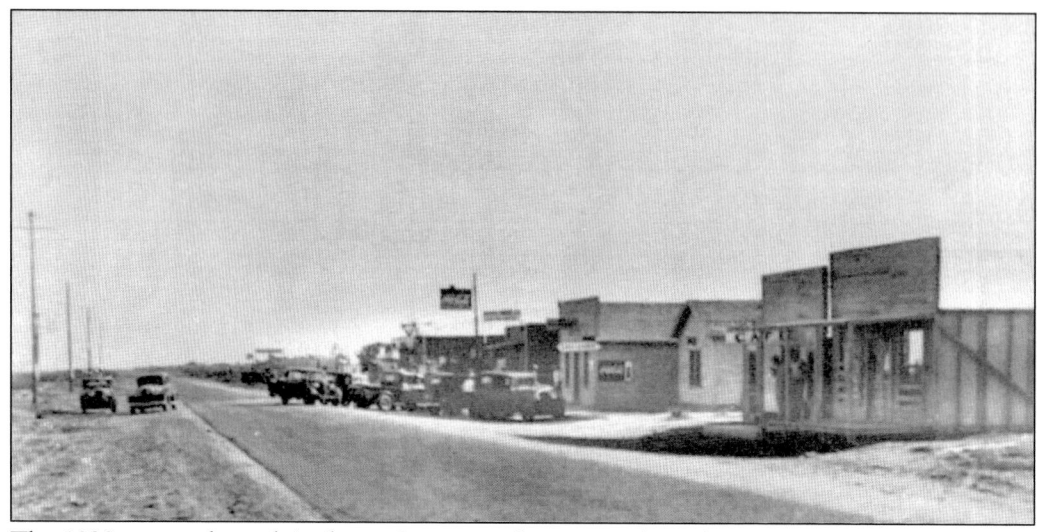

The 1930 census showed Andrews County with 736 people as the entire nation still struggled with the Great Depression. Slowly, oil companies began moving people into Andrews to fill positions needed for the exploration of oil. A decade later, 1,200 residents were recorded in Andrews, as oil resulted in much activity. The photograph above, taken in the early 1930s, shows little action on Main Street.

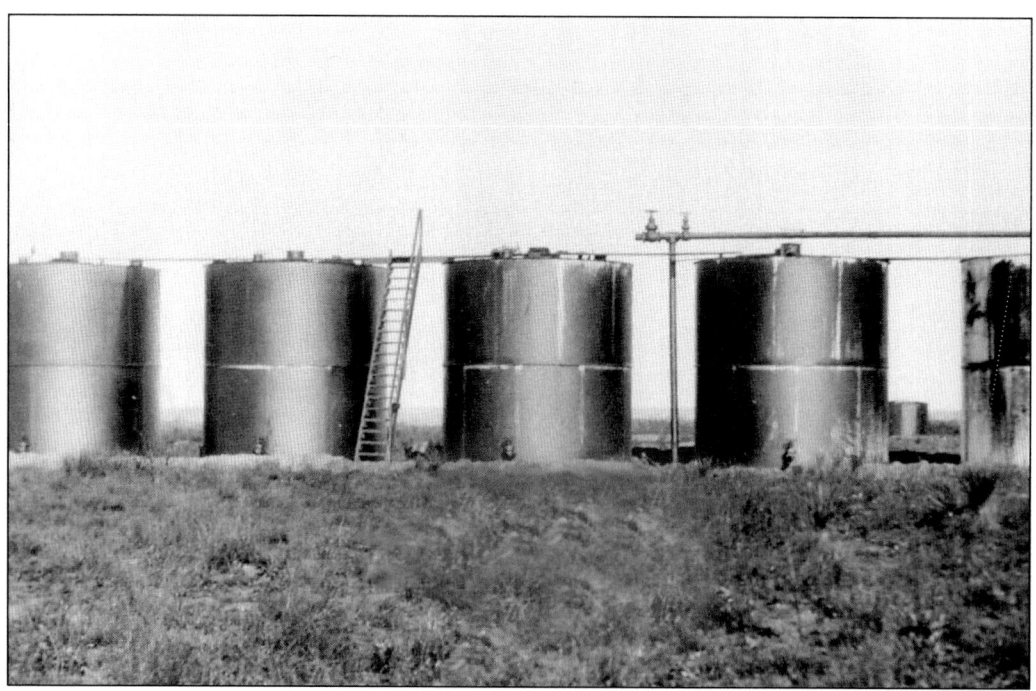

It took specialized equipment to drill for oil, including cable-drilling rigs in the beginning and later rotary drilling, and also an assortment of other equipment like storage tanks, as shown in this photograph. Once oil was found, it had to be stored in tanks like these until the crude could be sold to companies and hauled by trucks or pipeline to the owners.

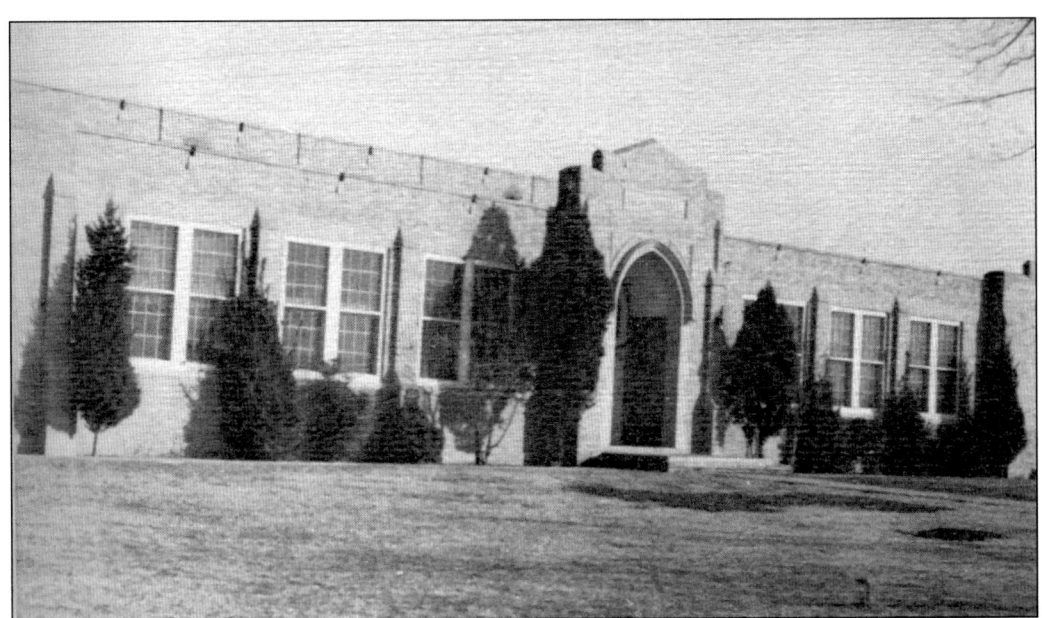

With the eventual consolidation of school districts and the population in Andrews growing, a bond was passed to build a new high school in 1930. The structure, shown here, cost $75,000. It was demolished in 1967 to make way for new tennis courts at the middle school. Additional growth resulted in another new high school constructed in 1945 costing $300,000, built just west of the other old high school.

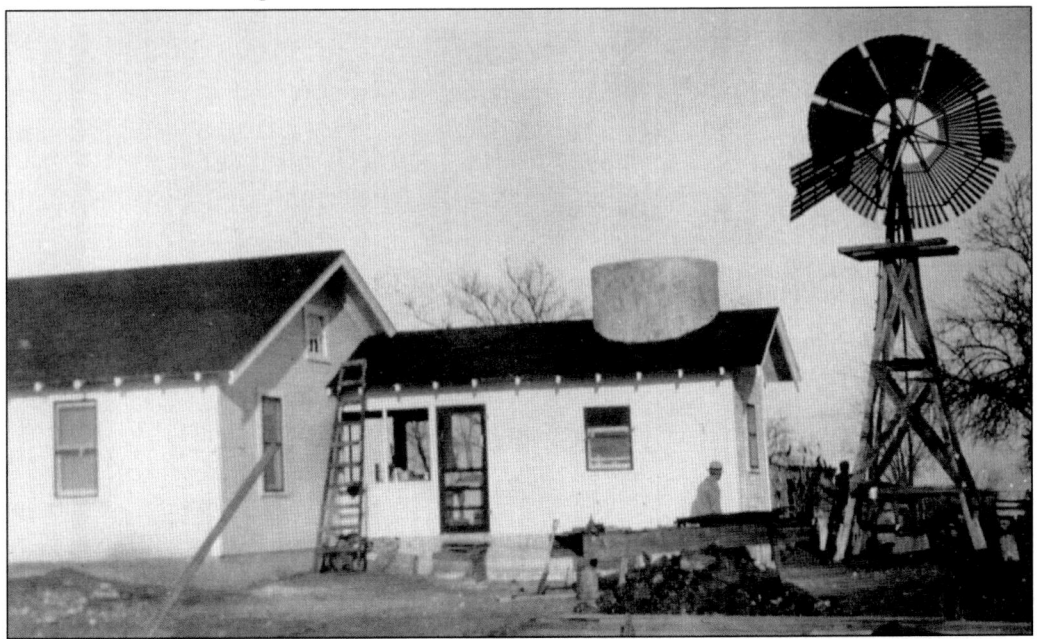

Advancements were beginning to occur during the early 1930s, including the use of windmills providing water to residences. The C. E. Ogden home piped water from an Eclipse windmill to a storage tank inside the home, as shown in this photograph. Water was sometimes piped into a wooden trough on a back porch where milk, cream, and butter were kept cool. The water then traveled outside to a ground tank.

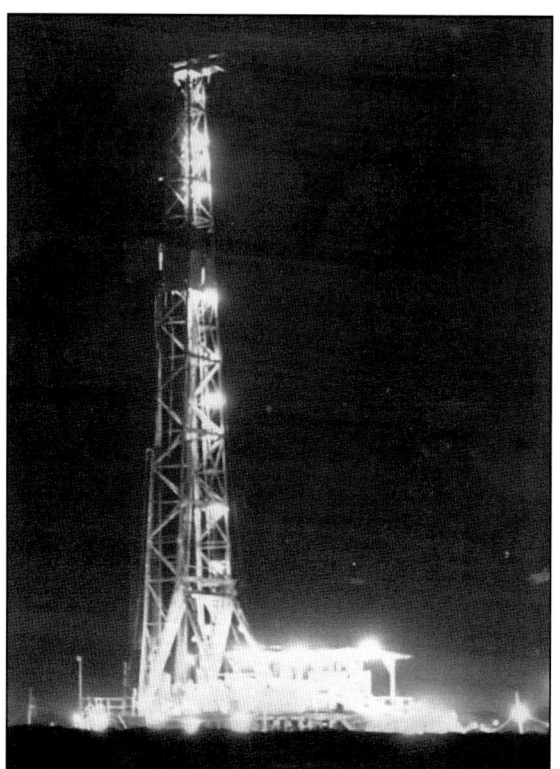

As more oil companies became aware of Andrews' oil reserves, they acquired leases on sections of land to drill oil wells. Property owners and oil companies benefited from the arrangement. Early on, workers were sent from different places to build derricks and run the rigs, but eventually it meant more permanent employees for Andrews. At left, an oil derrick is assembled so that a new well can be drilled.

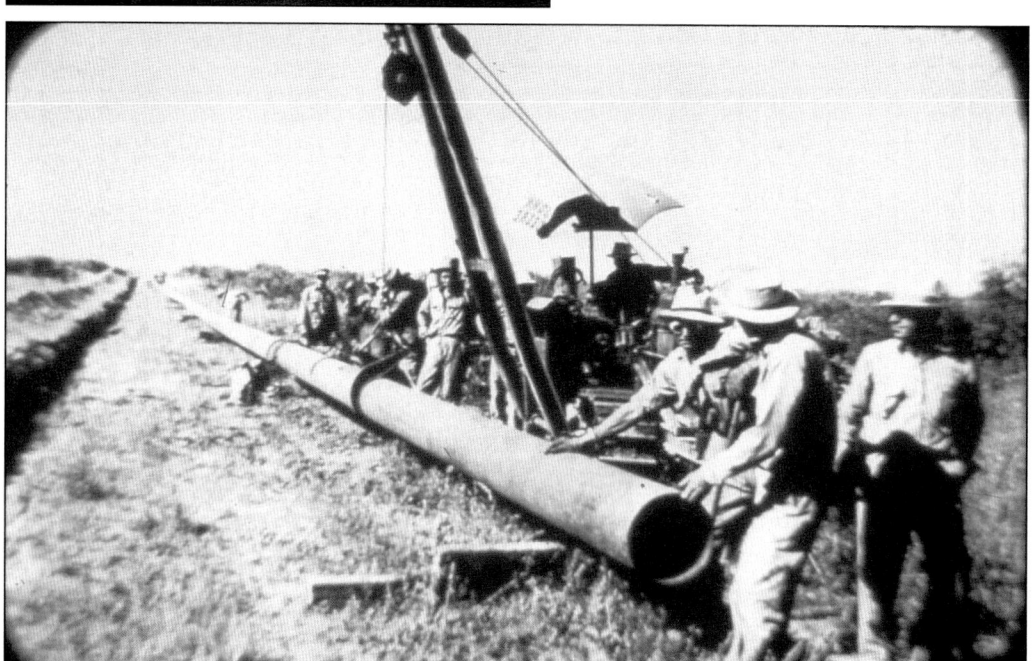

By the mid-1930s, additional attention was given to building a larger pipeline so oil that was being produced could be shipped to refineries in other parts of the country. It was a long, hard job but it kept many men busy during a time when jobs were still hard to come by. Humble Oil's pipeline opened up new production, as a means to get the oil to market was critical.

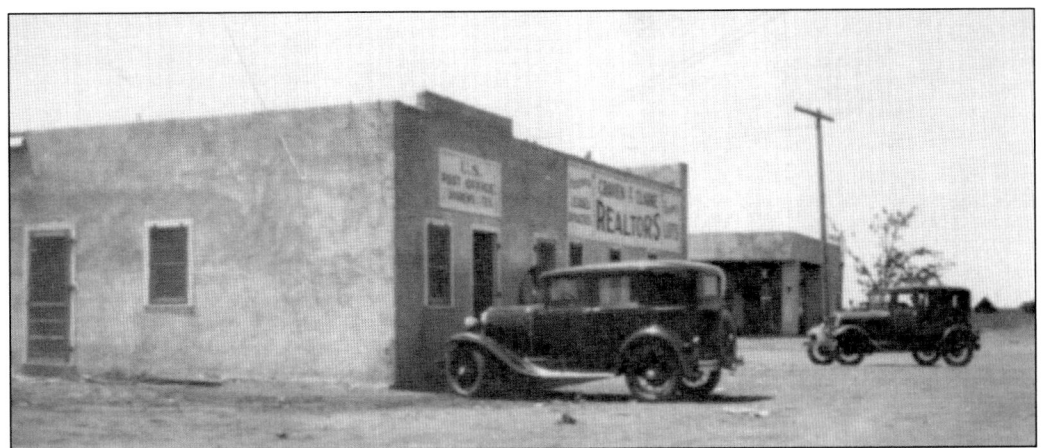

The first post office in Andrews was established in 1909. Aside from Shafter Lake, which also had a post office, there were no fewer than a dozen post offices that operated in the county during the early times at settlements and oilfield camps. Some of the early post offices were at Cal, China Pond, Chicago, Dollarhide, Florey, and Frankel City. Pictured above is the Andrews Post Office in 1936. (Courtesy Mark Hooper.)

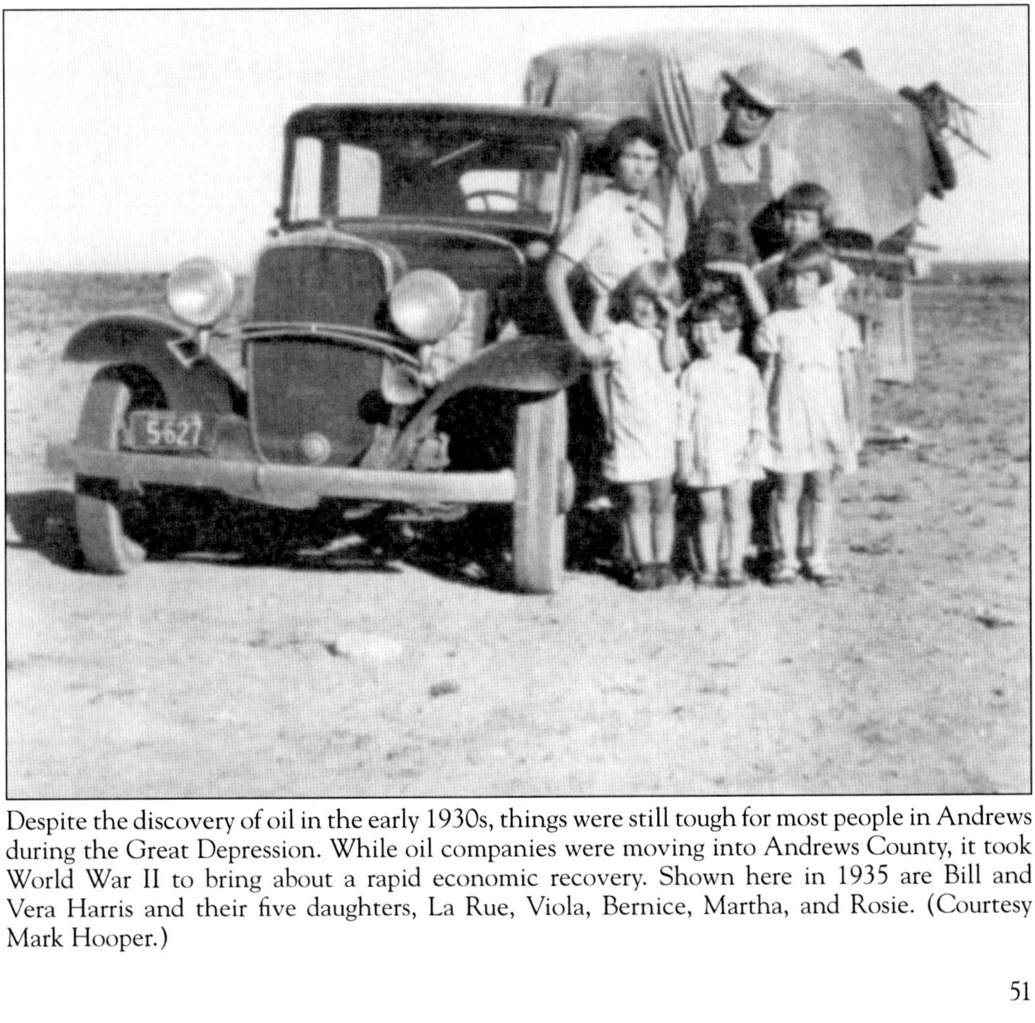

Despite the discovery of oil in the early 1930s, things were still tough for most people in Andrews during the Great Depression. While oil companies were moving into Andrews County, it took World War II to bring about a rapid economic recovery. Shown here in 1935 are Bill and Vera Harris and their five daughters, La Rue, Viola, Bernice, Martha, and Rosie. (Courtesy Mark Hooper.)

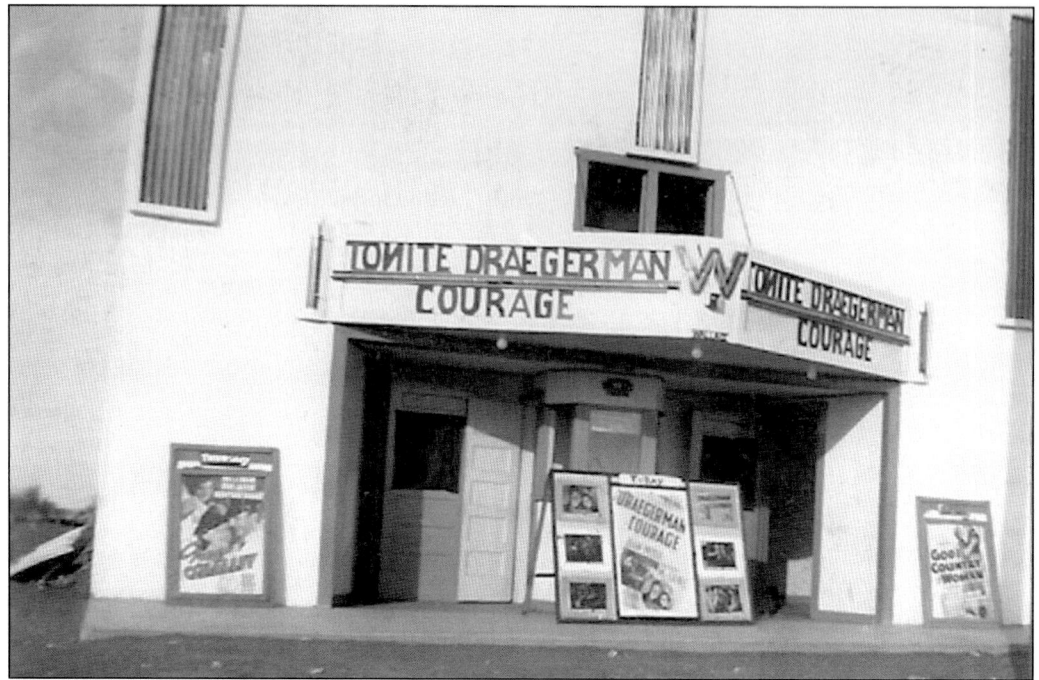

The Wallace Theatre in Andrews was located on Main Street just across the street from the Andrews County Courthouse. Based on the movies being shown, *Draegerman Courage* and *God's Country and the Woman*, this photograph was taken in 1937. The Wallace Theatre was later joined by the Rose Theater just down the street where the Andrews Police Department is now located.

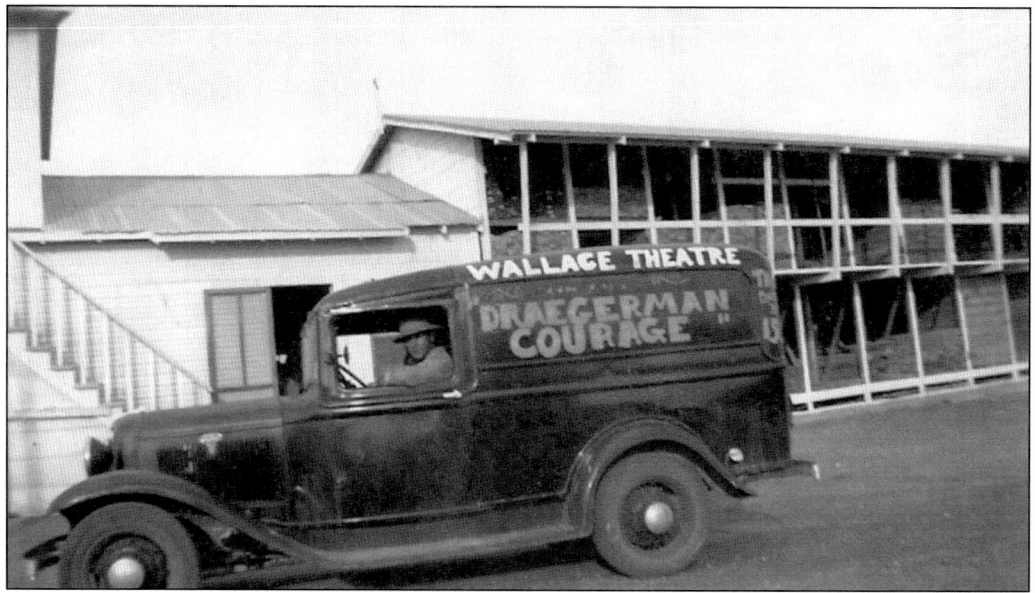

Early businesses used a variety of methods to advertise, as shown here with placards pasted across a truck, announcing the shows being played at the Wallace Theatre. The picture show was one of the main entertainment venues in Andrews for many years. The Wallace was the first theater in Andrews and was followed by the Rose Theater later on during the early 1950s.

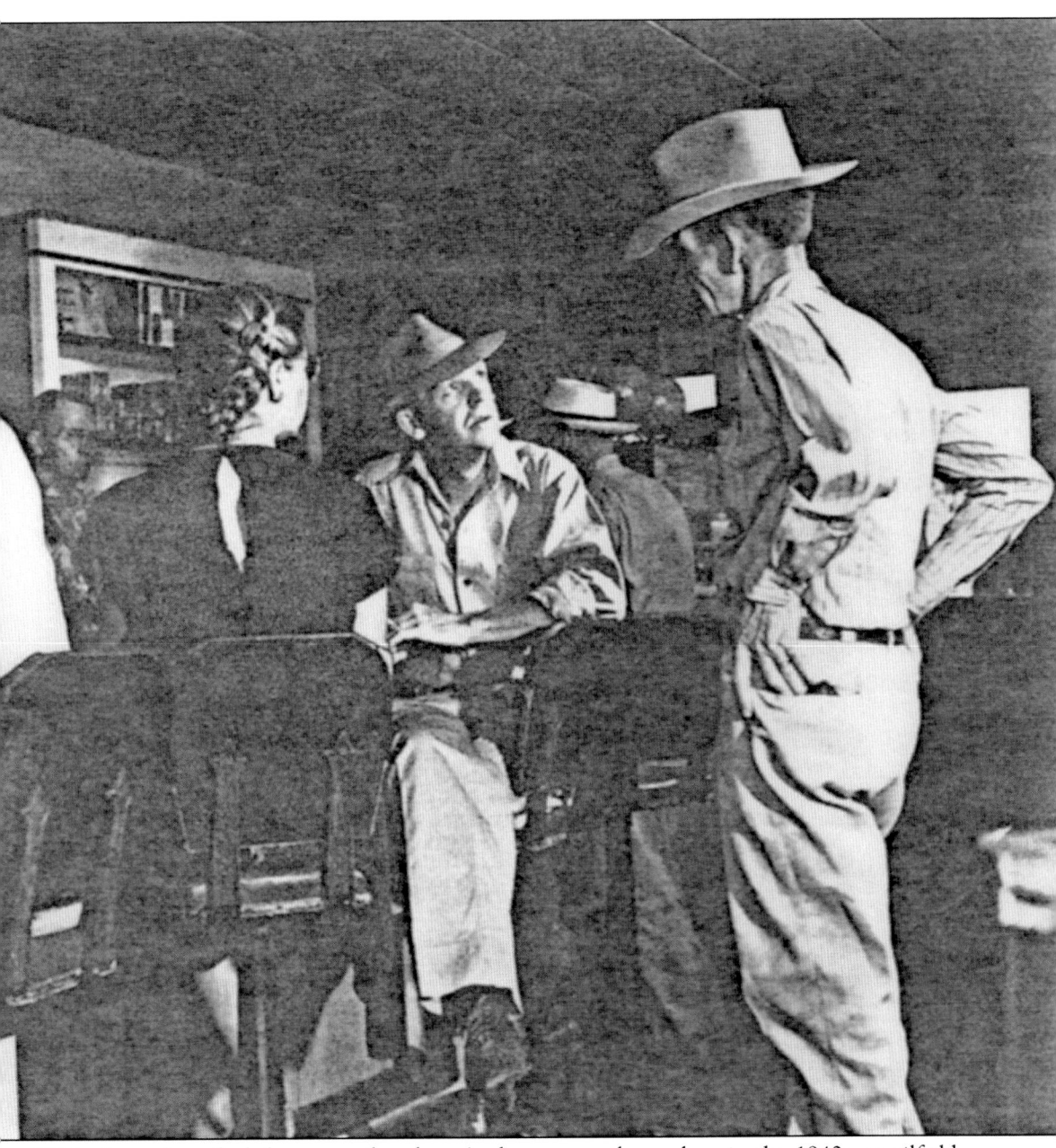

With the rush to find the next oil gusher, Andrews was a busy place in the 1940s, as oilfield workers, drilling crews, company scouts, geologists, and others in town sought information, help, or sometimes just a good meal. Here two men and a woman talk shop, probably about oil, land, or drilling activity. Overnight, lines formed at restaurants and other places as the small town suddenly found itself growing and its accommodations stretched to the limit. Things would not improve for several years, although most residents did not do much complaining, as they had experienced some lean years during the Depression. Meanwhile, restaurant owners found it difficult to find many foodstuffs and other wares, as the war effort was consuming everything. Besides silk, rubber, and gasoline, many types of vegetables, flour, and sugar were rationed and sometimes nonexistent. (Courtesy Martha Page.)

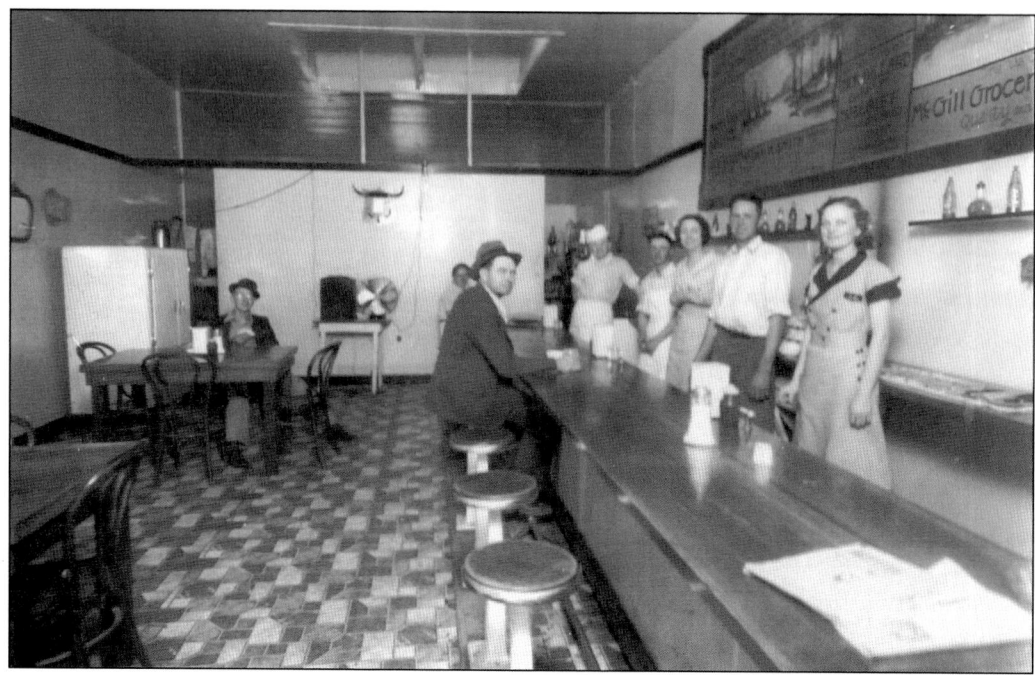

One of the popular eateries in Andrews during the 1930s was Coconaugher's Café, located approximately at Main Street and Broadway Avenue. The café was owned by Roy and Ina Coconaugher, who had converted a trailer house into a six-stool restaurant. Residents gathered at Coconaugher's for meals, while young people met there in the evenings for a soft drink and to listen to big band music on the radio. (Courtesy Martha Page.)

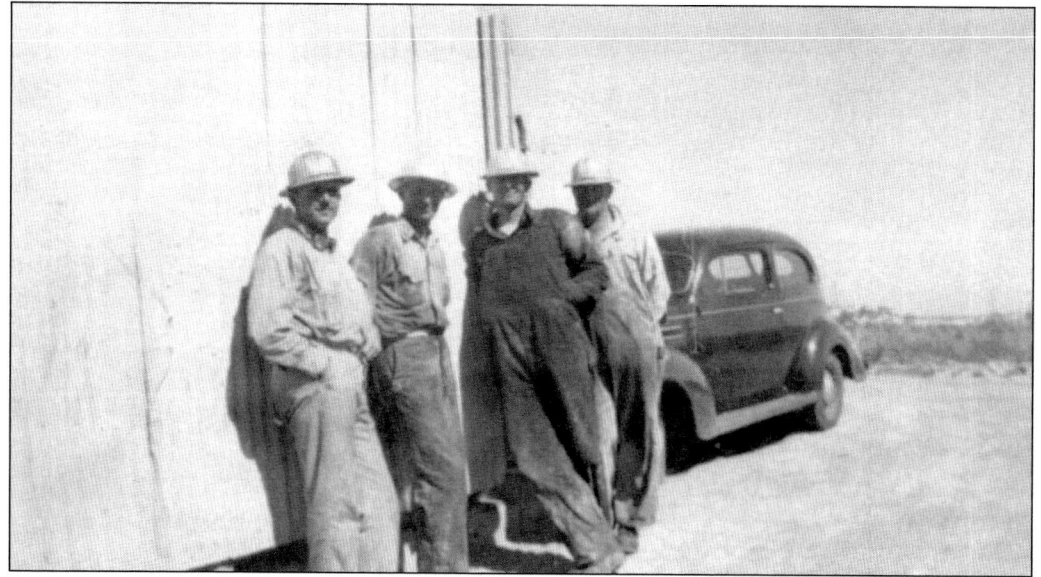

By 1939, nearly all areas of the county were being explored by oil companies. The major oilfield discoveries during the 1930s included the Fuhrman, Means, Parker, Emma, and Shafter Lake fields. The Shafter Lake Field was the last field to be discovered in the decade. Shown in the photograph are oilfield workers, from left to right, Mac Farmer, Clete Pope, Ham Pinnell, and George McLaughlin. (Courtesy Martha Page.)

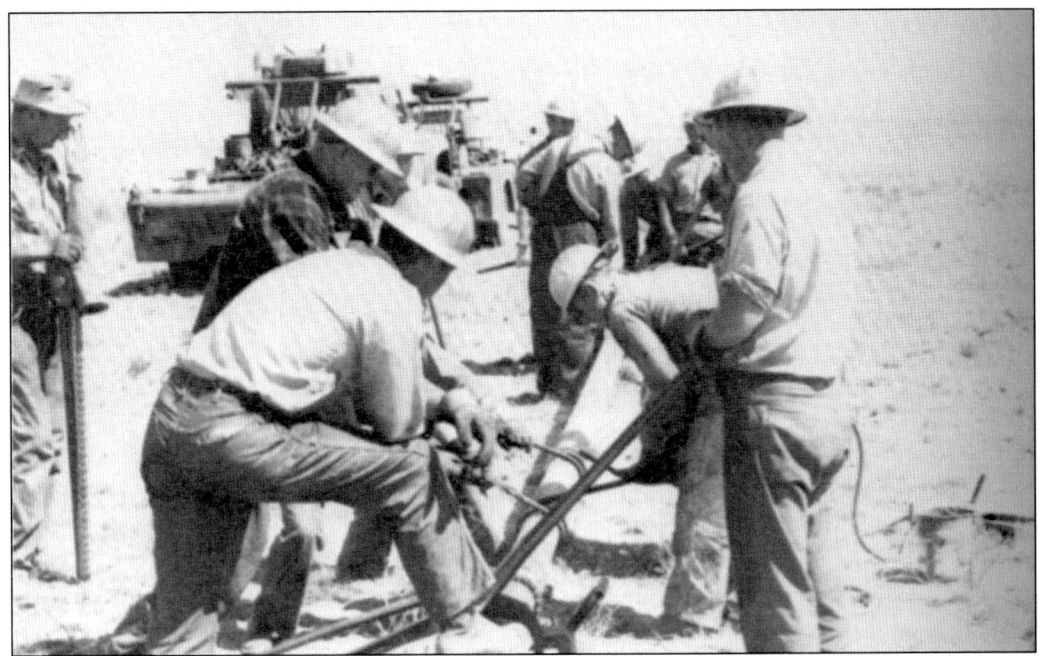

Oilfield work was and still is hard and dangerous in just about every aspect, as workers handle heavy equipment, sometimes under demanding conditions such as a blazing hot sun or frigid winter temperatures. Workers in the photograph include Ham Pinnell, J. B. McNeil, Kenneth Bartell, Bill Barnes, Jack Seay, H. Pilgrim, and Bill House.

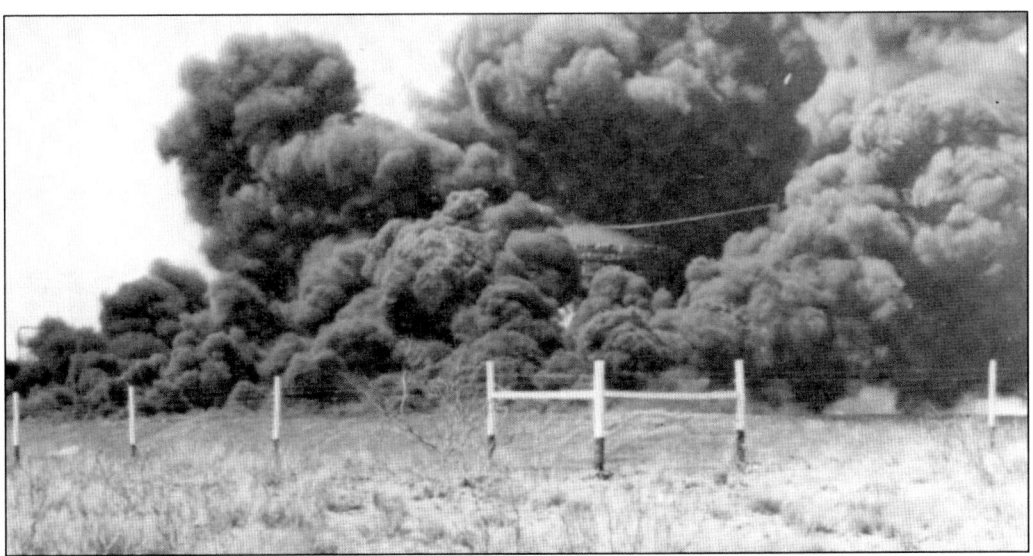

As the drilling and storage of crude oil increased in the county, so did the tendency for fires, as shown in this undated photograph taken on the J. S. Means Lease northeast of Andrews. Oil kept in storage tanks could ignite from the accumulation of gas fumes and fires could be sparked by lightning. Over the years, the Andrews Fire Department became known as specialists in combating oilfield fires.

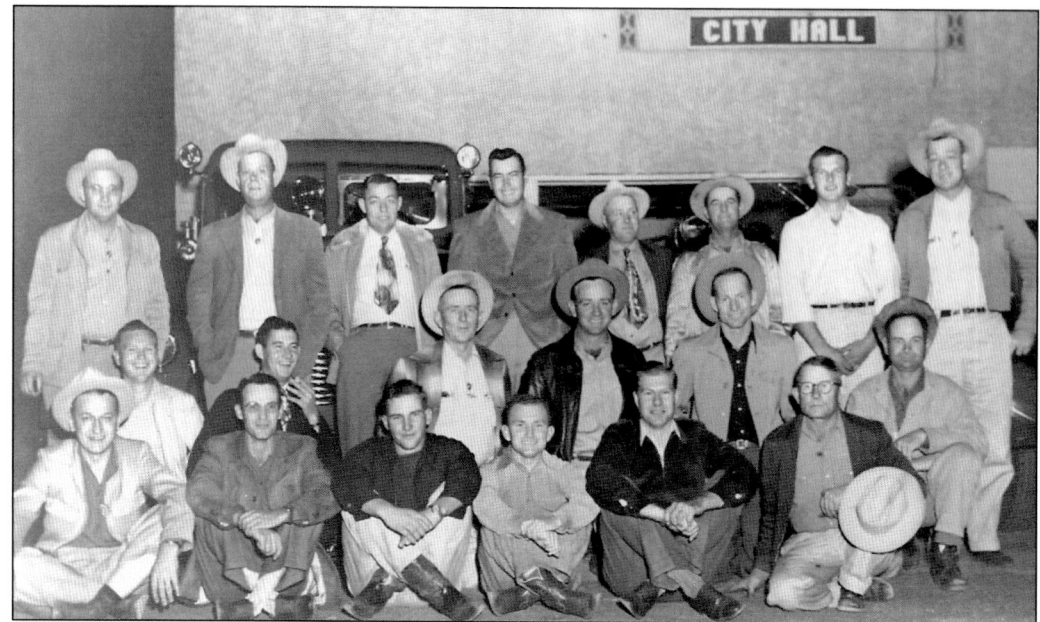

The Andrews Fire Department remains an all-volunteer outfit. In the late 1940s, members were, from left to right, (first row) Charlie Burkett, Laure Gregston, Blackie Smyers, Grady Kidd, Floyd Jackson, and Bill Wyatt; (second row) Glen Wieser, T. T. Carter, John Suggs, Cecil Mobley, Opel Nix, and Dick Underwood; (third row) Ray Phillips, Pat Wright, Virgil Lasater, Fred Swinney, Bob Dillard, Winiford Hudgins, Kenneth Jackson, and Dee Lunceford.

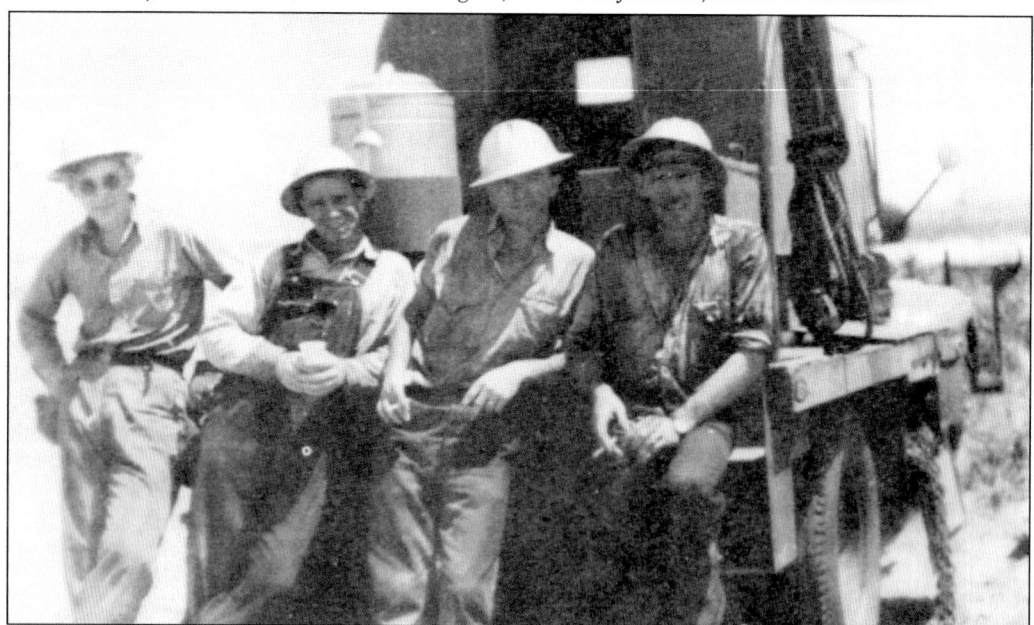

By the late 1930s, oil development had picked up along with the price of crude, but the start of World War II on December 7, 1941, resulted in a boom in Andrews. Among the work load were roustabout crews, which did basic maintenance on existing wells. Shown above are local men who worked back then, including Bennie Farmer, Van Ward, Curley Sharp, and gang pusher J. B. McNeil.

During the war years, Andrews County had more than 100 drilling rigs operating night and day as companies and men worked to find and provide oil for the nation's war effort. Andrews was experiencing its first oil boom, and while many more would follow, for the time being jobs and paychecks were plentiful, although housing was a different story.

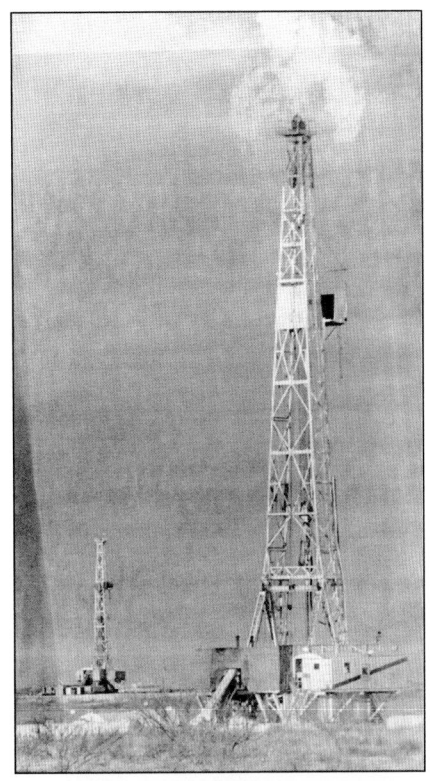

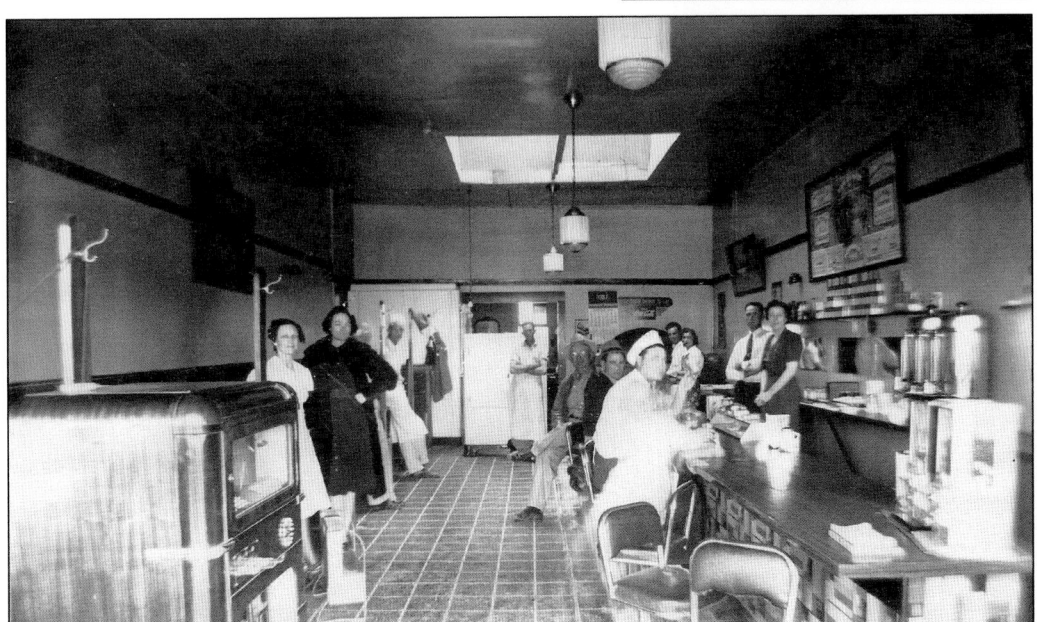

Cafés like this one on Main Street were usually filled during the booming conditions in Andrews. Not only could workers find a meal, but oftentimes a job by simply mentioning that they were looking for work. Of course, finding a job was one thing, but housing in the community was stretched to the limit. Eventually the government opened Deep Pay Village to accommodate the needed manpower in the oil fields. (Courtesy Martha Page.)

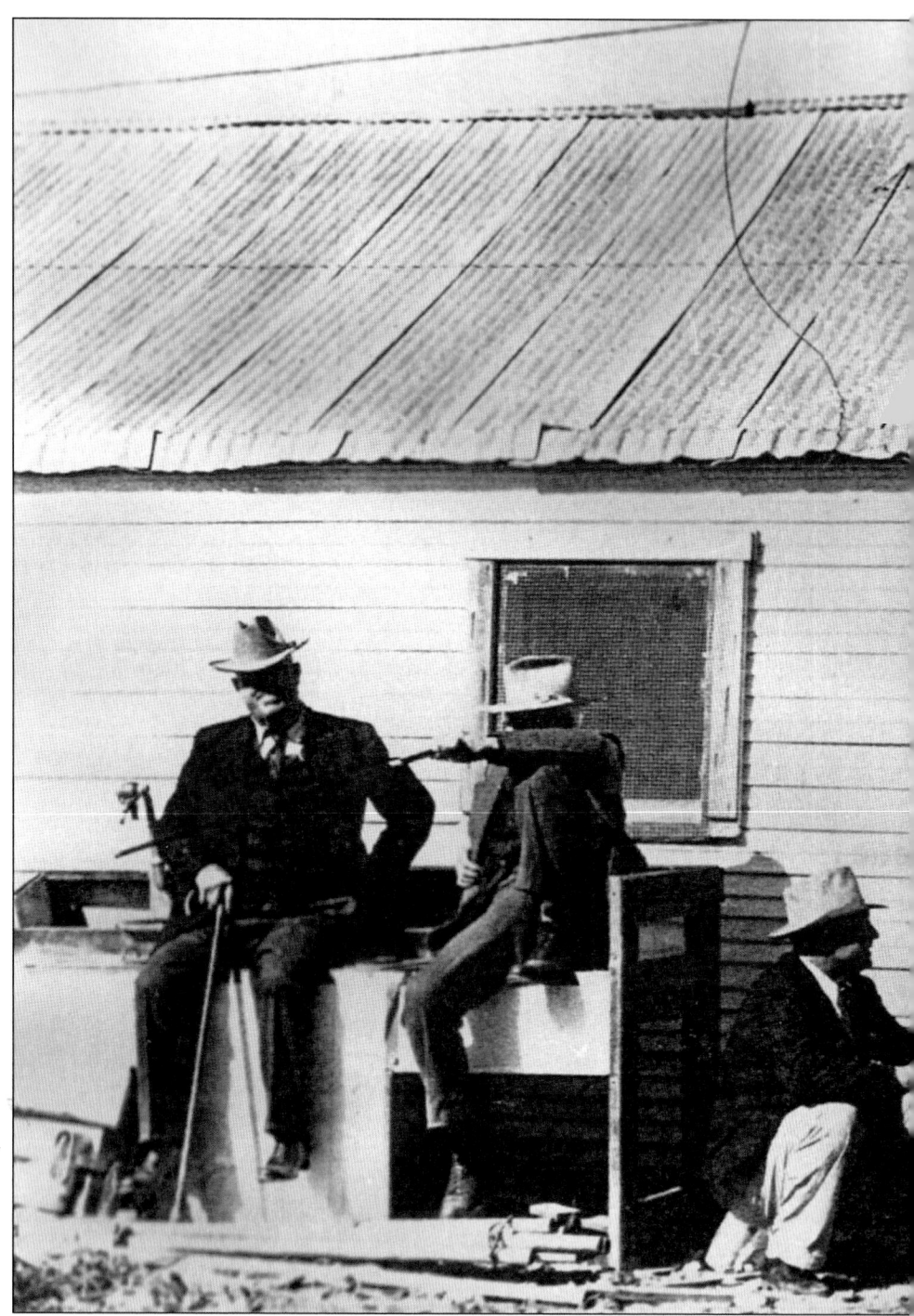

Andrews was bustling with activity in the early 1940s due to oil exploration and growth within the city. Twenty-six new oilfields were discovered in the county during this period. The rapid growth stretched the community's resources for providing housing, water, and other services. Almost overnight the town became a patchwork of tents, trailers, and shacks as job seekers came from all parts of the country. Most of the streets were still unpaved, but people still gathered

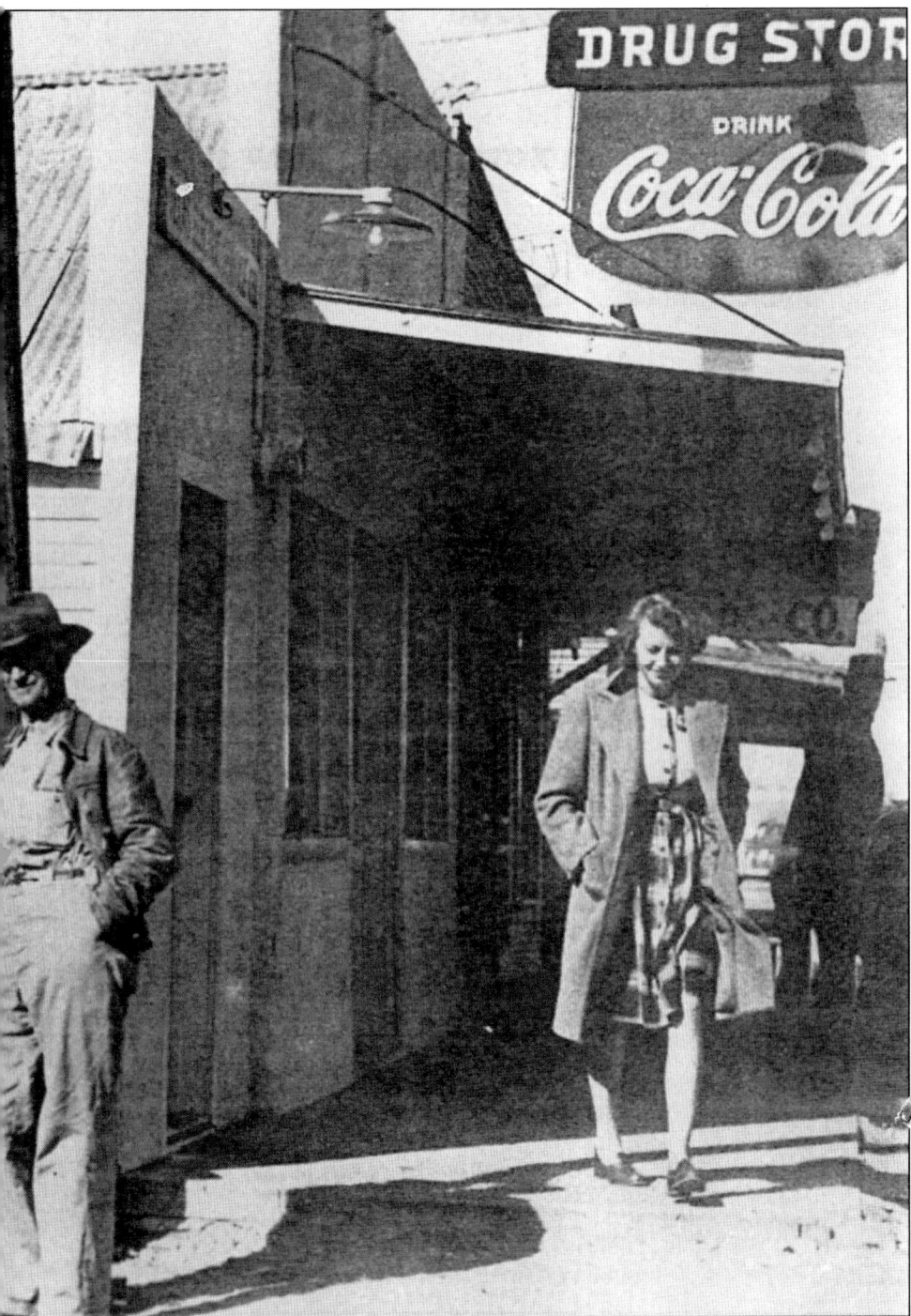

outside stores to visit, including outside City Drug Store, shown here on Main Street. Walking down the wooden sidewalk in front is Fern Heath. With more than 100 oil rigs operating during most of the early 1940s, there were standing lines in cafés and shortages of everything, including meat, coffee, sugar, tires, and gasoline. Baths were 25¢ at the barbershop. (Courtesy Martha Page.)

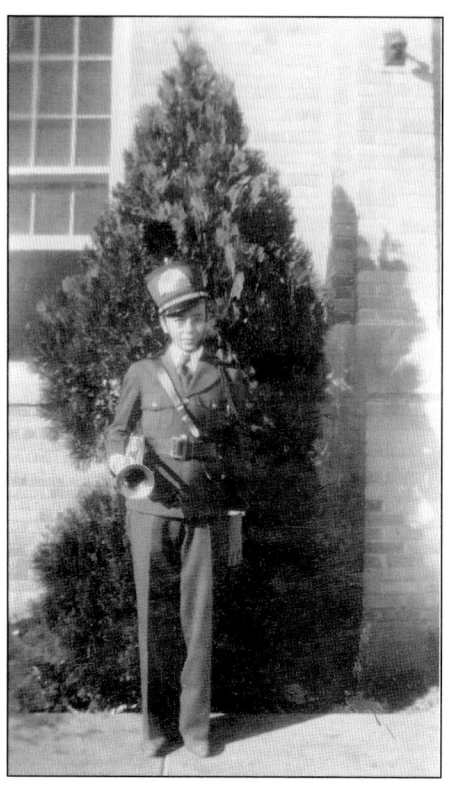

Not everything was all work in the 1930s; school activities prevailed for the youngsters. Shown here is Byford Sealy, who played in the Andrews High School Band and served in the U.S. Marines during World War II. Sealy, whose parents, Carl and Lurline Sealy, managed Andrews Abstract Company, also served in the Korean War and as an FBI agent before returning home to marry JoAnn Herring and manage the abstract company. (Courtesy Martha Page.)

Other students in the Andrews High School Band included, from left to right, (first row) Thomas Smith, Kathleen Davis, Mary Sue Stovall, and Patsy O'Neil; (second row) David Moore, Wesley Roberts, and Alvin Little. The band was a favorite pastime of students in Andrews and allowed many students the opportunity to show their talents.

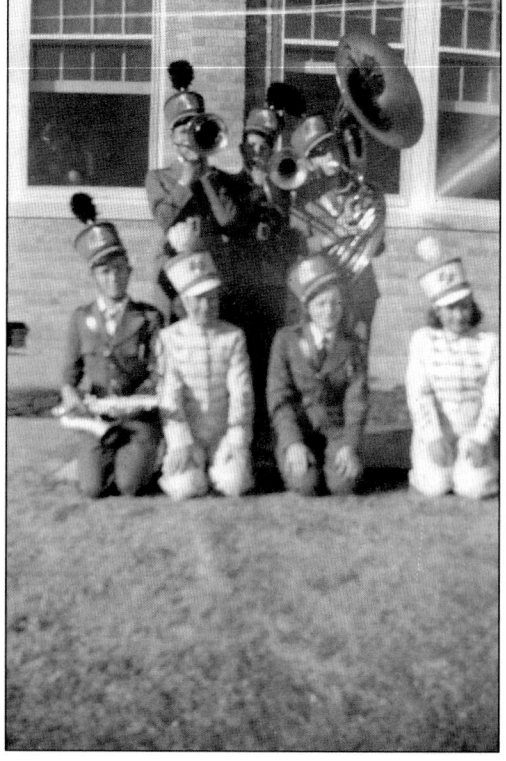

Taking time off from practice were these members of the Andrews High School Band. From left to right are Maxine Barnes, Sonny Tom, and David Moore. Since the school was small, some marching band members also played football for the Andrews Mustangs.

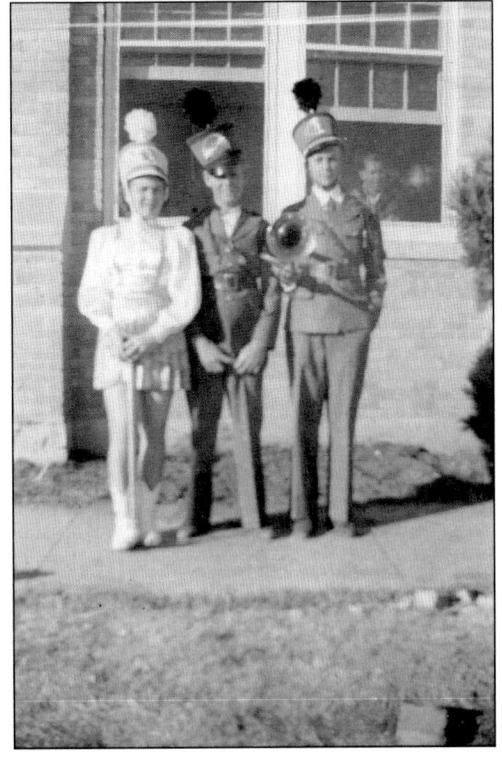

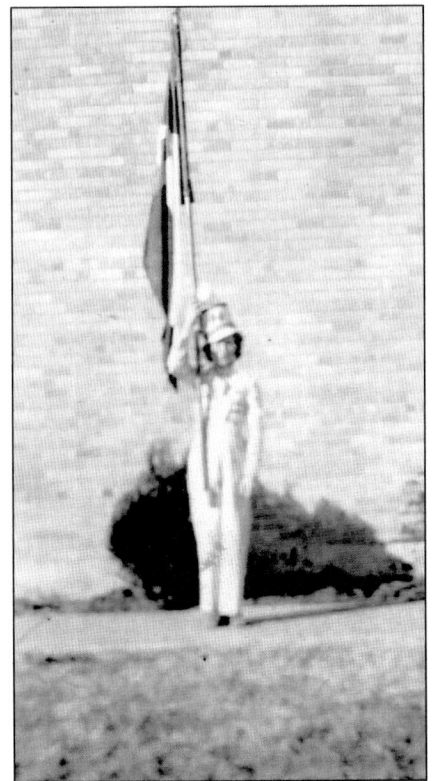

Being in the Andrews High School Band was a major commitment, even in the 1940s, as teachers expected students to still do their homework, show up for class on time, and do well academically. Pictured here is Ila Sue Burkett, the daughter of early residents Edgar and Maggie Burkett, practicing her band routine in the morning before school.

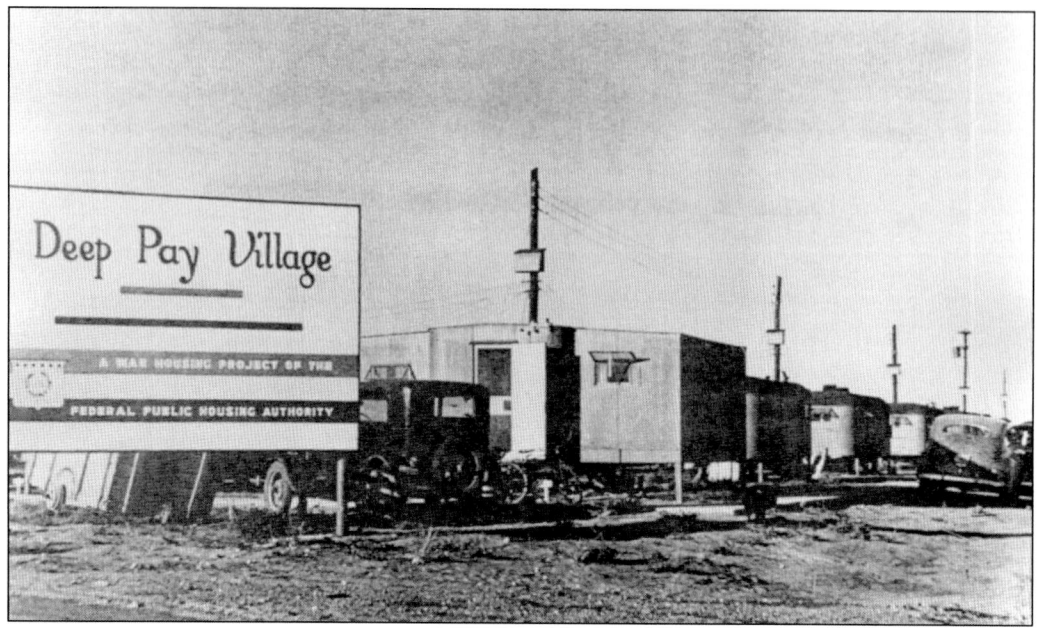

December, 7, 1941, changed America forever as the nation entered World War II after the Japanese attacked Pearl Harbor. Suddenly the oil reserves in Andrews were direly needed, but because of the lack of housing available, the federal government set up a housing district, Deep Pay Village, to accommodate oil workers and their families. The housing district was in northeast Andrews and provided temporary homes for families.

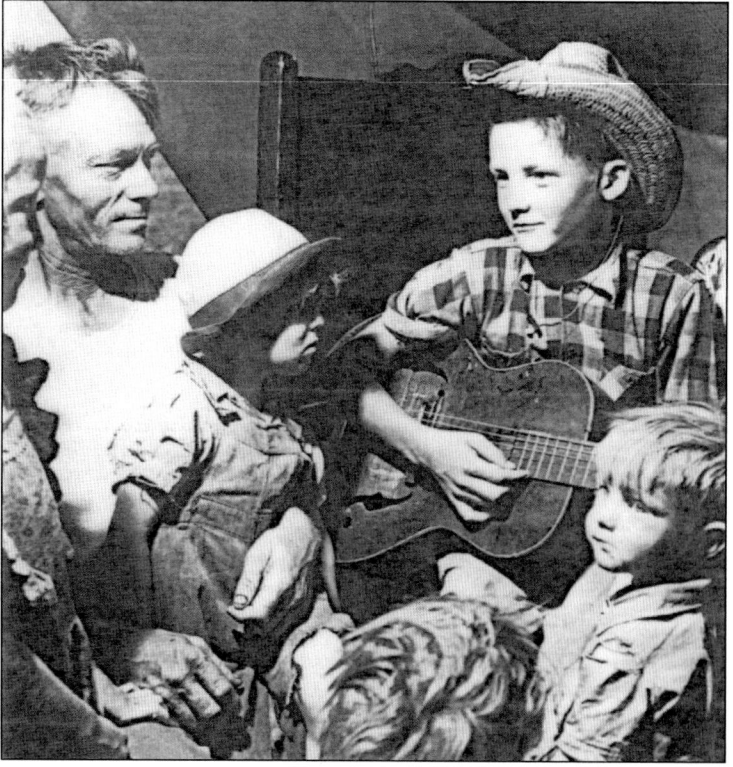

Housing in Andrews during the war was stretched thin due to boom time conditions and the multitude of workers and their families who moved to the community to take advantage of the situation. Companies were desperate for employees. In order to accommodate the overtaxed housing market, the federal government opened a low-income housing district, which helped alleviate the problem. This photograph shows a Timmons boy providing entertainment for his family.

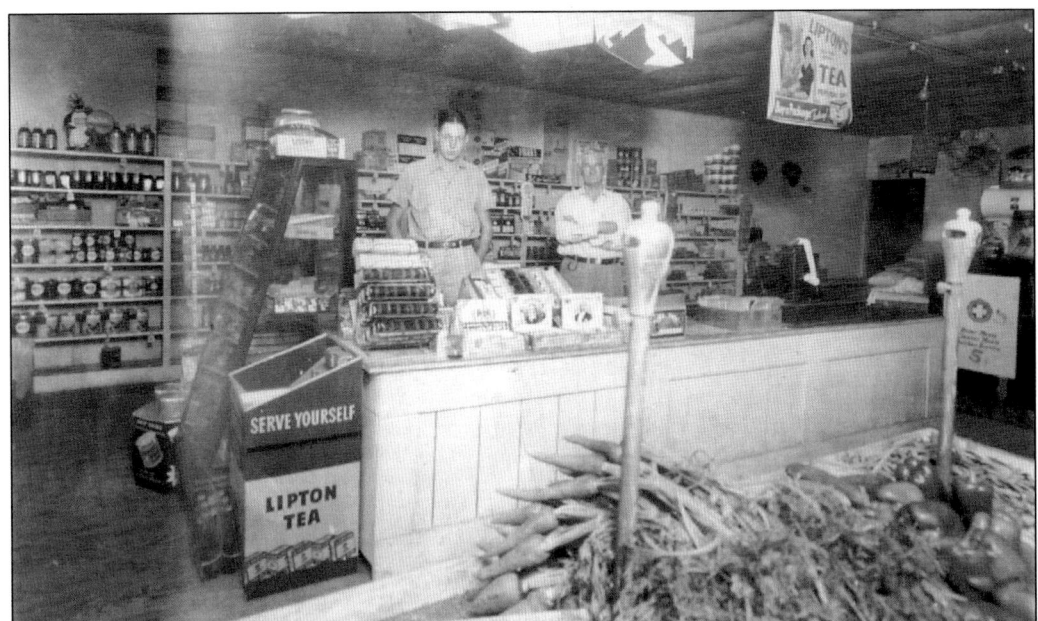

Supplying Andrews with groceries, dry goods, and vegetables in 1940 were Curly and John Underwood at the Underwood Market. Most of the vegetables came from the Underwoods' own farm, while other foodstuffs and items had to be brought or shipped in by freighters. Rationing during the war made getting many supplies difficult, as staple items like sugar, flour, and cigarettes were hard to come by.

Andrews began to see great change in the late 1930s and early 1940s as activity in the oil patch and the start of World War II brought much business and growth to the community. The sleepy West Texas town was suddenly transformed into a bustling little oilfield hub. Shown in the photograph are two longtime residents, Katherine McGill, left, and Ruby Lasater.

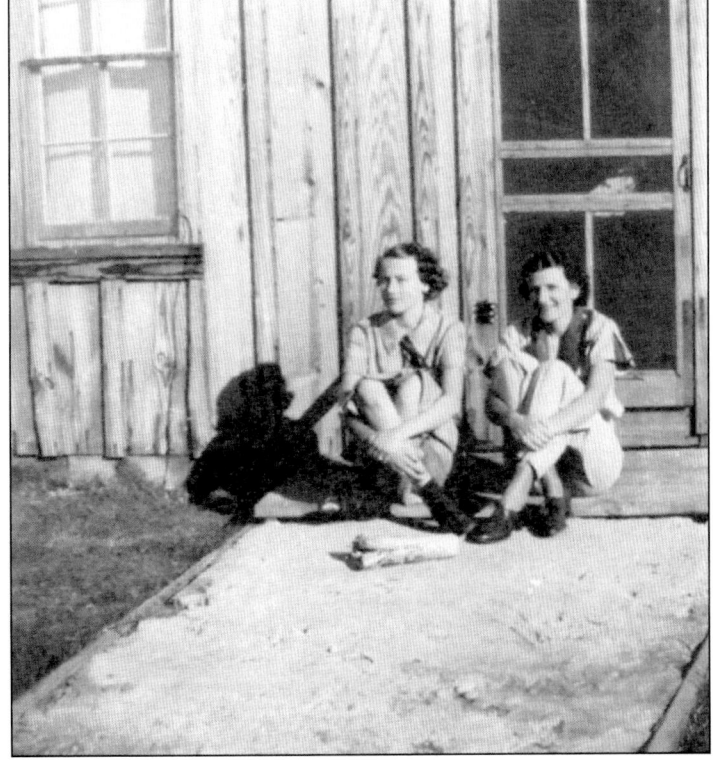

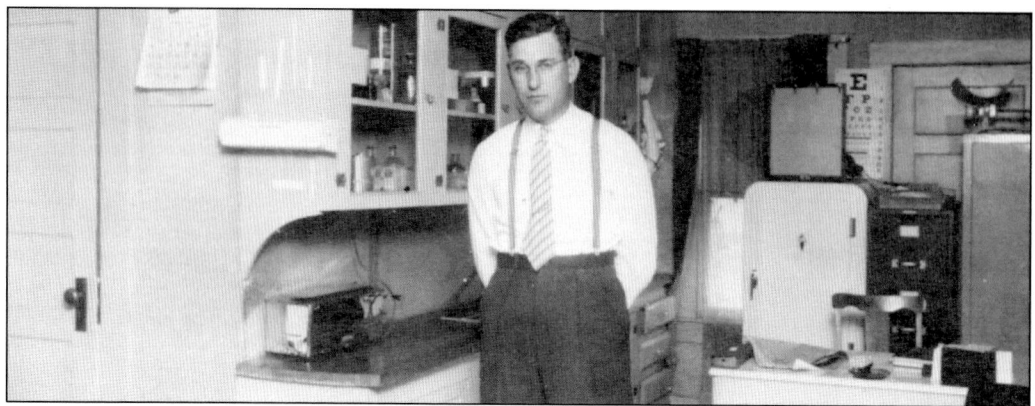

Dr. Murray Wood arrived in Andrews in June 1940 and began treating patients almost immediately because the need for a physician was so great. He lobbied for a hospital, which was built in 1941, and remained until the end of the war, when he left to resume his studies. Wood returned to Andrews in 1955 and stayed until his death in 1958. He was buried in the Old Andrews County Cemetery.

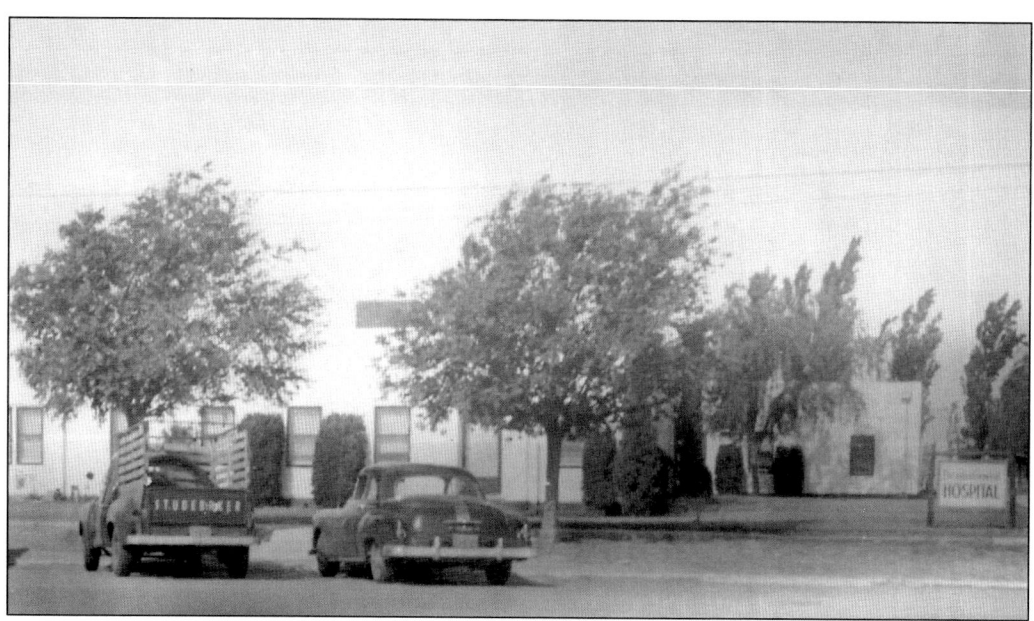

The Andrews County Hospital provided medical care in the 1940s and 1950s. It was located just across from the Andrews courthouse. The eight-room hospital was built in 1941 using material from the town's first courthouse. Doctors seldom stayed long due to the heavy patient load because of accidents in the oilfield. Dr. J. L. Cobb arrived in 1946 and was joined later by Dr. Z. W. Hutcheson, who remained for many years.

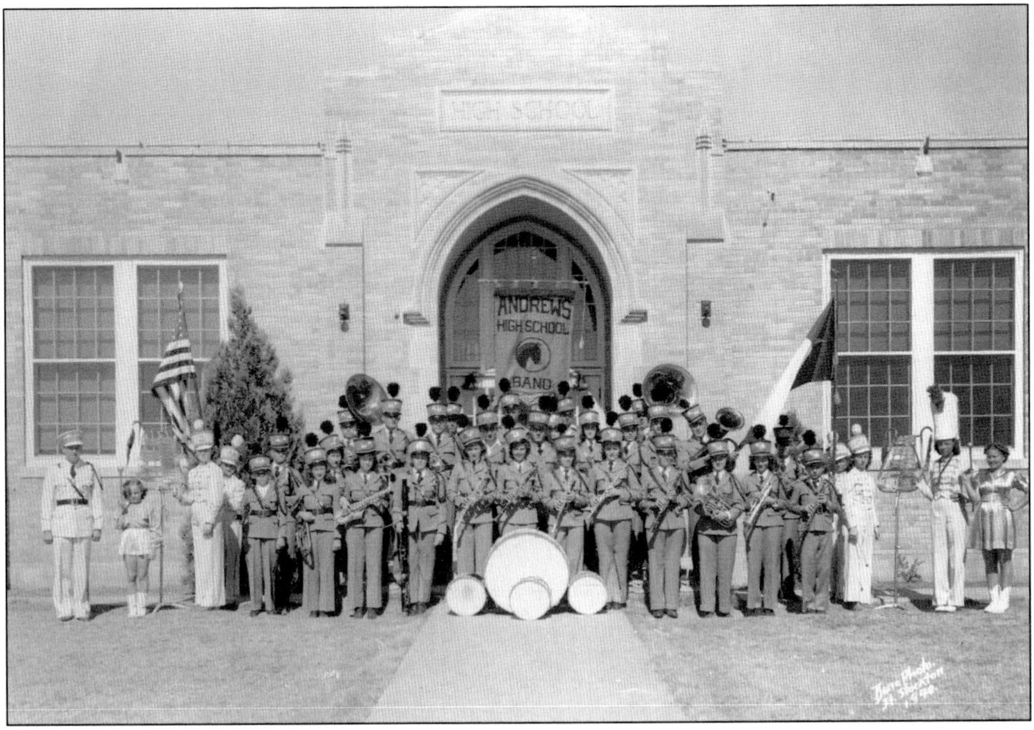

Thanks largely to oil exploration in the county, in 1940 the population of Andrews grew to more than 1,270 people. An increase in students had resulted in a new high school three years earlier, and a new county courthouse was also completed in 1940. This photograph shows the Andrews High School Band arranged in front of the high school.

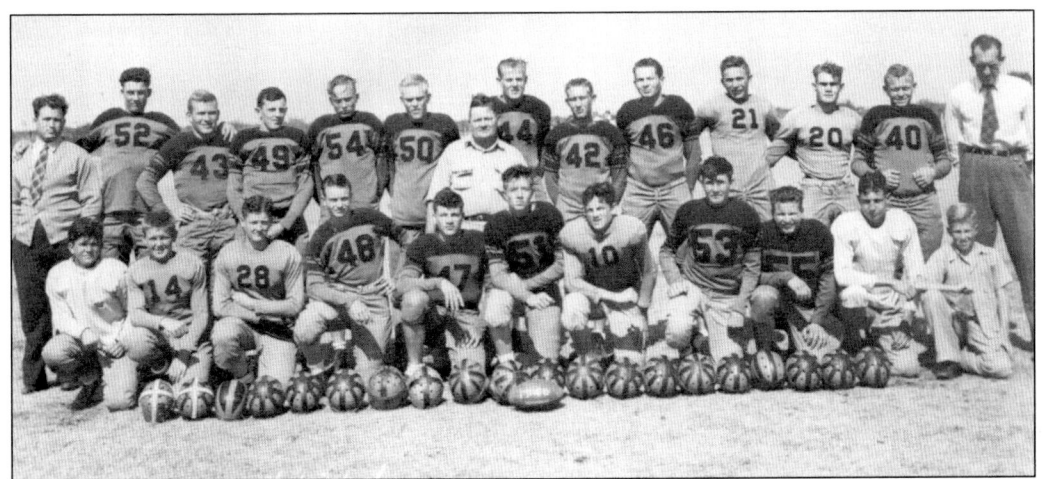

The 1940 Andrews football team included, from left to right, (first row) ? Fuson, Junior Embree, Red Cox, Leo Barnes, James Roberts, Max Evans, Wesley Roberts, Onie Allbright, David McMurray, Junior Underwood, and trainer Ben Donegan; (second row) coach J. Lee Smith, Robert Dillard, Dalton Echols, Gene Irwin, E. W. Williamson, Jack Fitzgerald, Hub Nixon (visitor), Joe Dillard, Kenneth Thompson, Bill Pinnell, Nelson Hitch, Warner McKinney, Bunkley Sanson, and coach Bob Anthony.

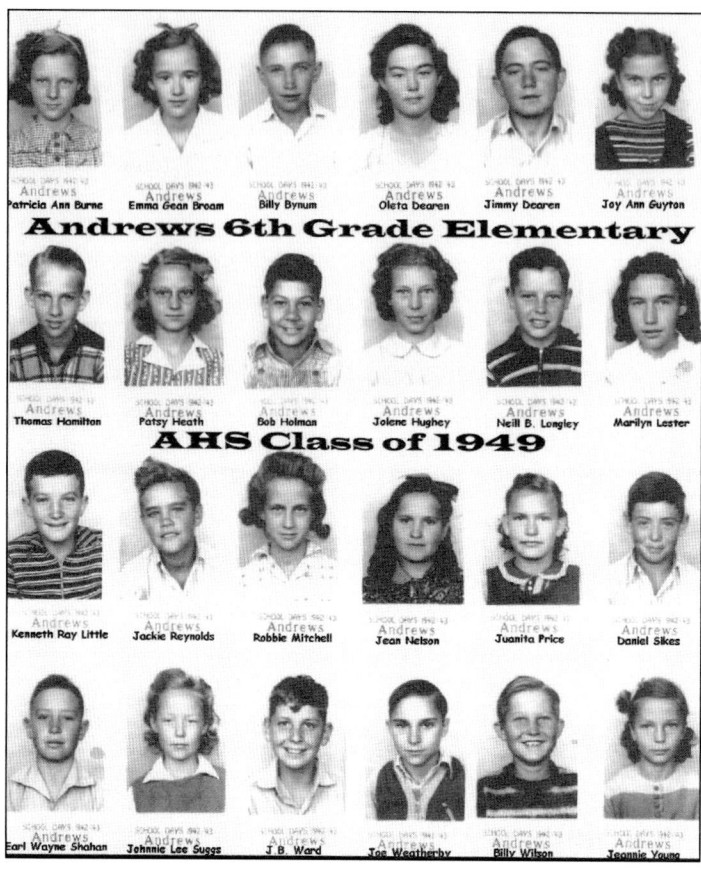

Andrews sixth graders in 1942 included, from left to right, (top row) Patricia Ann Burne, Emma Gean Broam, Billy Bynum, Oleta Dearen, Jimmy Dearen, and Joy Ann Guyton; (second row) Thomas Hamilton, Patsy Heath, Bob Holman, Jolene Hughey, Neill B. Longley, and Marilyn Lester; (third row) Kenneth Ray Little, Jackie Reynolds, Robbie Mitchell, Jean Nelson, Juanita Price, and Daniel Sikes; (fourth row) Earl Wayne Shahan, Johnnie Lee Suggs, J. B. Ward, Joe Weatherby, Billy Wilson, and Jeannie Young.

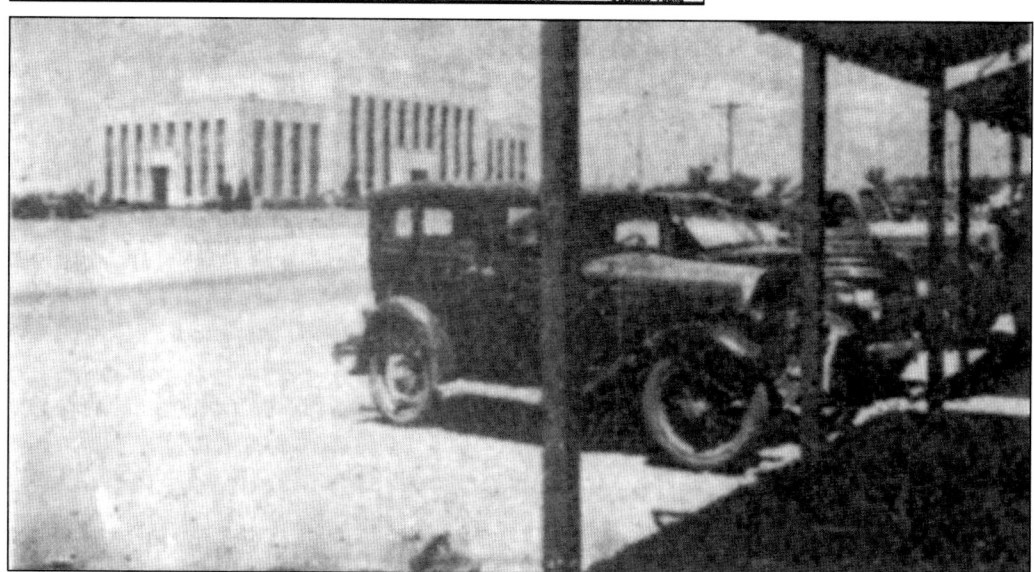

Downtown Andrews was a mix of new and old in the early 1940s, with a new courthouse now the dominate feature on Main Street. Twenty-six new oilfields were discovered, including the Fullerton, Dollarhide, Mabee, and Midland Farms. Lines were beginning to form at cafés and stores as the number of people in town grew rapidly. The boom was underway in Andrews.

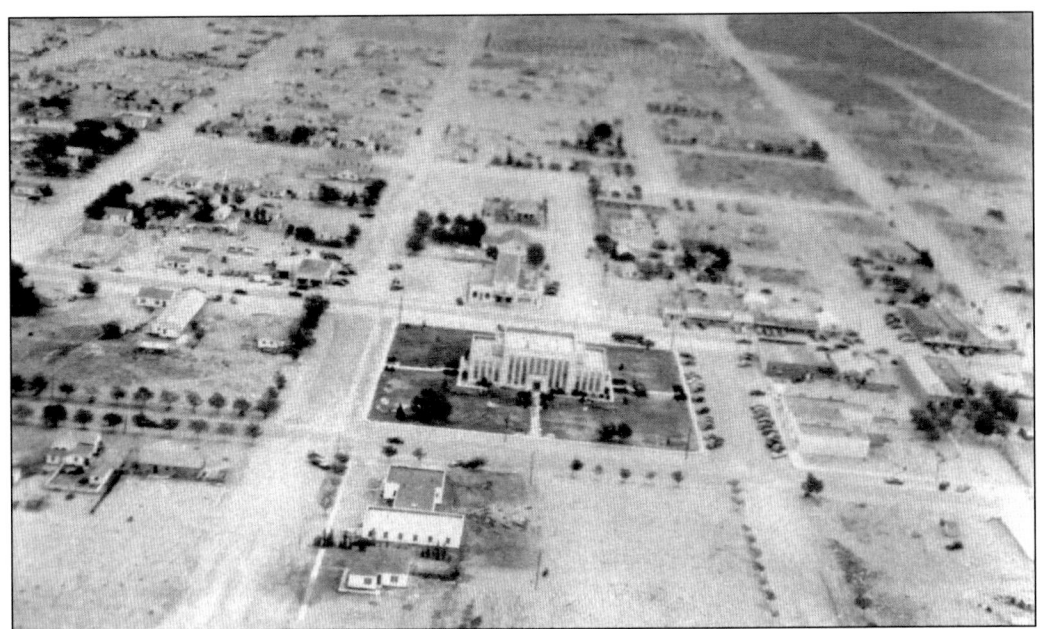

This aerial photograph of Andrews looking east was taken in the early 1940s and shows the Andrews County Courthouse on Main Street and the county hospital across the street, below and to the left of the courthouse. Main Street was the only paved street in town; the highway going to Big Spring was still a hard-packed dirt road. Oil exploration accelerated greatly at the start of the war.

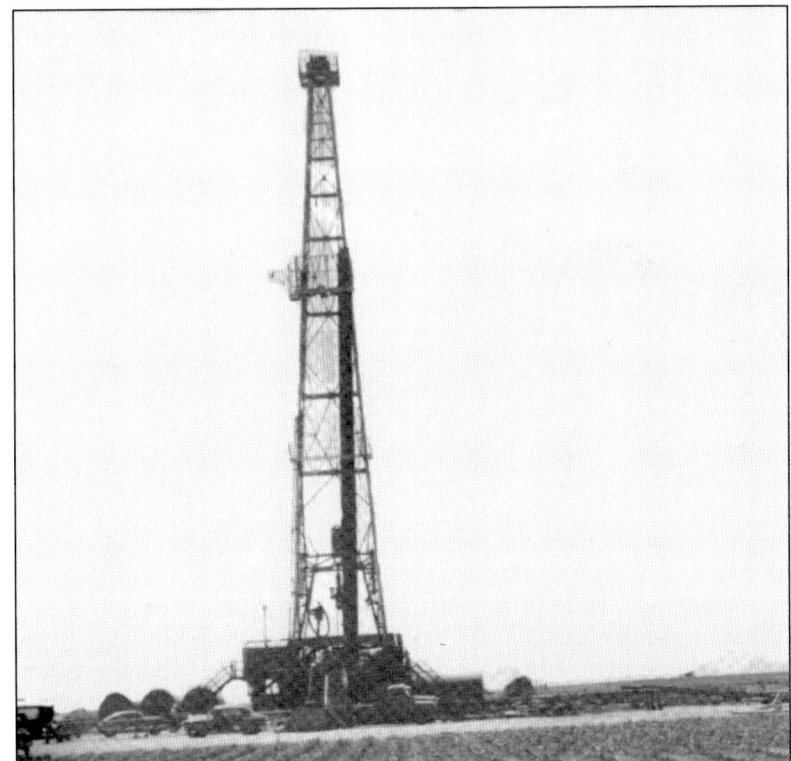

Rotary drilling rigs replaced the old cable tool rigs during the late 1930s, and once the war started in December 1941 there were more than 100 rigs operating in Andrews County. The need for oil increased the population, stretching the already thin housing market and causing lines at stores and cafés.

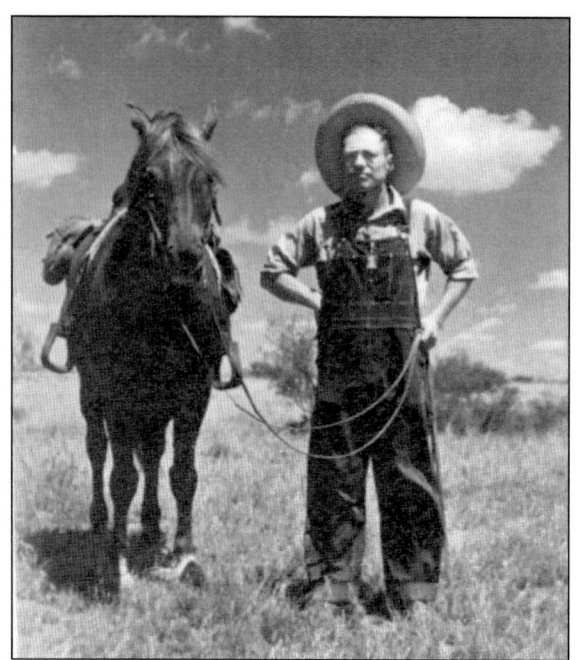

The start of World War II not only increased the need for crude oil, but it caused many shortages in both tools and supplies needed in the oil patches as well as staple items needed for average people. Oil companies had difficulties finding equipment, while tires, sugar, and gasoline were rationed to citizens. Taking the initiative to conserve gasoline was resident Red Sikes, who rode his horse to work daily maintaining existing oil wells.

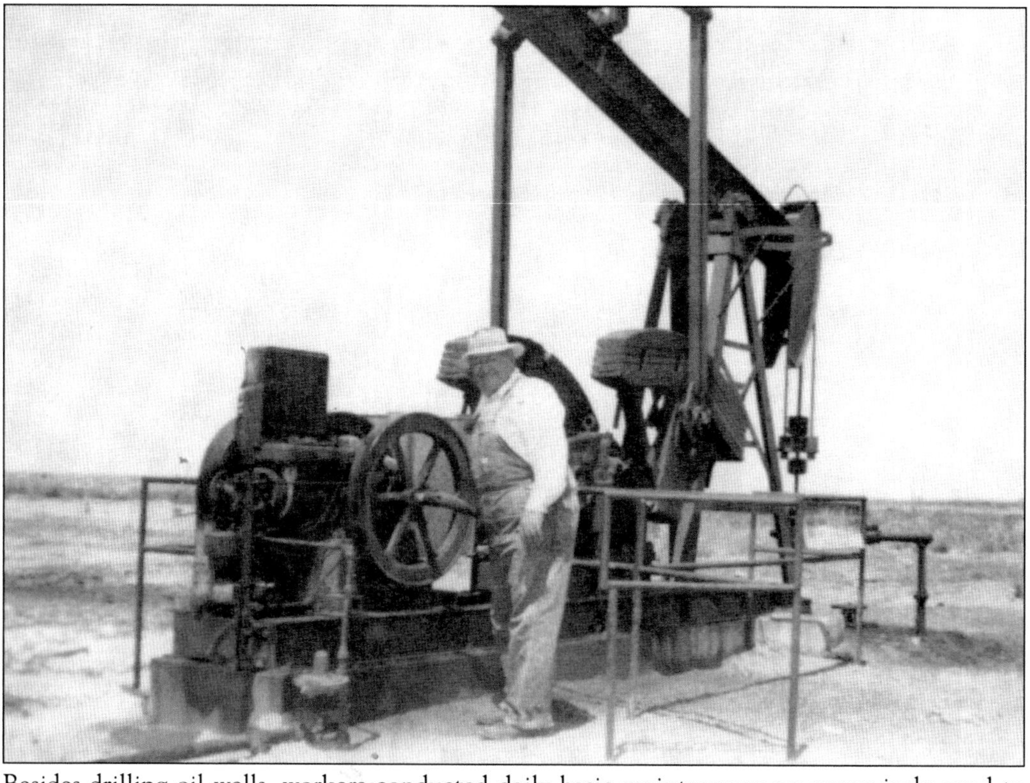

Besides drilling oil wells, workers conducted daily basic maintenance on pump-jacks used to pump the oil up to the surface once a well was completed. After the oil reached the surface, it was piped to storage tanks, then either hauled or piped to refineries. In this picture is Andrews resident Clat E. Robertson at a University "P" Lease, Oil Lease No. 4.

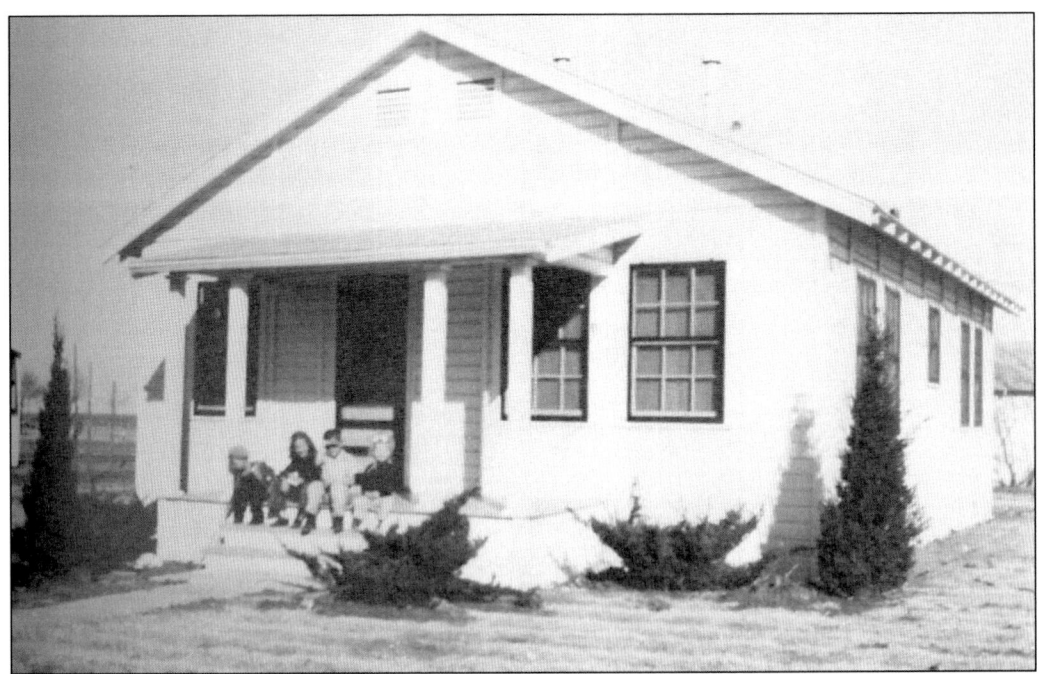

During this period is when oilfield camps, established by oil companies for their employees, flourished across the county, including camps like Humble Oil's Means Camp or Florey, Phillips, Magnolia, Pure Oil Gas Plant, Three Bar Gasoline Plant, El Paso Natural Gas, and many others. Florey was among the largest oil camps in the area and today exists as a county park.

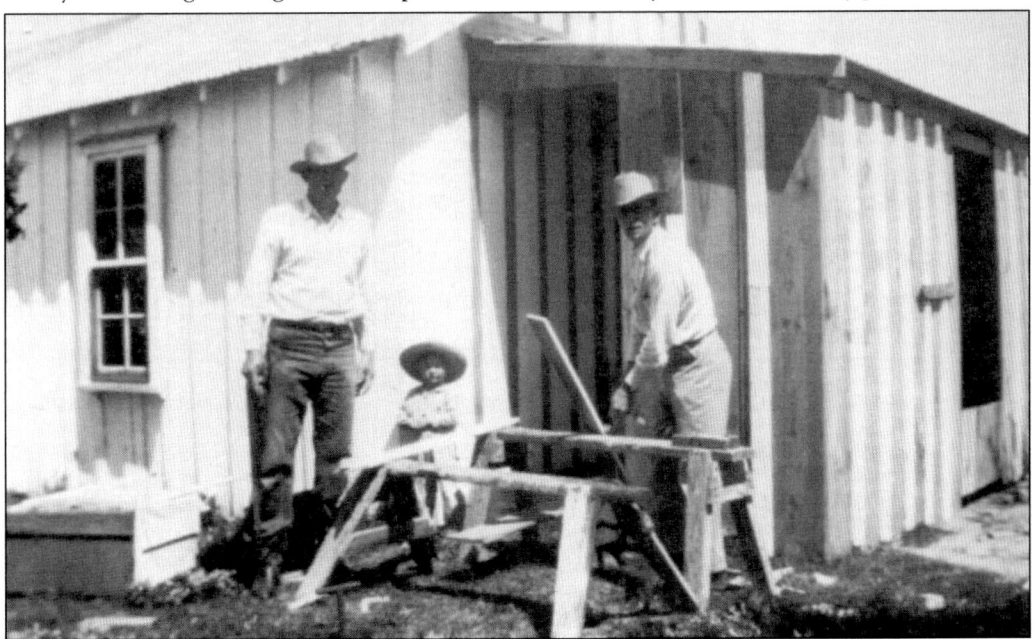

Because housing was so hard to find, oilfield camps were established to provide necessities for employees. Some of the camps, like the Humble Oil Camp at Florey, were mini-cities with grocery stores and cafeterias, housing for families, and bunkhouses for single men. The camps also made it convenient for employees, as it meant their job was often nearby.

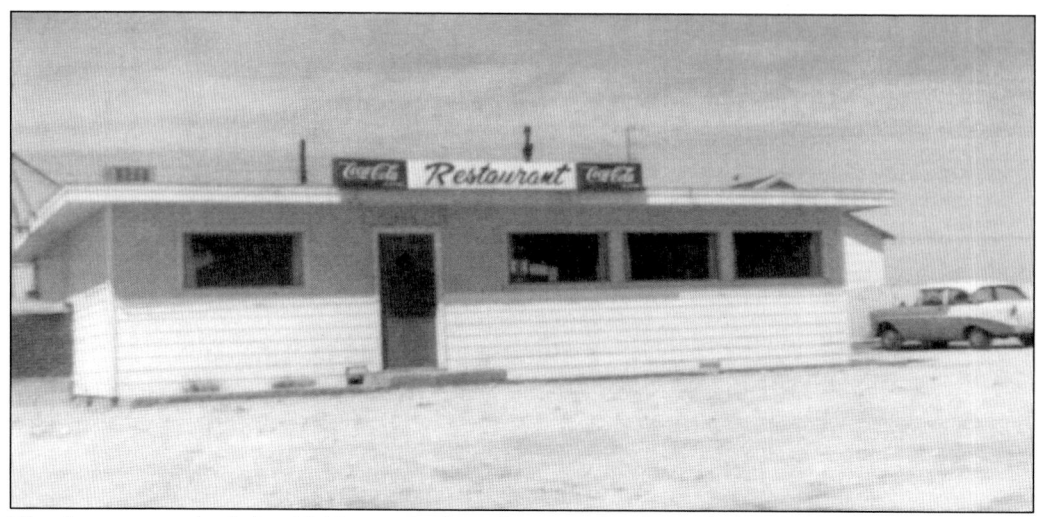

The boom period of the 1940s resulted in the growth of Frankel City, originally known as Fullerton, 15 miles west of Andrews. The discovery of oil in 1941 by Fullerton Oil Company of California and later by Magnolia Petroleum, later to become Mobil Oil, led to the influx of more companies and workers and the start of Frankel City. The upstart community survived for years until its population finally dwindled.

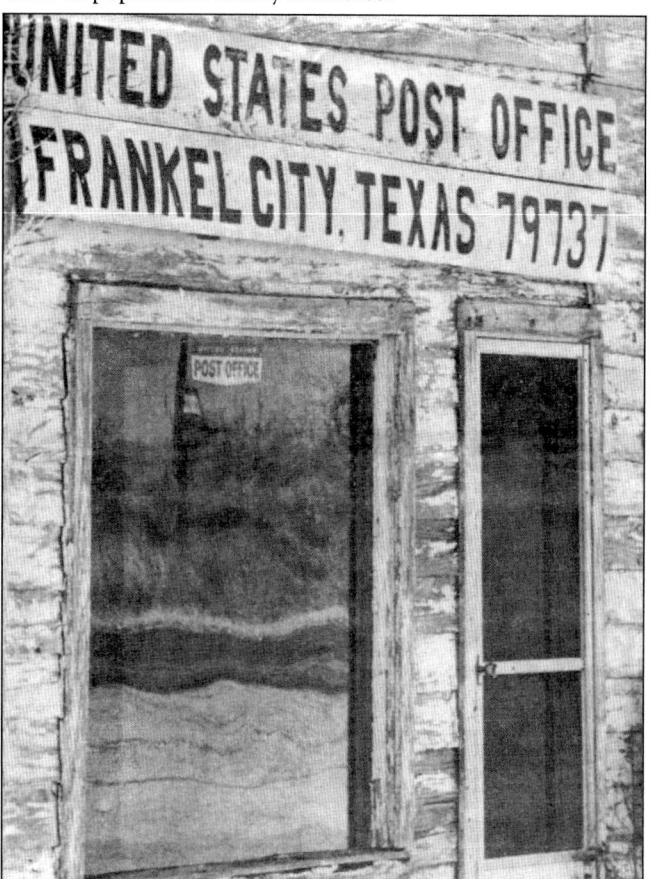

Frankel City in western Andrews County had its own post office to serve the 500 or more families that lived and worked in the Fullerton area during the oil boom of the 1940s. At one time, the community, now a ghost town, had two cafés, two gas stations, a grocery store, delicatessen, beauty shop, two churches, and a telephone exchange. The post office closed in 1976.

During the heydays of Frankel City, one enterprising individual was Ray Porter, who moved his family, including wife, Tiny, from Oklahoma to take advantage of the growing little oilfield town. Porter built his first grocery store in Frankel City and later moved to Andrews, where he operated Modern Grocery on West Broadway Avenue. His family still runs the supermarket in Andrews and other groceries in West Texas managed by grandchildren.

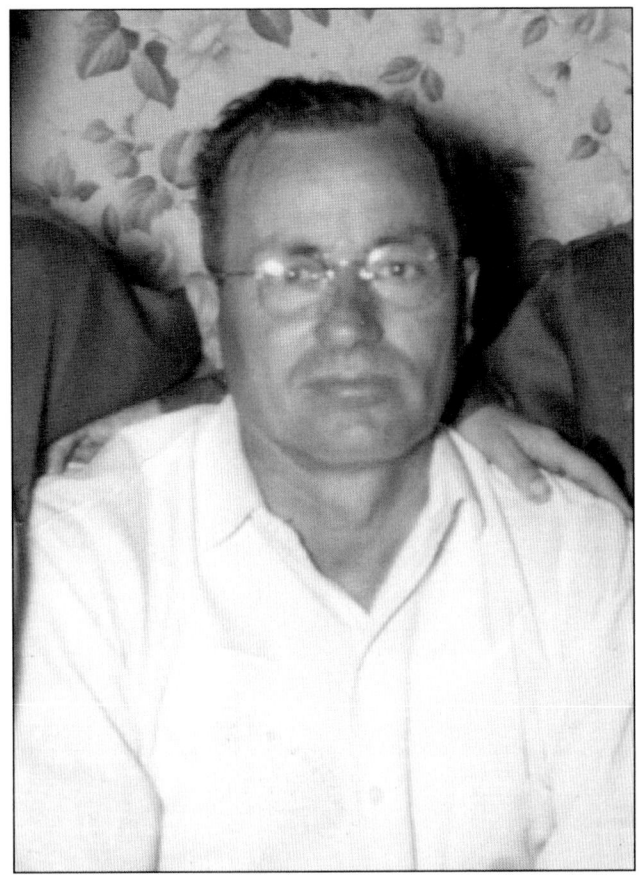

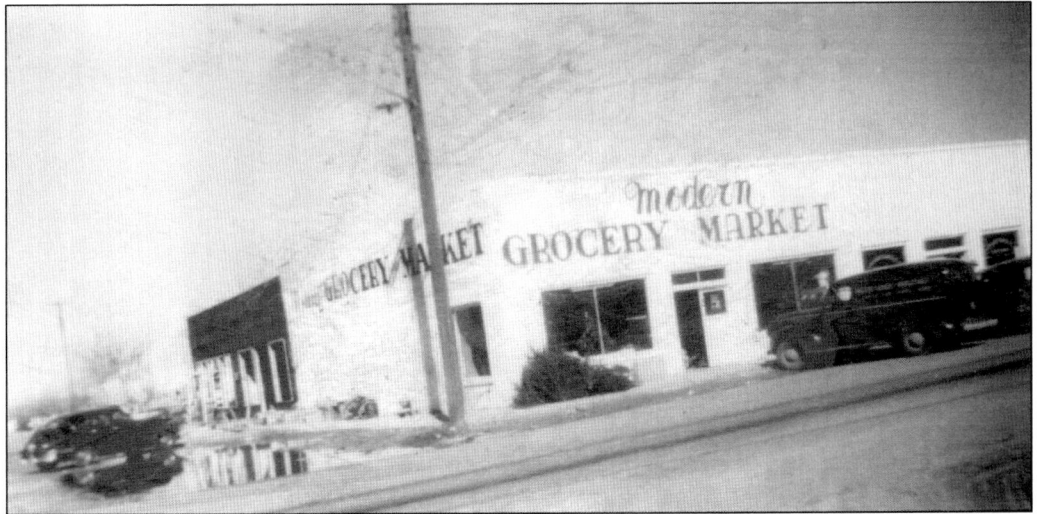

The Porters moved to Andrews from Frankel City where they operated Modern Grocery on West Broadway Avenue. The store was at this location first and moved across to the opposite corner, where it remained for many years. In the early 1980s, the store moved to a much larger facility just a block further west on Broadway Avenue. Then a larger Porter's Thriftway opened on North Main Street in 2000.

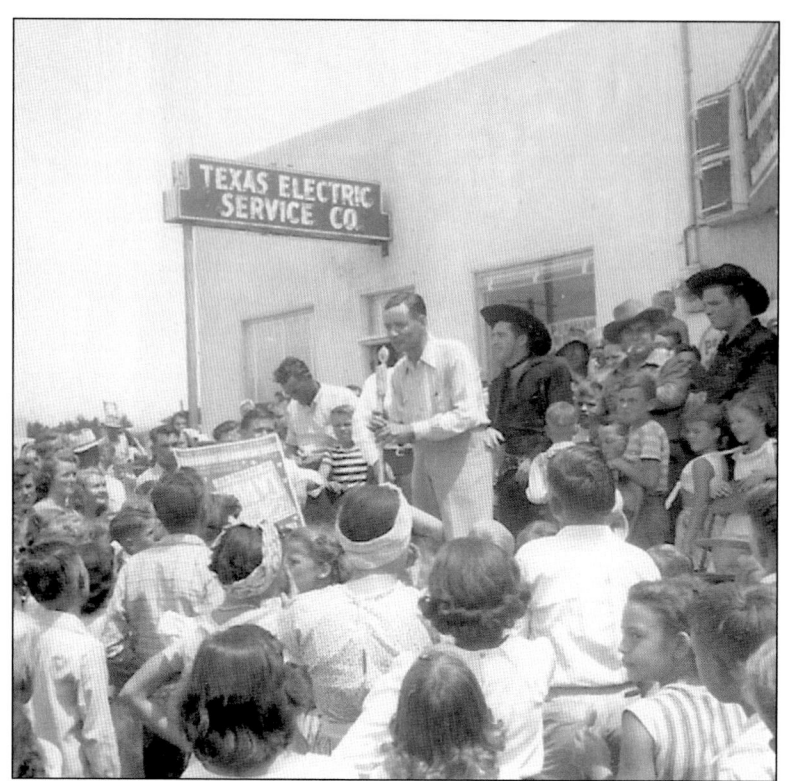

Entertaining moviegoers during the 1940s was cowboy star Lash LaRue, whose movies were popular. LaRue's stopover in Andrews was to promote a new movie and he did demonstrations using the bullwhip that had made him popular in the movies. Following a brief introduction, the crowd went inside the Wallace Theatre to see the actor perform on stage with his whip. Accompanying the actor was sidekick Gabby Hays.

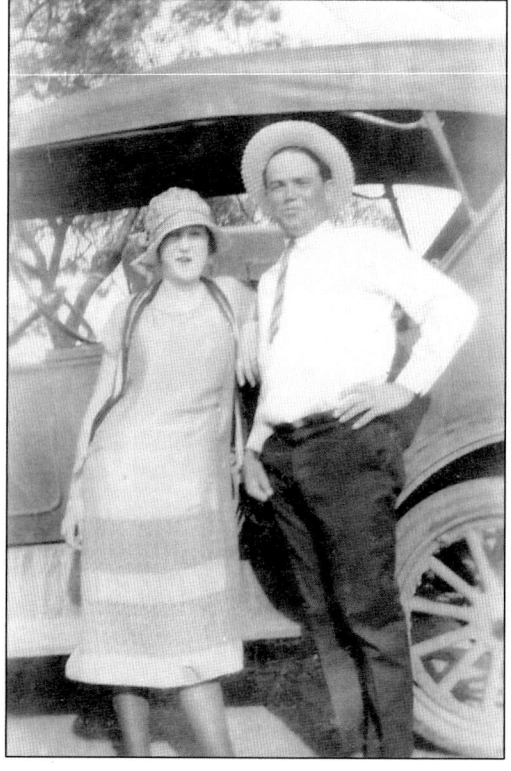

Tom and Ina Jeffreys moved from Odessa to Andrews in 1944 to open and manage a series of restaurants. They opened their first restaurant, Jeffrey's Café, at the start of the 1940s oil boom. Because building materials were scarce, Tom recycled lumber from an old ranch in Graham. They built T. J.'s Ranch House in 1956, which was a popular eatery until it was sold to K-Bob's in 1976.

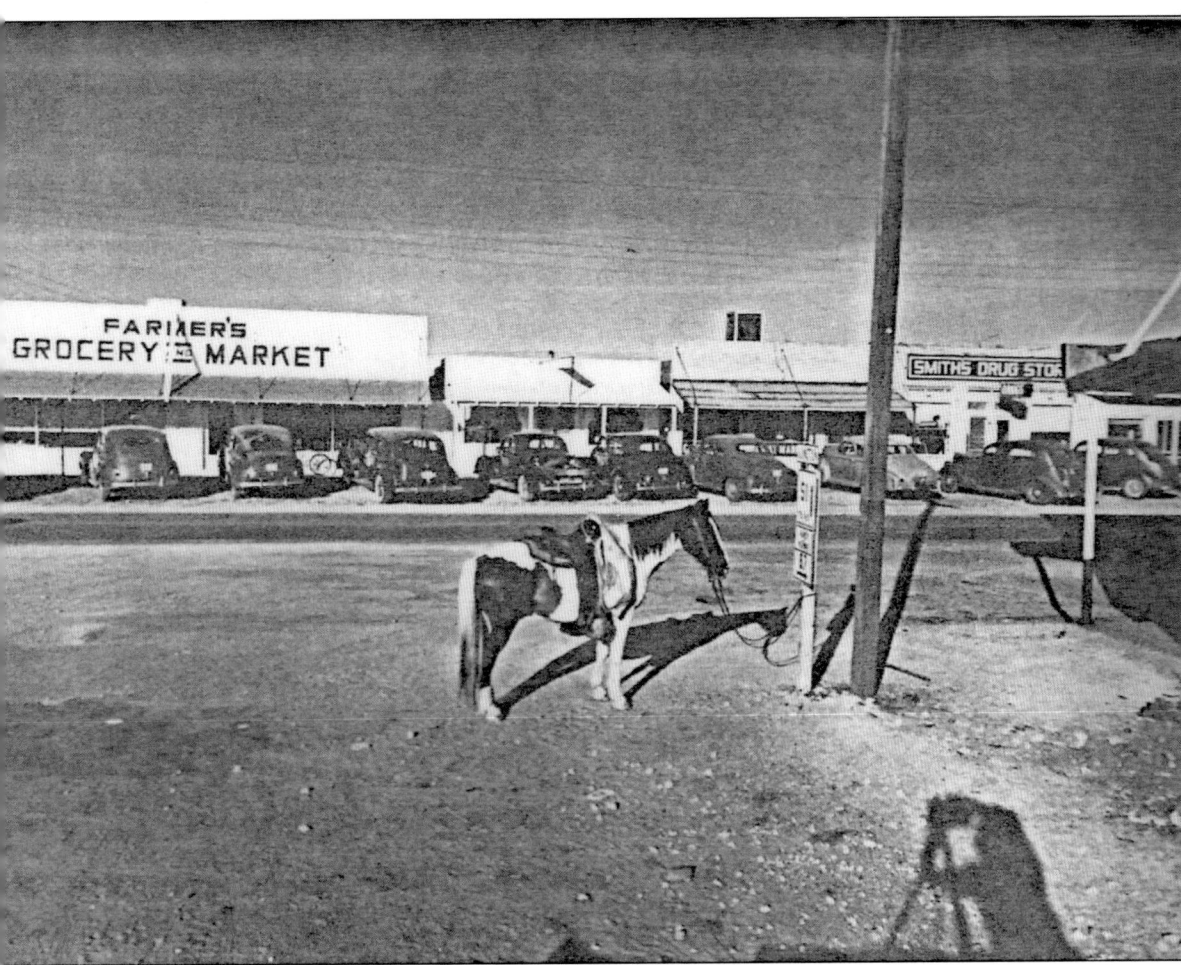

While downtown Andrews was undergoing changes during the war years, it still was not that uncommon to see horses in town tied up outside businesses. This picture, which looks west on Main Street or Highway 51, was taken in 1945 by Esther Bubley for Standard Oil of New Jersey. The horse, Bulldog, belonged to rancher Bill Price. It had been a rapid transition period for the small West Texas town, from a slow, easy-going community to a sudden town full of workers, company men, and others crowding the storefronts looking for a place to eat or stay the night. Lodging was next to nil and many times people went together to rent rooms or otherwise went without. Even after the war ended, the pace in Andrews did not let up, as the exploration for oil continued, now to accommodate peacetime and the sudden return of servicemen and women looking for work and housing. The pace would not let up for several more decades, as oil was big business.

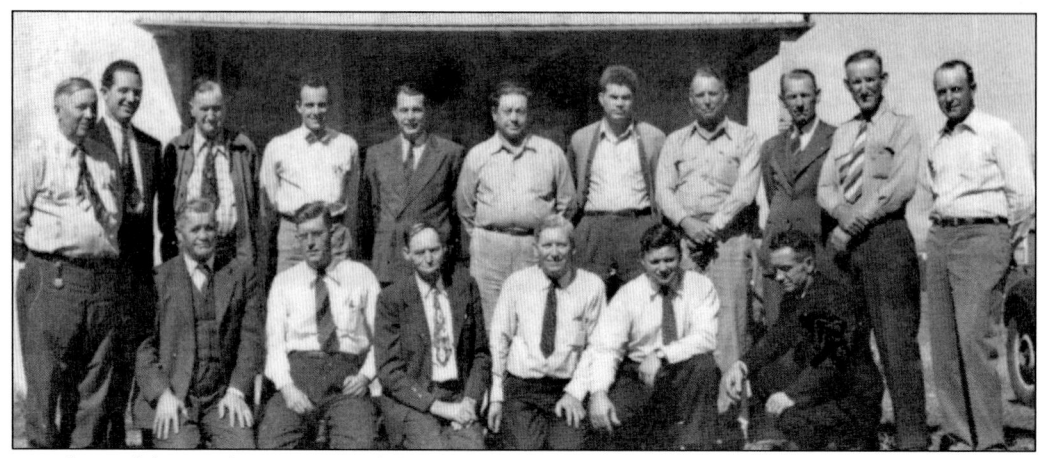

Members of the Andrews Lions Club in 1945 were, from left to right, (first row) C. W. Roberts Sr., A. L. Rhodes, Henry Heath, Rev. P. B. Story, Frances Tubb, and unidentified; (second row) H. T. Wilson, L. L. Taylor, Carl Betenbough, Jim Rogers, unidentified, Dennis Nix, Charles Roberts Jr., Guy McGill, T. D. Hamilton, Bill Blair, and Homer Rentz.

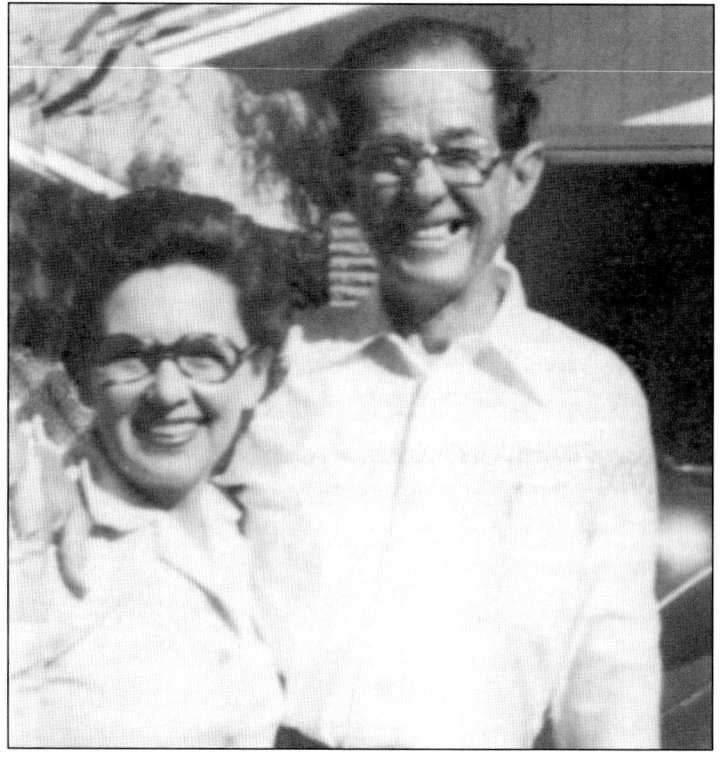

Russell and Maurene Austin arrived in Andrews in 1946 after Russell served in the air force during World War II. He was a POW for 15 months before the war ended. He taught math at the high school and eventually obtained his law degree and later served as 109th district court judge while Maurene worked at the library. They had three children, Bill, Sherry Kay, and Sylvia Gay.

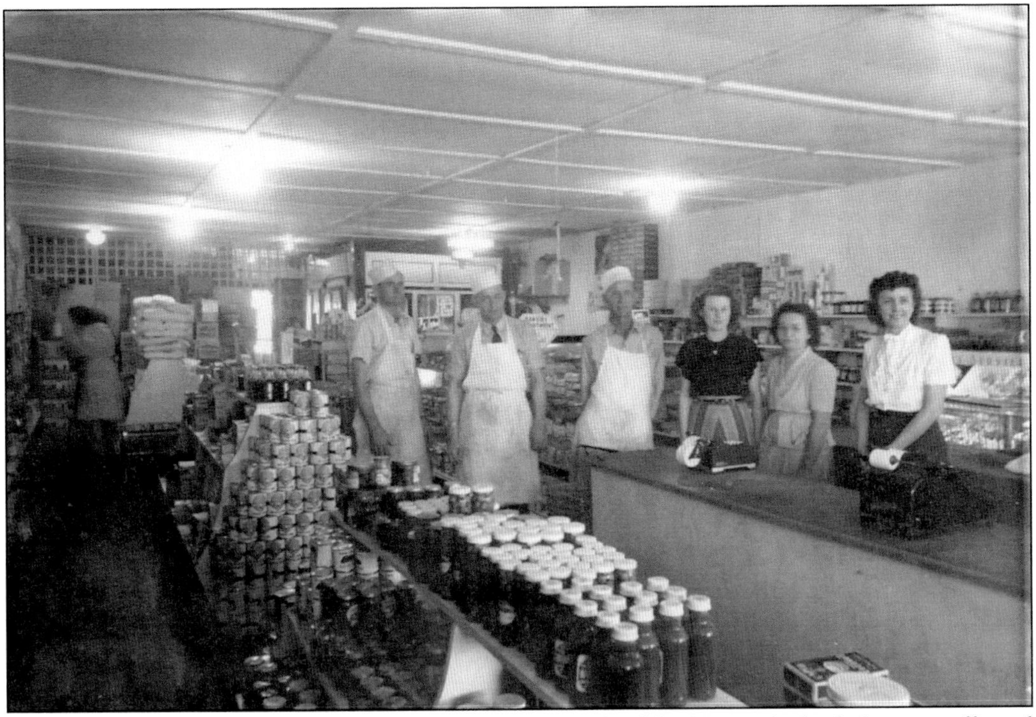

By the end of the war, Andrews had changed considerably. Not only had the war affected the town, but the huge quest for oil to supply the military had changed it, too. City Grocery had opened during the period to supply a growing population. Included in this picture are Oron Price, Virgil Lasater, Roy Coconaugher, Ruby Lasater, and Ina Coconaugher. (Courtesy Martha Page.)

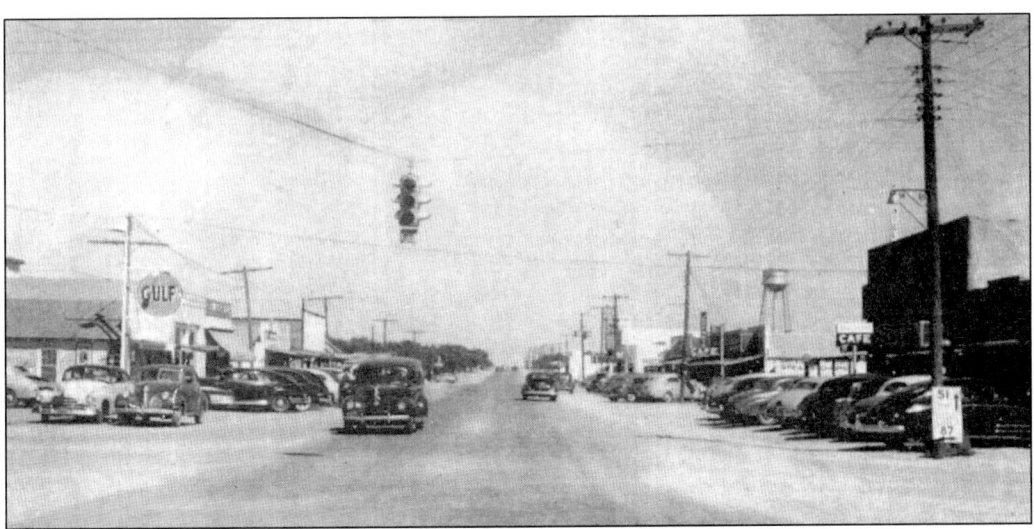

This is an after-the-war view of downtown Andrews looking north on Main Street or Highway 51. Though World War II had been won, it did not appear the boom was over, as oil companies were still discovering new reservoirs of oil. Stanolind Oil's Grayburg formation discovery on Fasken property and the opening of the Dollarhide Field by Magnolia and Humble kept drilling at a brisk pace.

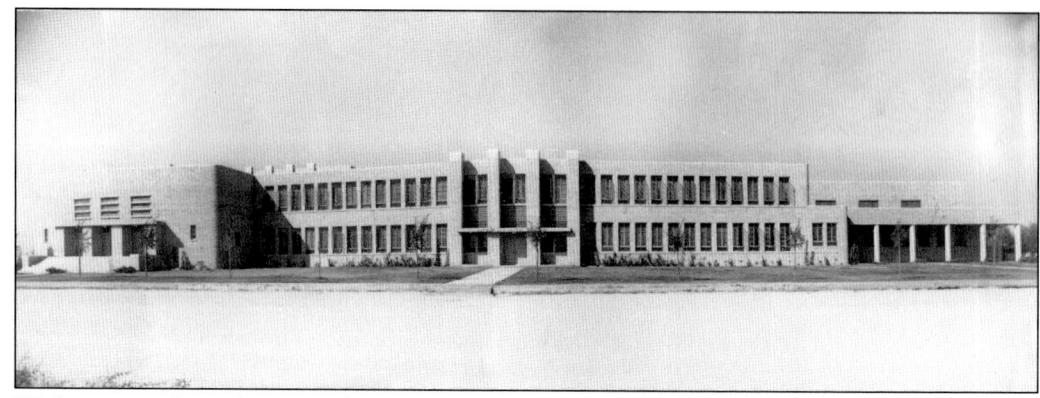

With more students than ever, $300,000 was spent in 1945 for construction of a new high school. The facility was built west of the old high school and a new football field, Hamilton Field, was built in 1949 just behind the new high school. In 1950, $223,000 was spent on building Mustang Gymnasium, located east of the high school. In 1956, to accommodate growth, five elementary schools were built.

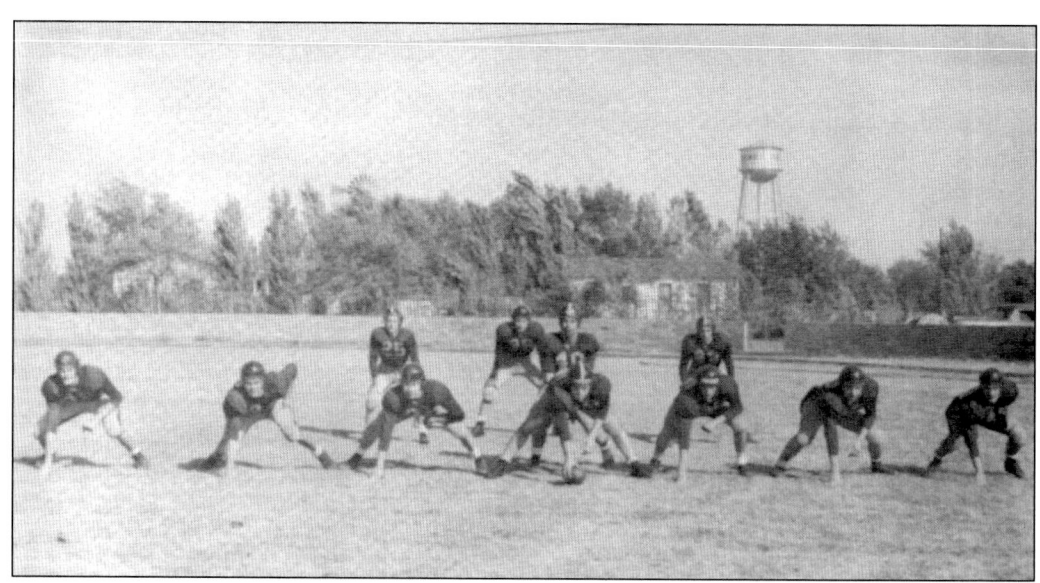

Members of the 1949 Mustang varsity football team included, from left to right, down linemen T. D. Hamilton, Max Short, Sonny Helvey, Robert Forbes, Allen Humphery, Billy Phillips, and John Corley. The quarterback was Bob Holman and the backfield included running backs Johnny Walker and Joe Weatherby and fullback Wayne Graham. The coaches included Francis Tubb, Neal Taylor, Vernon Payne, and Max Goldsmith. The football team manager was Billy Bynum.

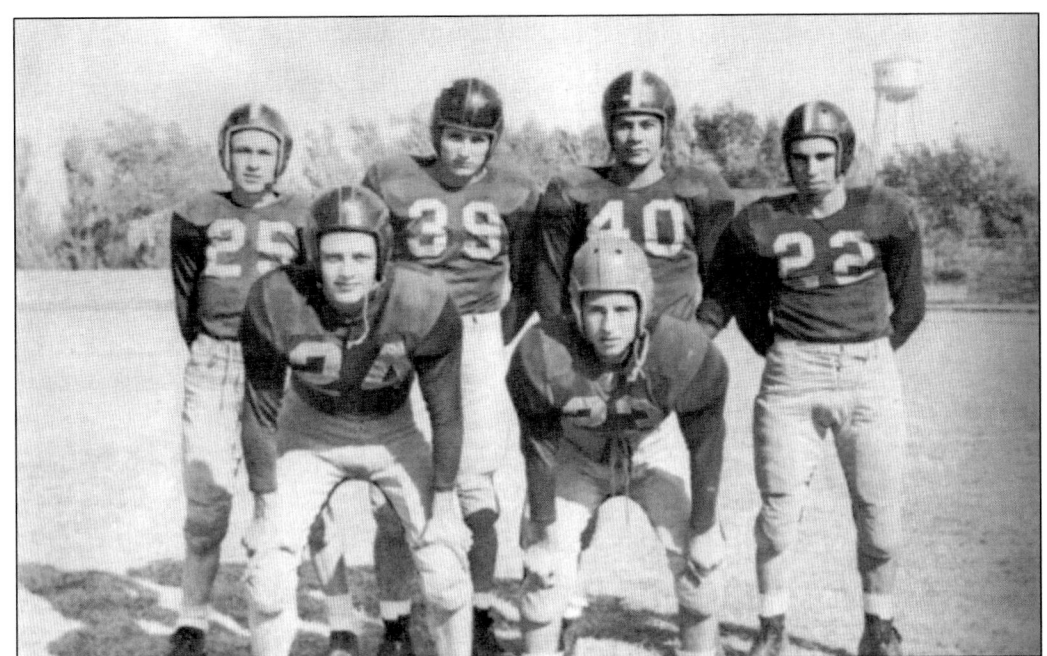

The backfield of the 1949 Andrews High School football team consisted of quarterback Bob Holman, left halfback Johnny Walker, right halfback Joe Weatherby, and fullback Wayne Graham. The Andrews Mustangs team had a new football stadium to play in with Hamilton Field, which was built near the new high school. Cocaptains were Holman and John Corley.

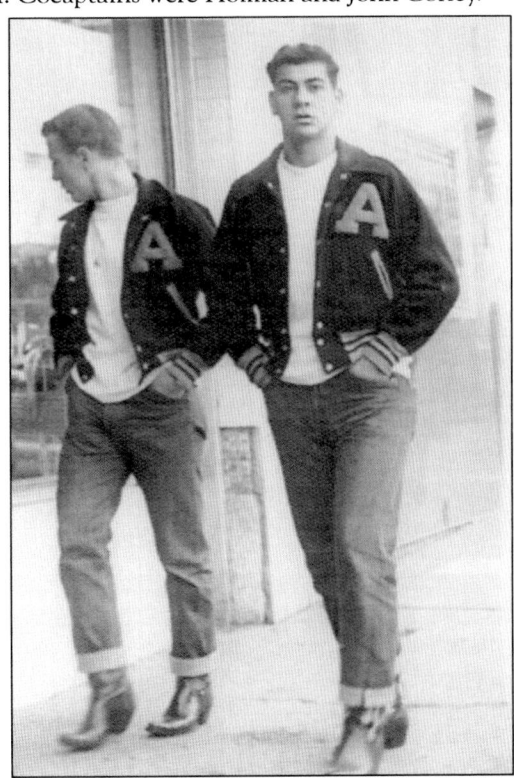

Showing off the latest fad in 1949 are two Andrews Mustang varsity players, Sonny Helvey, left, and Bob Holman. The two were likely heading downtown to City Drug or another café for a soda or milkshake after practice to socialize and visit with other high school students.

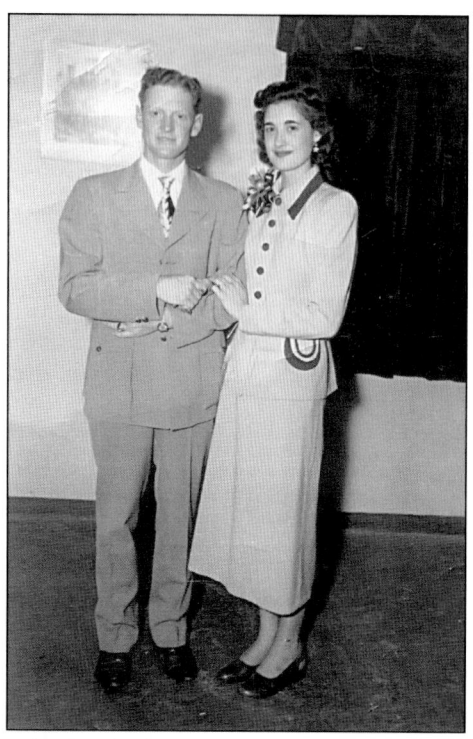

Billy Cox returned from World War II in 1946. He and Nell Floyd were married in 1949. Billy grew up in Andrews after his family moved there from Brown County. As a youngster, he worked for Virgil and Hazel Reed in their drugstore. After the war, he worked for Andrews Telephone Company while Nell ran a beauty shop. Later the couple operated a flower shop for years.

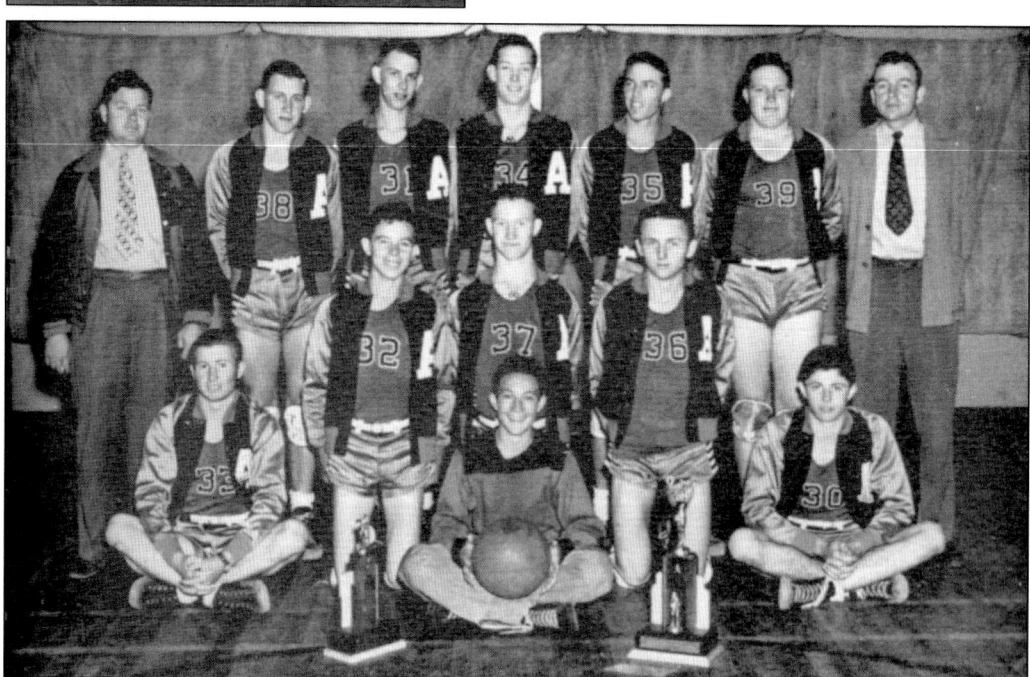

The 1946–1947 Andrews High School basketball team included, from left to right, (first row) guard H. T. Wilson, guard Billy Stell, guard James Smyers, forward Tex Collins, forward Jimmy McAuley, and manager Johnny Walker; (second row) coach Francis Tubb, guard Ferris Hamilton, center T. D. Hamilton, center Charles Pinnell, forward Jack Young, forward Ferrell Nixon, and coach Vernon Payne.

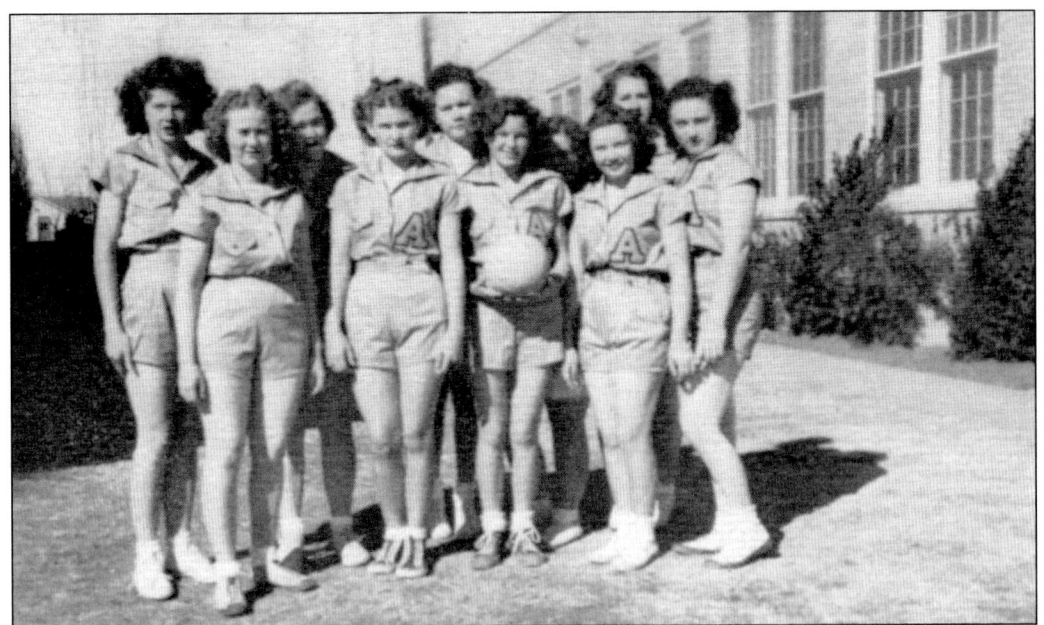

The Andrews High School Volleyball "B" Team in 1947 consisted of Coza Ree Nix, Charlene Greaves, Zeanna Henry, Patty Jenkins, Margaret Duncan, Virginia Robertson, Betty Turner, Jo Postelle, Rose Mary Stewart, and Alla Ree Eastman. Although not shown, the "A" team consisted of Dorsie White, Helen Cotton, Lola Turnbow, Geneva Hitch, Joyce Cotton, and Norma Phillips.

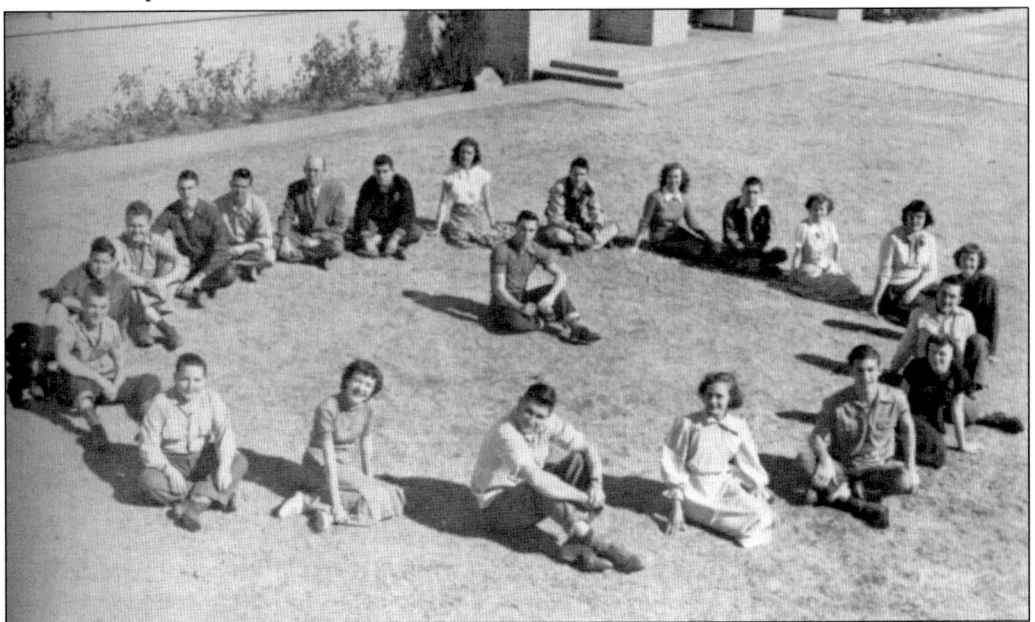

The Andrews High School Student Council in 1949 consisted of, going left from center, Wayne Graham, Charlene Goodall, Donald Nolan, W. E. Cain, Edward Lewis, Bobby Joe Barnes, Bob Summerwell, Jack Neely, sponsor M. O. Woolam, Bob Holman, Mildred Cotton, Gilbert Madison, Charlotte Landon, Billy Bynum, Lavada Alldredge, Phyllis Cercy, Joan Price, Johnny Walker, Connie Pruett, John Corley, Jean Price, and Joe Weatherby in the center.

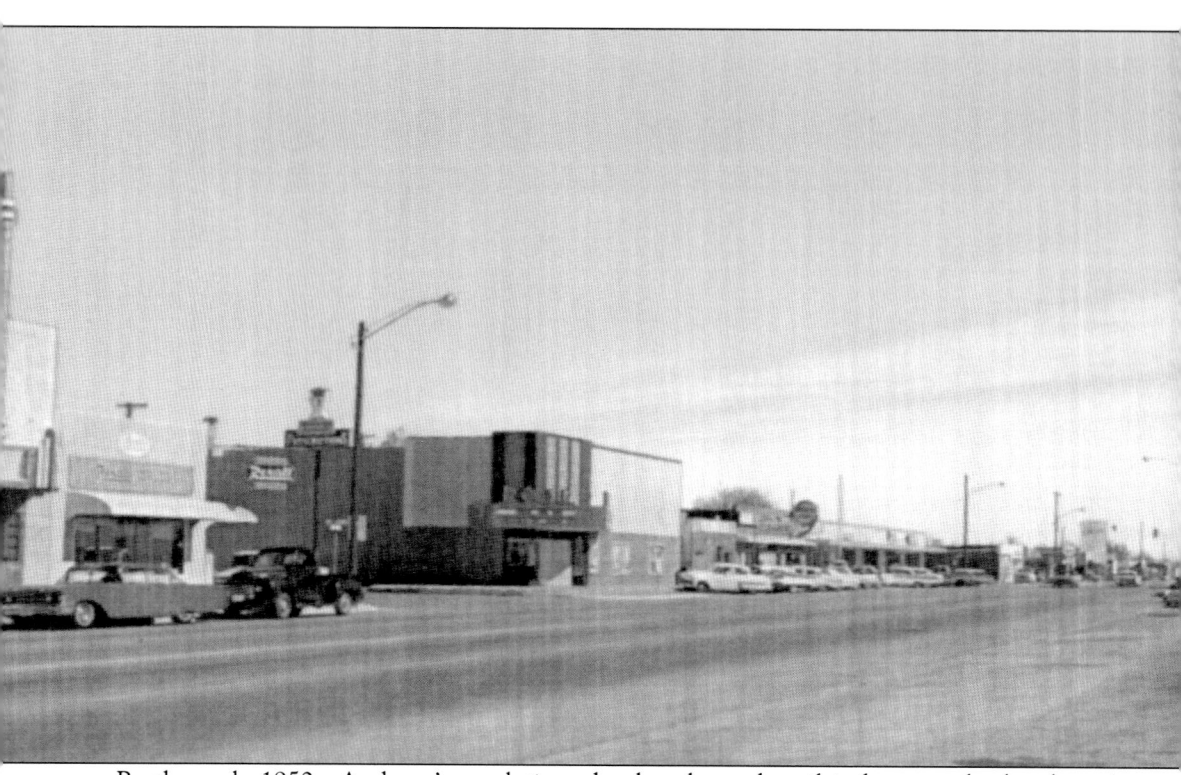

By the early 1950s, Andrews' population, due largely to the oil industry and related service companies, had grown to more than 5,000 residents as the face of the community changed drastically from just 10 years prior. Considerable construction had occurred downtown, more residential homes were built, and there was growth in the school system. Since 1940, construction projects included a new courthouse, airport, library, and community building, to name a few. Looking eastward on Main Street in front of the Andrews County Courthouse was the Rose Theater, while just barely visible to the left is the Wallace Theatre and Corner Drug, which was run by Elmer Hurley. Corner Drug's soda fountain was a favorite of high school students, and students frequented the business for several decades, including eventually under the guidance of pharmacist Jerry Trower and his wife, Jerri. To the right of the Rose Theater is the Western Auto store and farther right, looking southward, is Hulen's Jewelry. Past the intersection of Main Street and Broadway Avenue is Forrest Lumber Company.

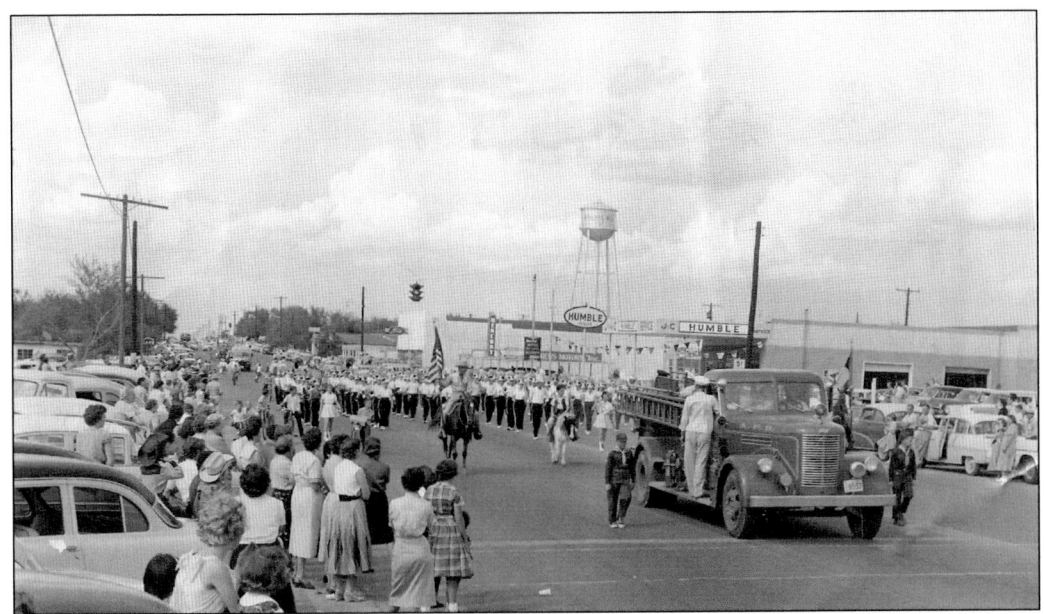

Another picture showing off downtown Andrews is this 1953 photograph of the annual Andrews County Fair Parade, looking north on Main Street. The man on horseback holding the American flag behind the fire truck is O. D. Huckabee. The county fair parade was eventually dropped and replaced with the annual homecoming parade.

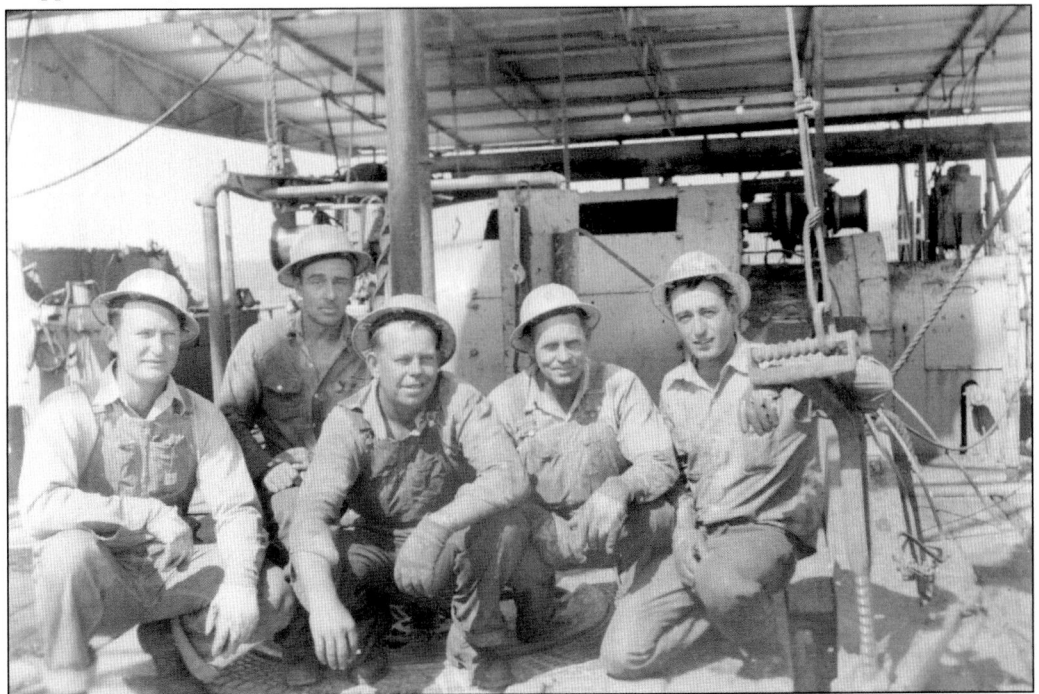

The 1950s saw 90 new oilfields discovered, more than any decade in the history of the county, a result of no slow down in activity following World War II. Shown in this 1953 picture are roughnecks with the oil drilling company owned by Henry Black. They included W. A. Heath, driller W. L. Baird, E. M. Deni, J. W. Arnold, and R. L. Gaines.

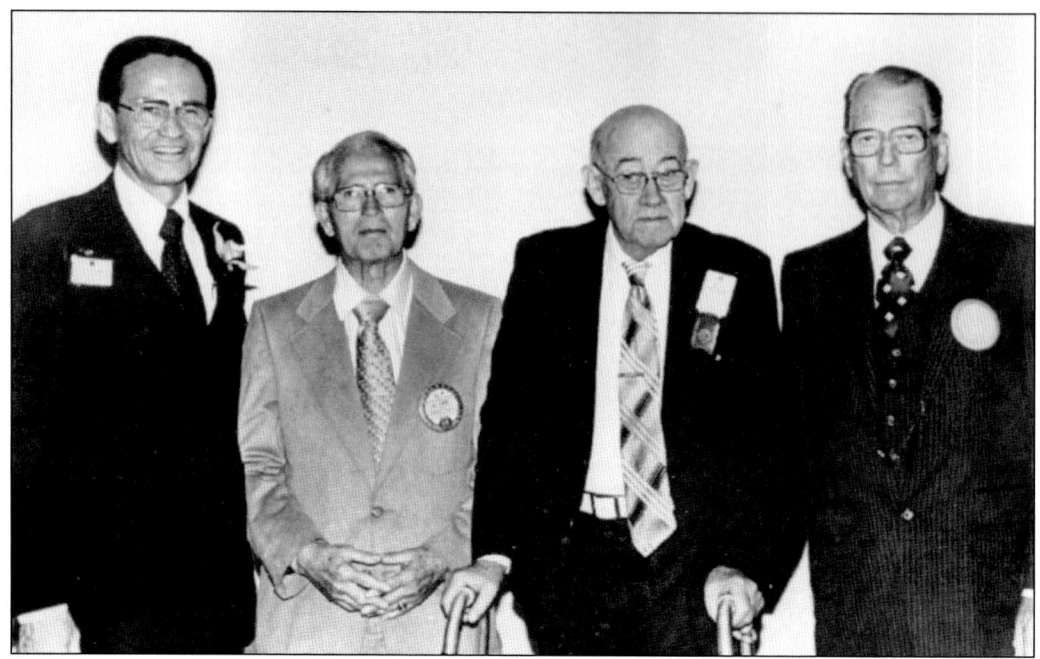

Three notable residents and Andrews Lions Club members were J. Lee Smith (second from left), longtime teacher and principal with Andrews School District whose wife, Juanita, also taught in the school district; M. O. Woolam (third from left), who moved to Andrews with his wife, Newell, in 1941 to teach; and Guy McGill (far right), operator of the local natural gas company. The person at the far left is unidentified.

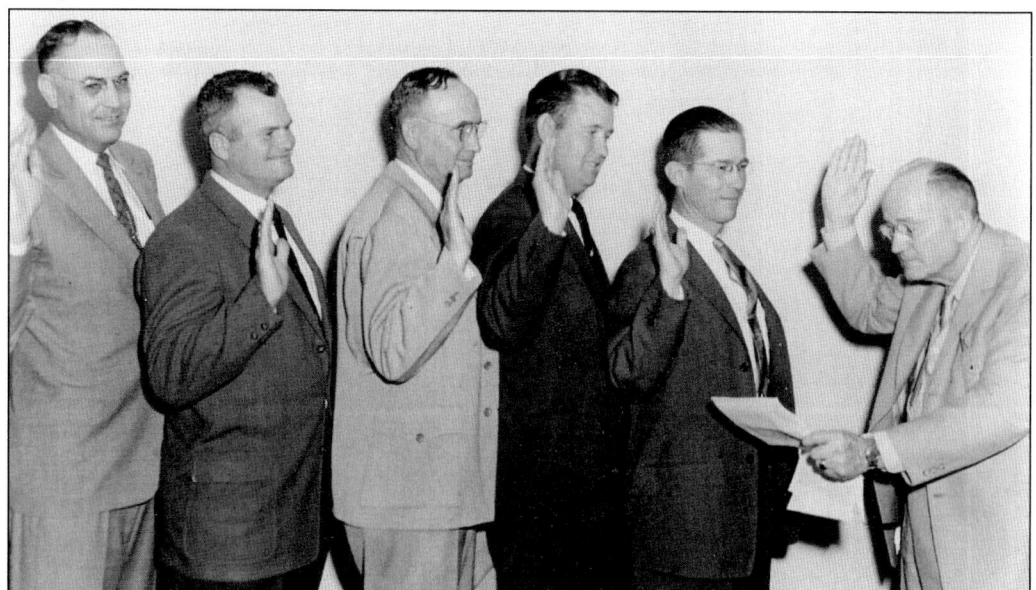

Being sworn into office as Andrews County officials on January 1, 1957, are, from left to right, tax assessor-collect Floyd Peacock; county commissioner of precinct No. 1 Joe Allbright; county sheriff Ray Phillips; county commissioner of precinct No. 3 J. W. Moxley; and Russell D. Austin, 109th District Court Judge. Administering the oath of office is longtime district clerk Sam Smith, pictured at far right.

Sandra Price was responsible for riding Old Snip, the Mustangs' mascot, during football games. The horse and rider were a favorite at football games at Mustang Stadium, where the duo led the players onto the field, helped stir team spirit, and entertained the crowd. During the 1950s and 1960s, the Mustangs' mascot was a crowd pleaser. Ultimately, the tradition ended due to state regulations from the University Interscholastic League that banned large mascots from participating in high school events, citing dangerous conditions with the animals. Andrews County schools have enjoyed considerable success in various sporting events for years, including girls athletic sports, which expanded in the 1980s. Andrews also maintains a successful academic record, winning 17 consecutive literary titles, including debate, math, journalism, and others, first beginning in 1962.

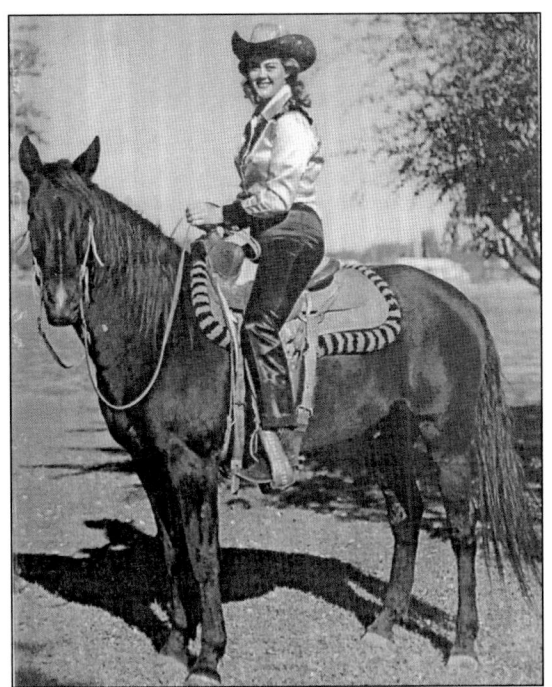

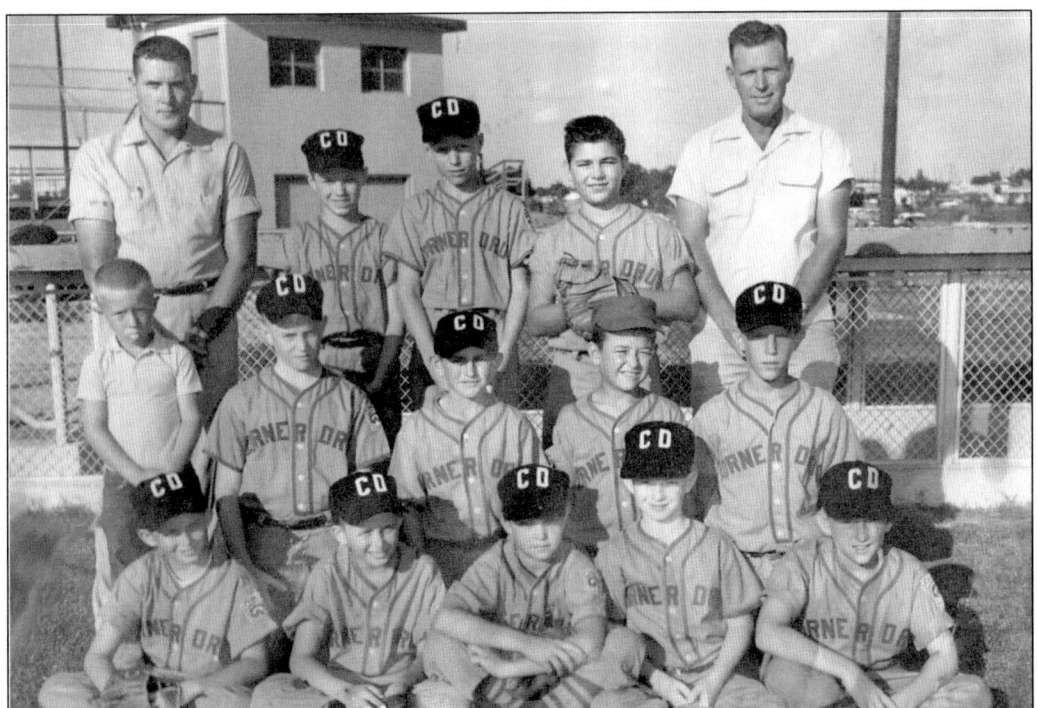

Little League baseball was important in the lives of local youngsters. Pictured here is the Corner Drug team, which came in third in 1959. From left to right are (first row) Jimmy Osterhout, Danny Osterhout, Doug Ham, Lynn Taylor, and Jerry Averyt; (second row) Terry Turner, James Flugham, Billy Neal, Roy Parker, and Jimmy Ryan; (third row) Tommy Jackson, David Horn, Mike Turner, Ronnie Caudel and coach Pete Turner.

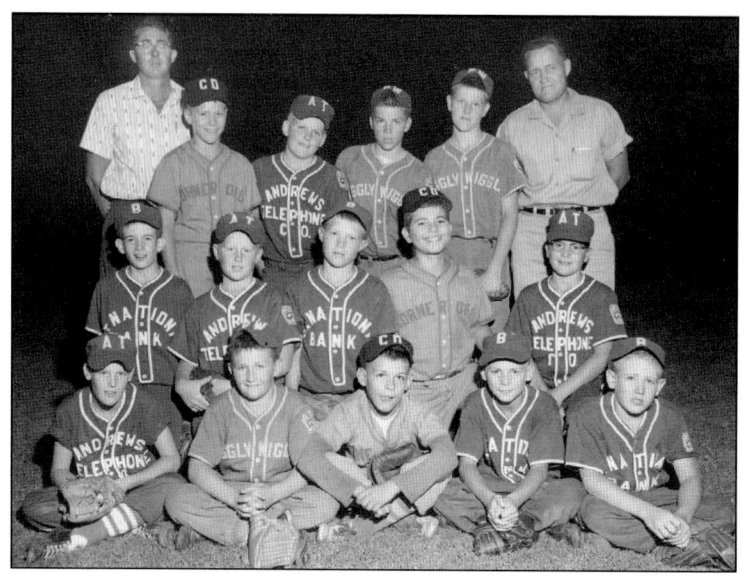

The Little League All-Star Team in 1959 included, from left to right, (first row) Vin Bentenbaugh, Douglas Jenkins, Rickey Camacho, Jimmy Newman, and Kenny Thompson; (second row) Jimmy Nelson, Gene Alley, Dwain Matthews, Ronnie Caudel, and Earl Scott; (third row) coach Curtis Nix, Mike Turner, Kip Sanders, Bobby Smith, Clayton McLauren, and coach John Jenkins.

During the late 1950s and early 1960s, Andrews dominated in track and field, receiving state and national recognition. At the 1960 Mustang Relays, the Andrews team set a new national record in the 440-yard relay with a time of 41.5 seconds. The team consisted of, from left to right, (first row) Darvis Carmier and Larry Shoemaker; (second row) R. C. Merritt, coach Max Goldsmith, and Ted Nelson.

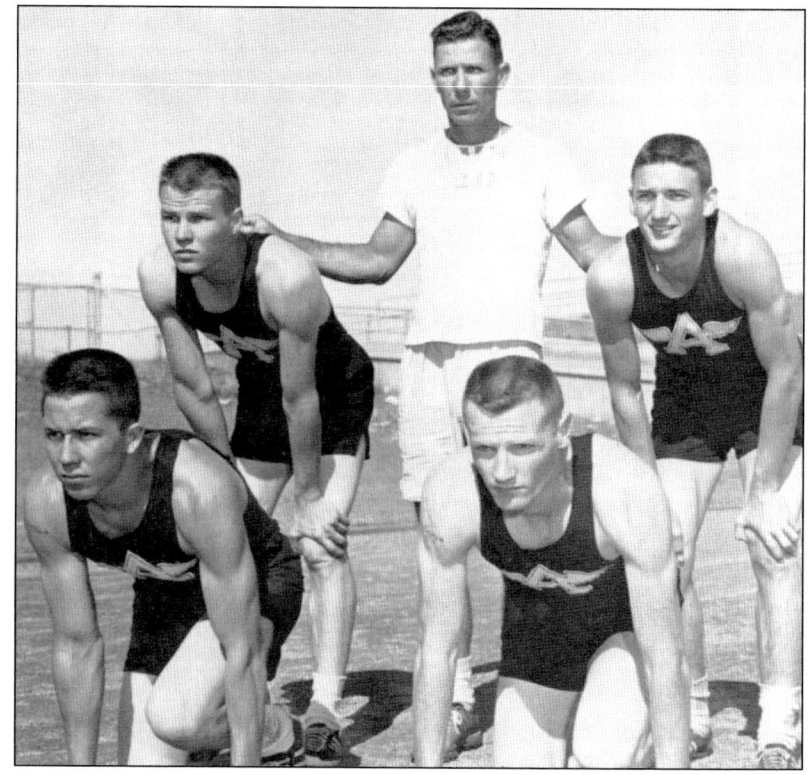

Three
A GRAND JUBILEE

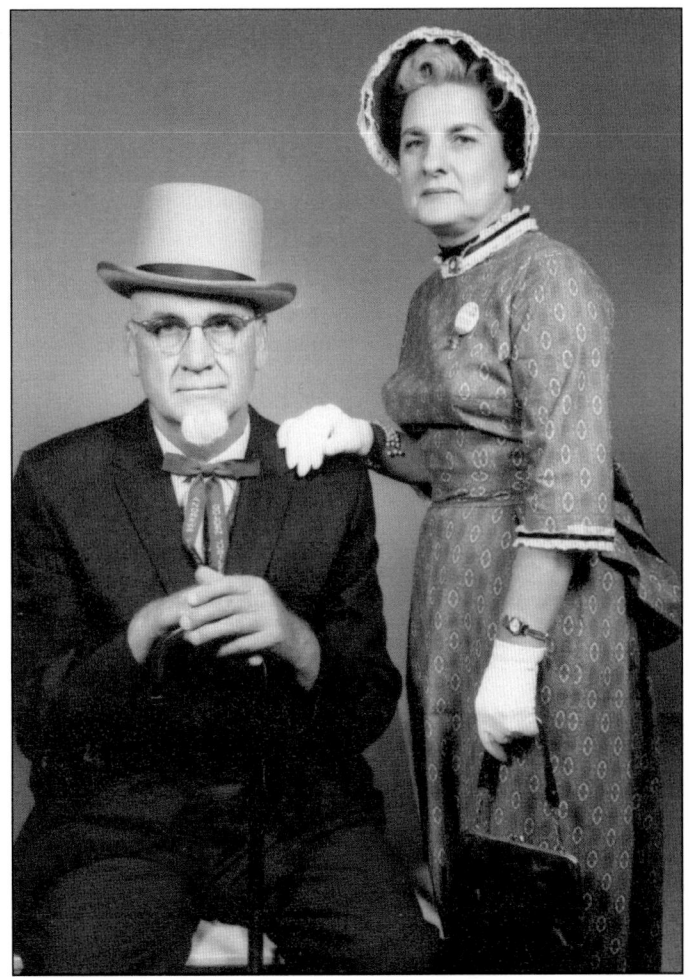

In 1960, Andrews celebrated its 50th anniversary with a celebration that spanned an entire week and included contests, musical shows, beauty contests, and dances—an extravaganza to honor and recognize the community's past and celebrate the future. Participating in the celebration were Andrews residents Charlie and Quida Carruth (right), who raised two children, Chock and Kendall, in Andrews and operated an oilfield trucking company, which still exists today.

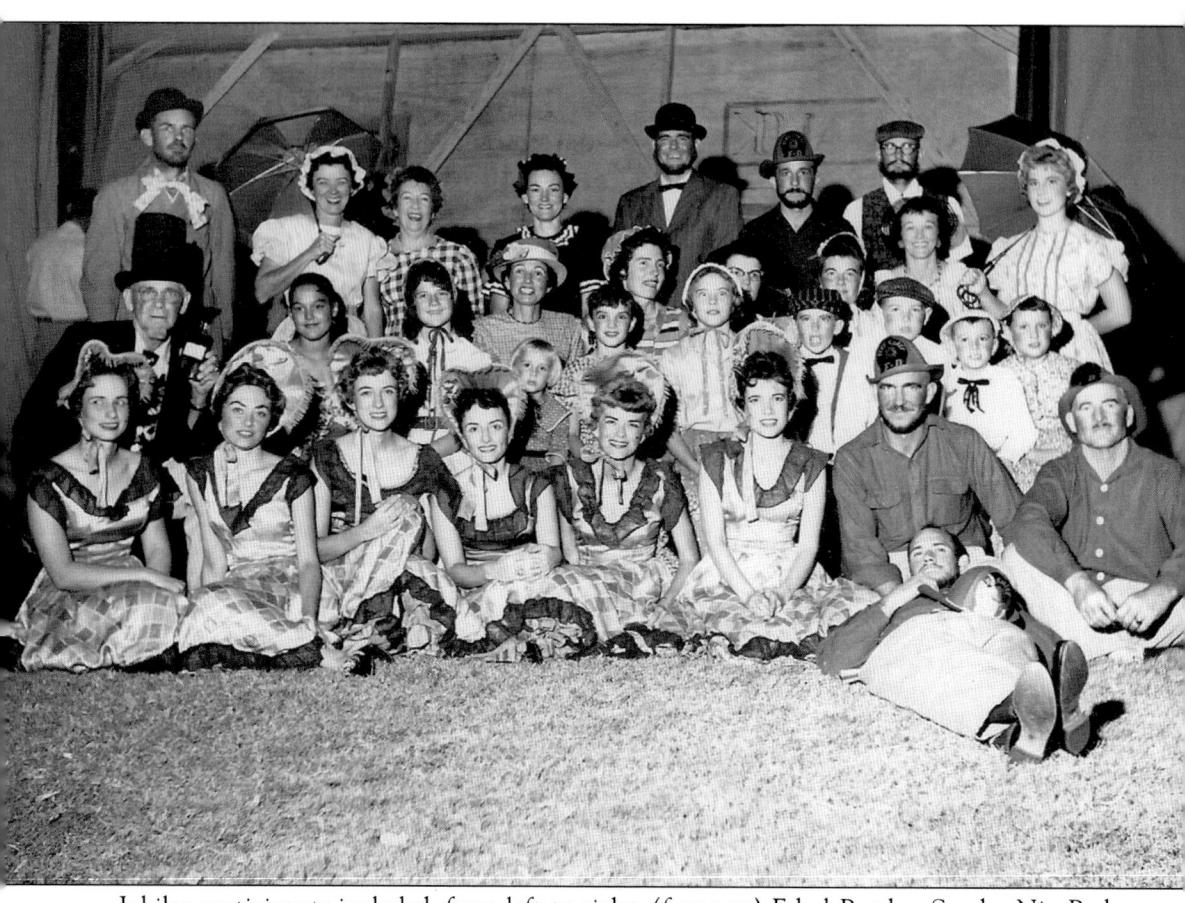

Jubilee participants included, from left to right, (first row) Ethel Porche, Sandra Nix Parker, Frances Deen, Nadine Black, Jo Green, Carolyn Green, Roy Cypert, O. A. Nix, and Gayle Morrow; (second row) Jack Newman, Cheryl Thomas, unidentified, Wanda Raburn, Brenda Hamilton, Becky Shepherd, Gladys Sharbutt, Peggy Shepherd, Richard Hamilton, Mona Hamilton, Rock Raburn, unknown, Chuck Raburn, and Ginger Raburn; (third row) Raymond Sharbutt, Margaret Shepherd, Lovie Newman, Ruth Thomas, O. B. Raburn, George McDaniel, Leland Hamilton, and Annette Elkins.

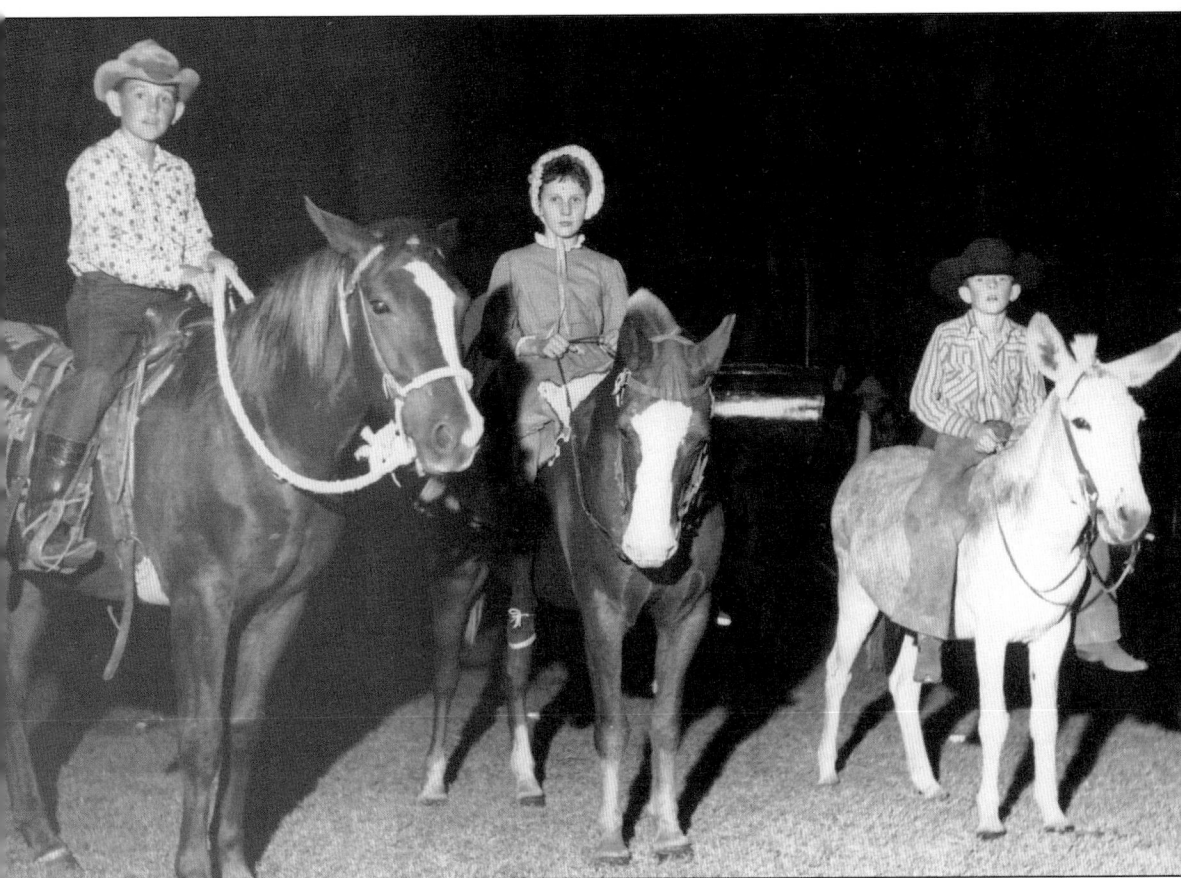

From left to right, Billy Neal, Susan Irwin, and Doug Irwin look the part of early county pioneer youths aboard their animals. Young Doug rode a burro for the occasion. Locals dressed like those from years long ago during a trip down memory lane as the community-wide jubilee celebrated the town's 50th anniversary.

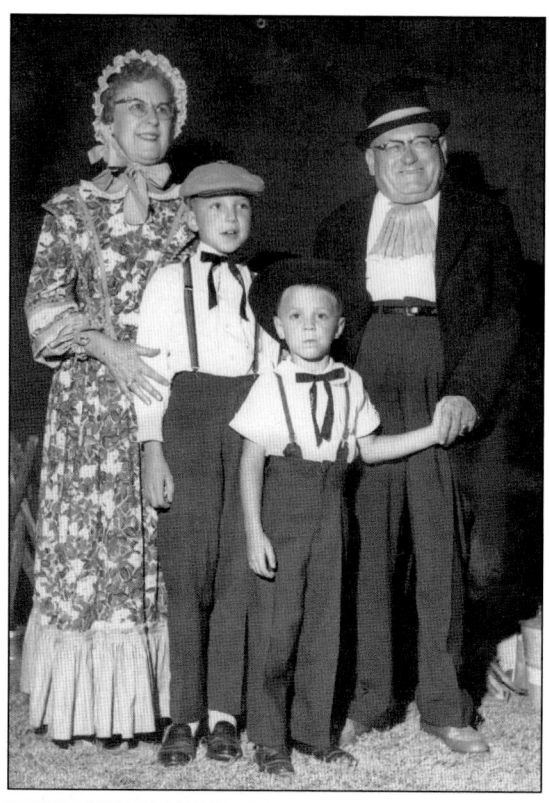

Cleo Doggett, left, and Owen L. Doggett enjoy spending time with their grandsons, Gordon Ramsey, second from left, and Matt Ramsey, third from left, during Andrews County's Golden Jubilee Celebration in 1960. It was a time for families to celebrate the county's historical achievements during its 50 years in existence.

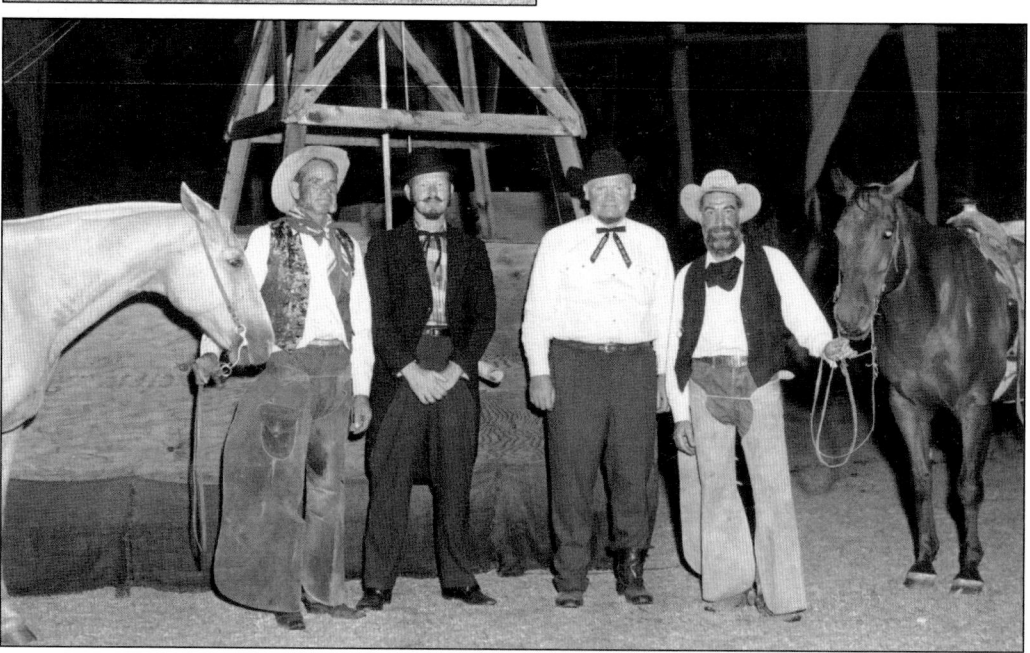

From left to right, Oron Price, Ken Wilson, Bud Duncan, and Frank Stickney thoroughly enjoyed themselves during Andrews County's Golden Jubilee in 1960. The goal of the celebration was to create an atmosphere complete with clothing and lifestyles similar to those in 1910. Promoters of the jubilee were serious about the event and even fined men 25¢ for not growing a beard.

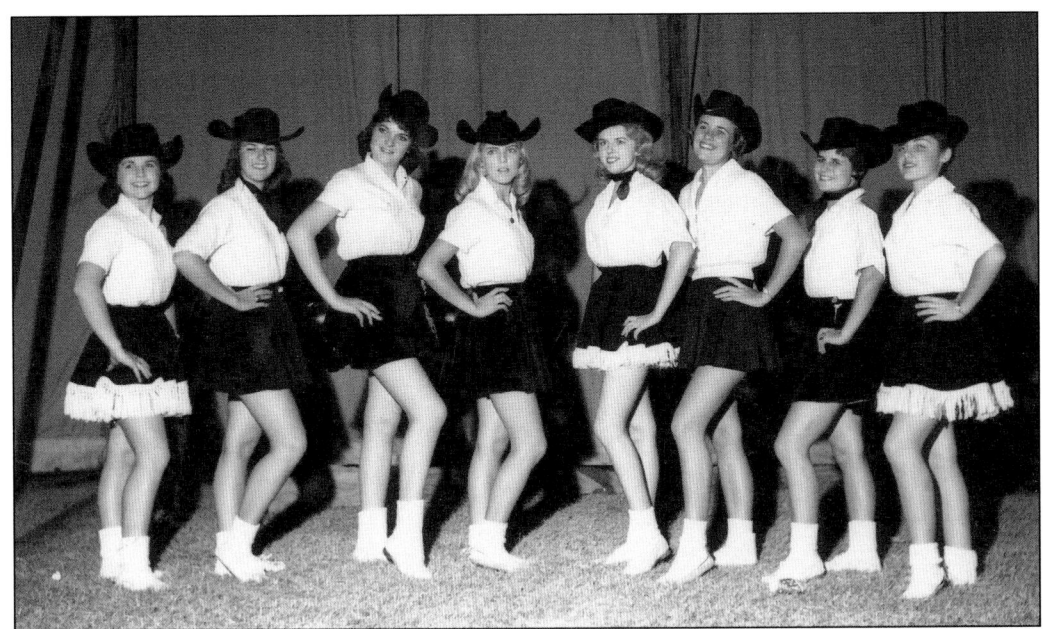

The Andrews Western Girls came out in force during Andrews County's Golden Jubilee Celebration in 1960. The weeklong celebration included numerous plays, pageants, and contests all related to the county's heritage. The western girls included, from left to right, Nancy Lyons, Jo Beth Payne, Pat Ryan, Sharon Perkins, Dorenda Alcorn, Connie Beilue, Saundra Norman, and Diane Thompson.

One of the popular traditions of the 50th jubilee celebration in September 1960 included residents donning clothing from 1910, when Andrews County was officially organized. Many couples dressed in stylish attire were captured in photographs during the weeklong festivities. Ernest and Grace Hensley, pictured here, were among them.

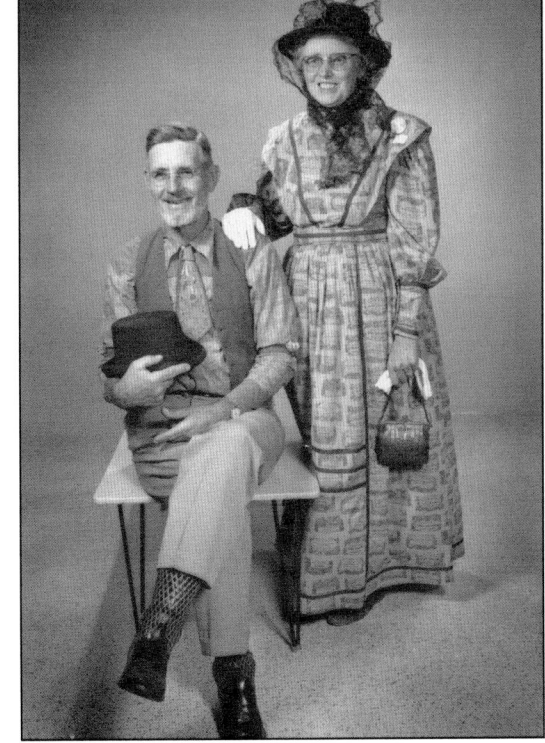

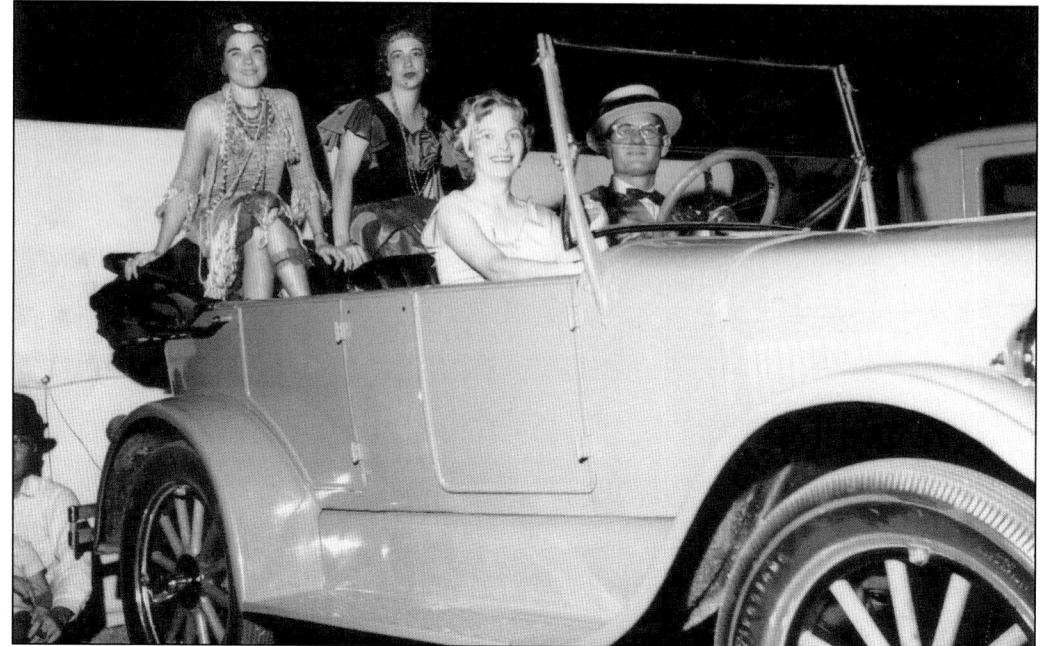

Several Andrews County residents hopped aboard a vintage vehicle during the Golden Jubilee Celebration held in 1960. Driver Bobby Wilson, Ann Smart, Ann Thomas, and Burleigh Donahue are enjoying the activities. The jubilee was a big hit that ultimately led to the 100th anniversary celebration in July 2010.

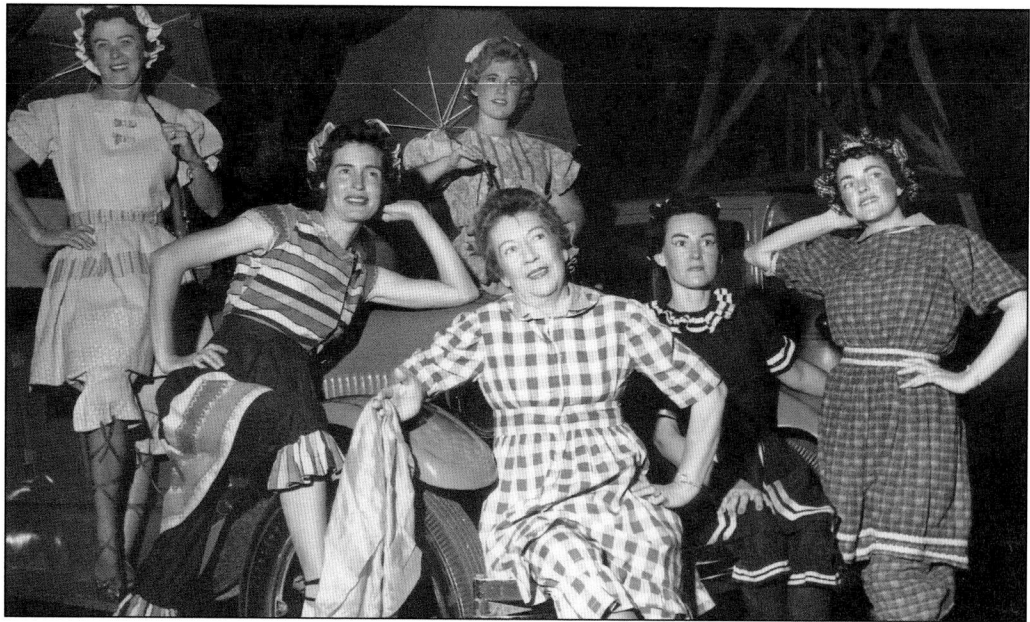

Damsels striking a pose during the Golden Jubilee are, from left to right (first row) Gladys Sharbutt, Margaret Shepherd, Ruth Thomas, and Charlene Hulen; (second row) Lovie Newman and Annette Elkins. The women were photographed with a vintage vehicle from the era in which Andrews County was officially organized. The community staged a pageant including music and skits at the old Hamilton Field.

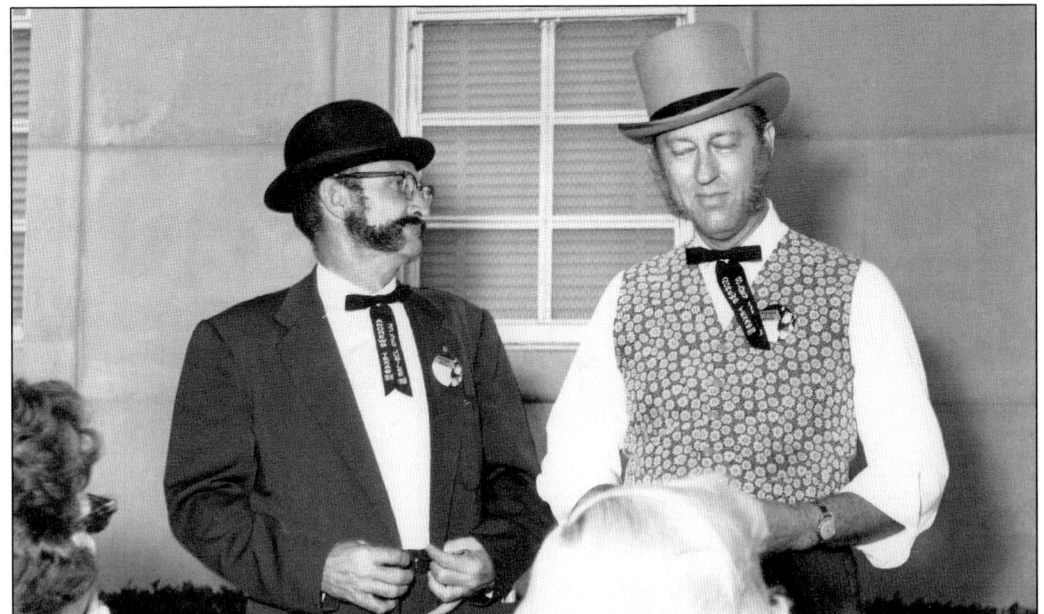

Frank Elkins, left, and Dave Foreman grew sideburns and facial hair akin to those that were stylish in 1910. Derbies and top hats were also popular among men who were celebrating Andrews County's Golden Jubilee in 1960. For many, the celebration included blasts from the past with clothing and styles. Jubilee deputies often levied small fines against those not participating in the beard growing festivities.

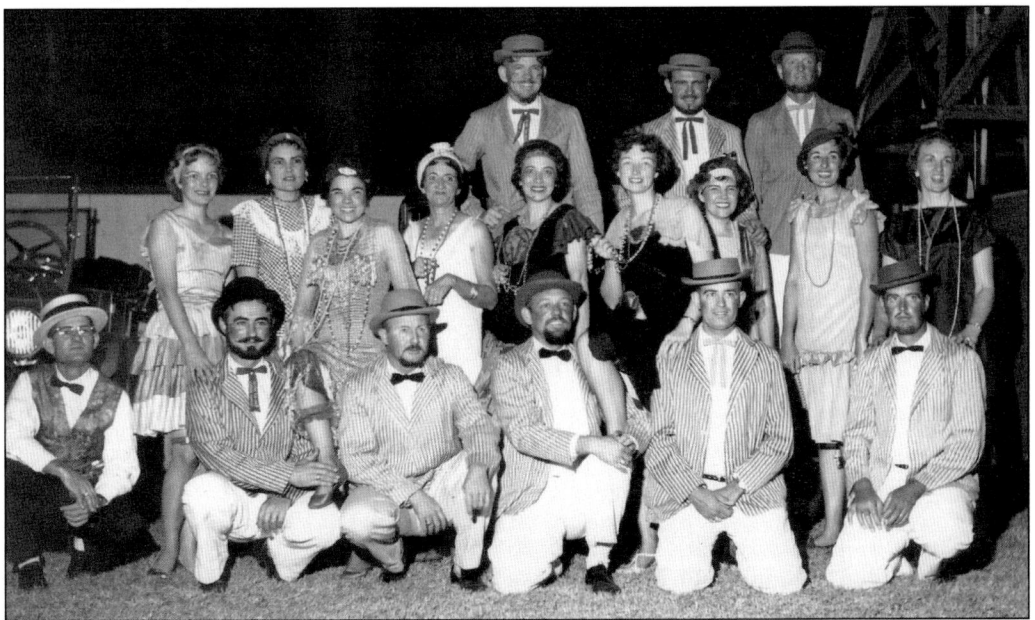

Some of the gals and guys who celebrated the jubilee in 1960 include, from left to right, (first row) Burleigh Donahue, Bill Sanders, Corky Wilson, Jack Smart, Cliff Blackwelder, and Jake Donaldson.; (second row) Ann Thomas, Jane Sanders, Bobbie Wilson, Gertrude Averyt, Ann Smart, Joan Blackwater, Mary Hart, Nell Cox, and Jean Donaldson; (third row) Elmer Hurley, Bill Hart, and Billy Cox.

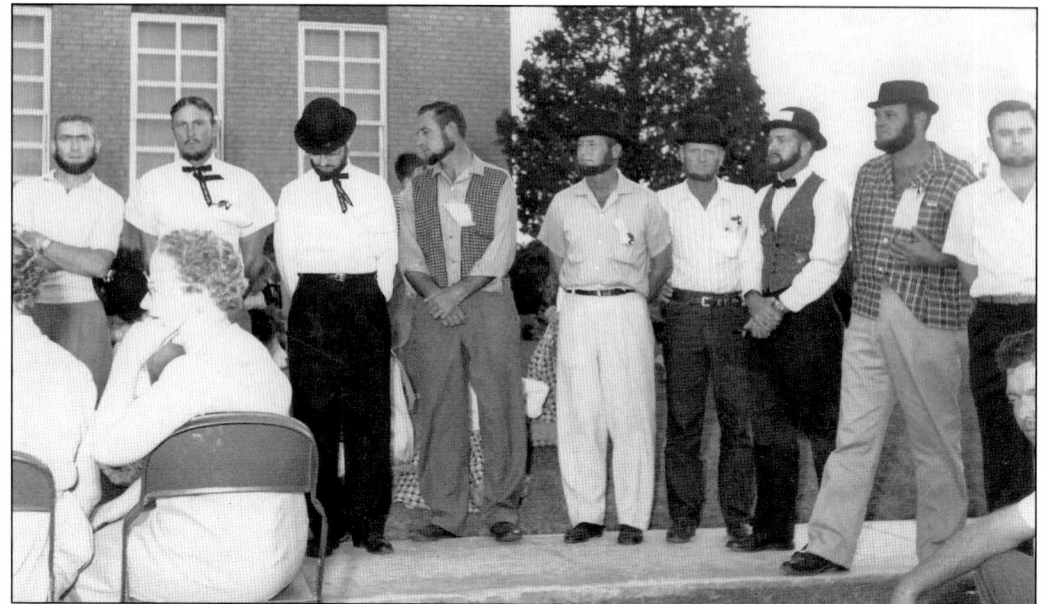

The 50th jubilee beard contest was popular among men during the 1960 celebration. The beards were required to be reflective of an earlier time, when Andrews County was organized. The contest kept some men that did not participate in growing a beard on the run, as fines for not growing a beard were steep—25¢. Some of the men who participated include those pictured here: unidentified, J. D. Whiteside, Don Gilliland, unidentifeid, Clovis Bostick, Billy Cox, and three unidentified.

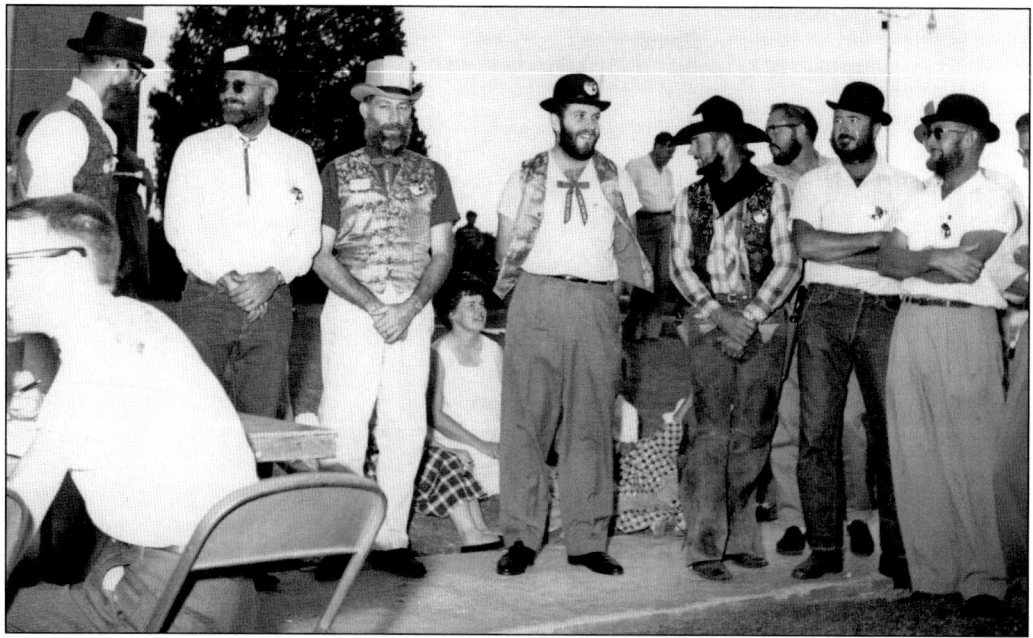

The beard growing competition was a popular event among men during the county's 50th anniversary celebration in September 1960. Some of those involved in the jubilee contest include Frank Stickney, C. L. Abernathy, Gene Irwin, Curtis Nix, and James Foster. Men who did not participated in growing whiskers were fined and some were dunked in a water tank.

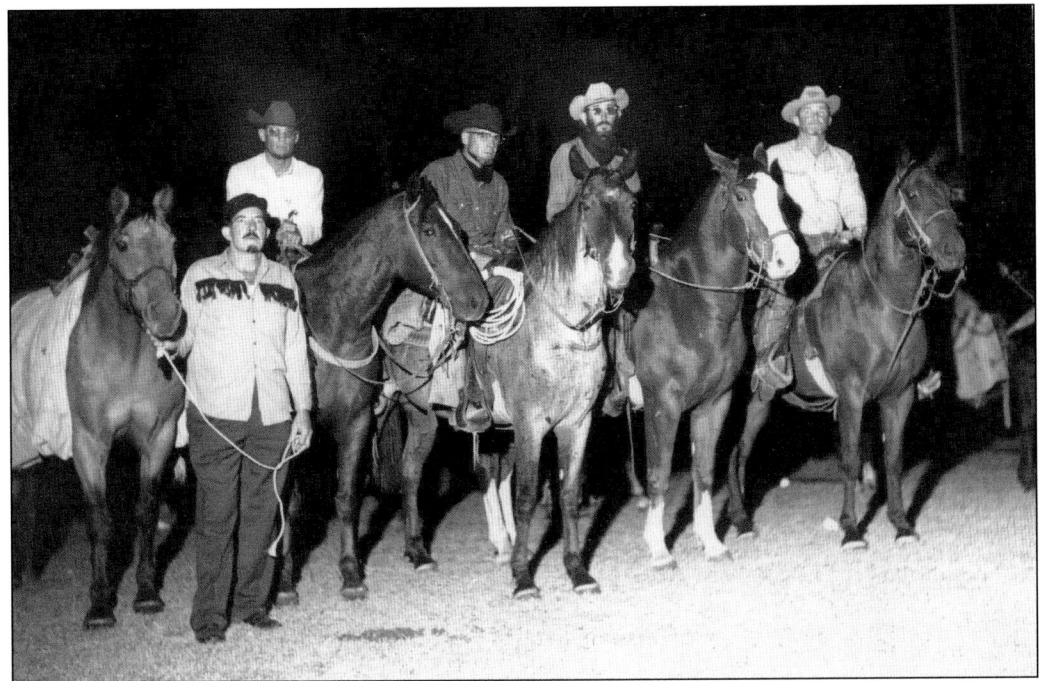

Johnny Roberts, Ken Helvey, Cecil Moore, Bill Neal, and Harold McGraw took part in the county's golden anniversary celebration in 1960. The event featured many contests and competitions that ranged from beard growing to costumes.

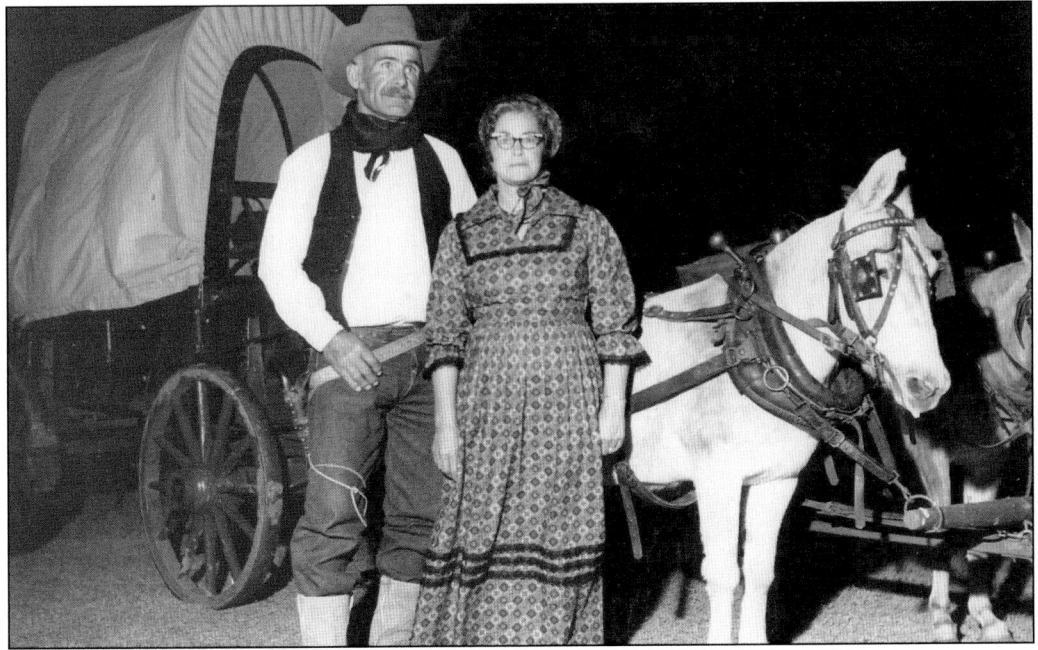

Mr. and Mrs. Jody Kemper went all out with a covered wagon and horses during the county's 50-year anniversary. The Kempers dressed the part of Andrews County pioneers who settled the land and began ranching operations. A weeklong schedule of events included a pageant, contests, and fireworks at Hamilton Stadium.

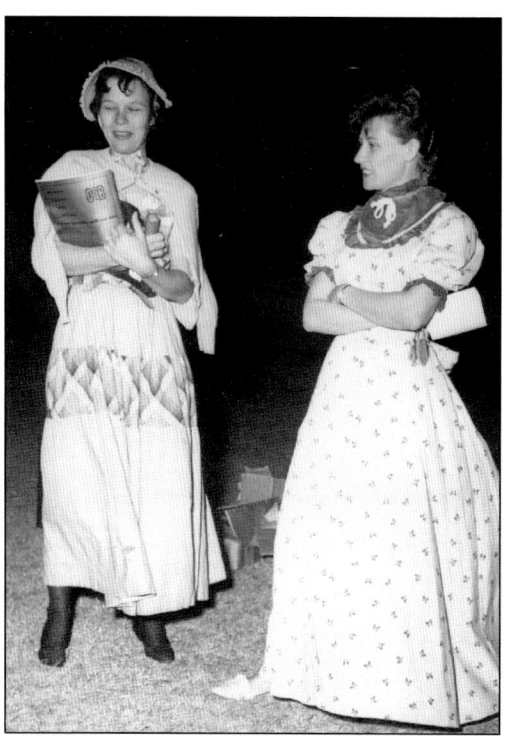

Elaine Goldsmith, left, and LaRue Hutchinson share a moment together during the jubilee. The town of Andrews was actually formed in 1908 and was elected the county seat in 1910 during a contentious election with Shafter Lake residents.

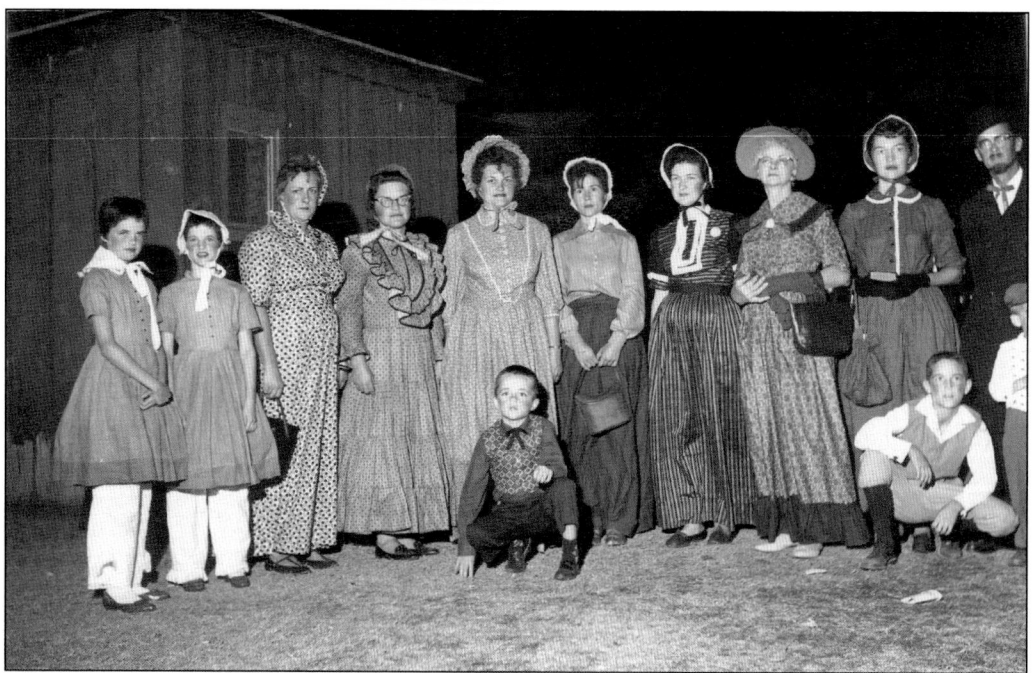

The jubilee was enjoyed by just about all of Andrews County's residents—including youngsters and older citizens alike. Shown in this photograph are, from left to right, (first row) Ronnie Williams, Paul Williams, and John Williams; (second row) Marilyn Williams, Carolyn Williams, Juanita Leatherwood, Phyllis E. Hawes, Helen Williams, Barbara Hogard, unidentified, Eulelia Ogden, Ruthie Williams, and Roy Smith.

June Stevens was the winner of the Jubilee Belles competition. She wore an appropriate outfit for the occasion that depicted the style of dress worn in the early 20th century. Many local women competed for the prestigious honor, which occurred during the jubilee in September 1960. Many events were held during a weeklong schedule celebrating Andrews and its residents.

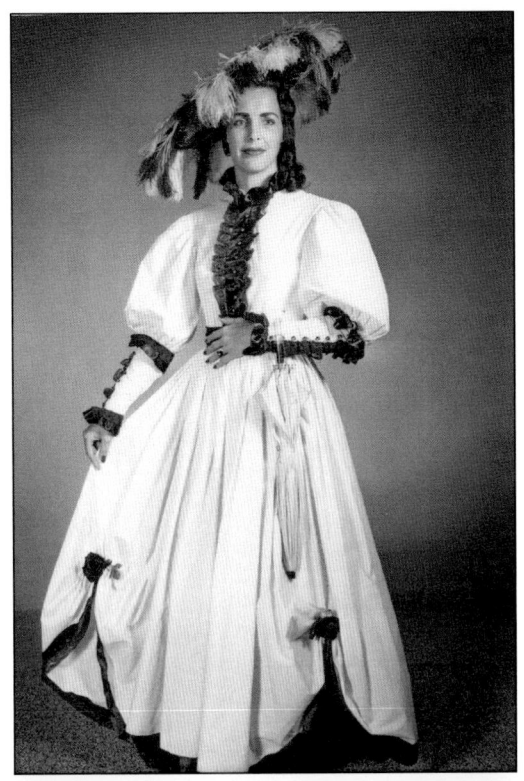

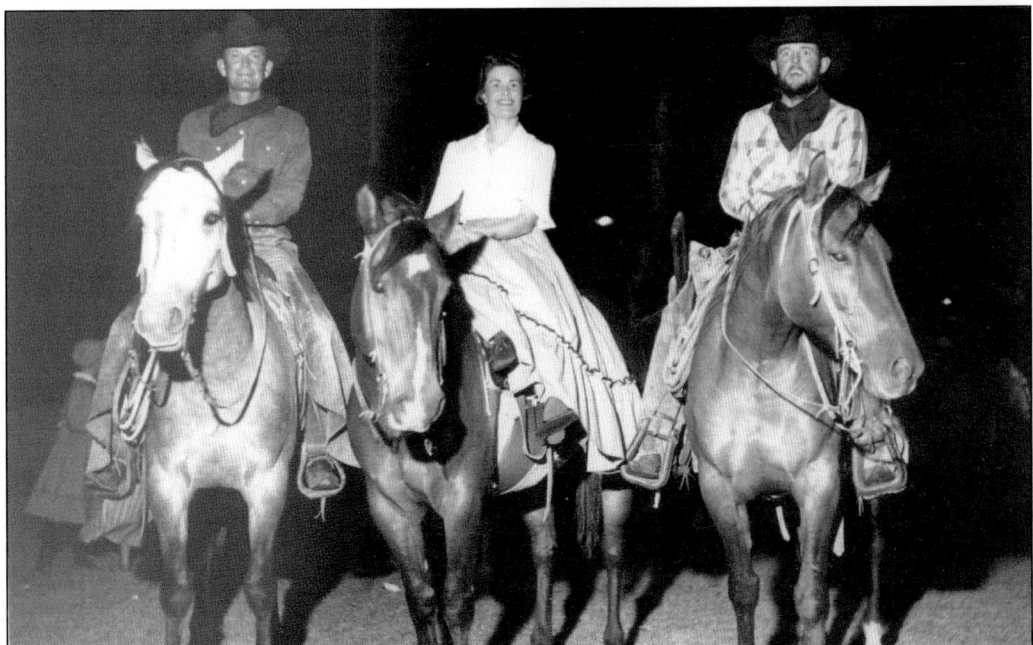

Ranching was Andrews County's economic staple for years before oil and gas came into play in late December 1929. Cowboys and cowgirls abounded, as did the rodeo crowd in years to come. Pictured from left to right, Bubs Price, Sue Jo Lindsey, and Gene Irwin rode horseback during the county's 50-year celebration in 1960.

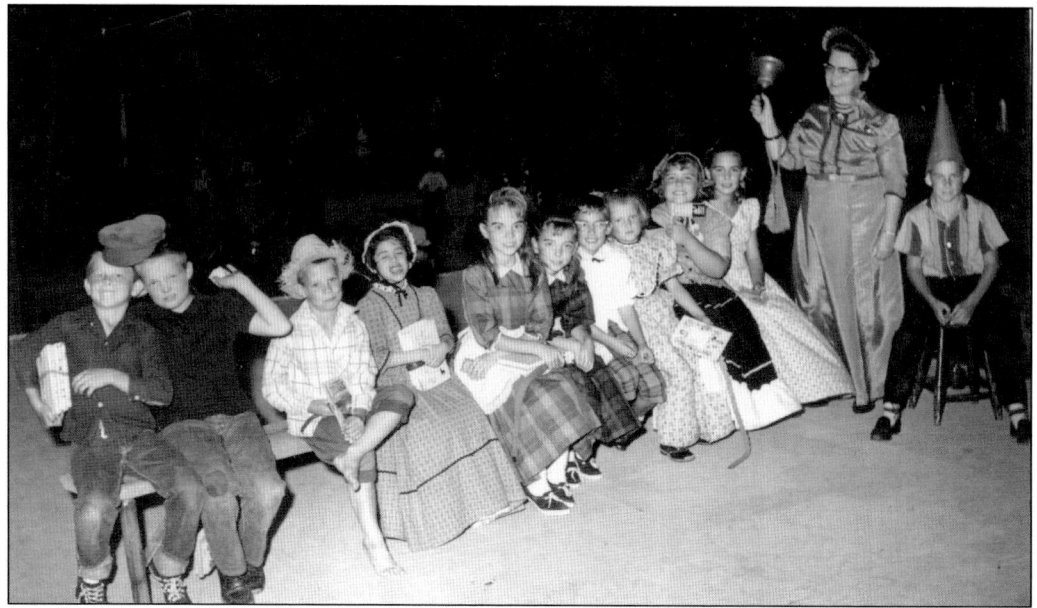

Getting into the spirit of the jubilee was a make-believe class from the early 20th century. Among those students representing schooling in the old days were, from left to right, Brodie W. Hutchinson, Gary Goldsmith, Roger Goldsmith, Becky Partridge, Paula Piper, Pam Piper, Carolyn Brenholtz, Nedra Hutchinson, Jeannie Mills, Lynne Gordon, and David Brenholtz. Newell Woolam was attempting to maintain order with the school bell.

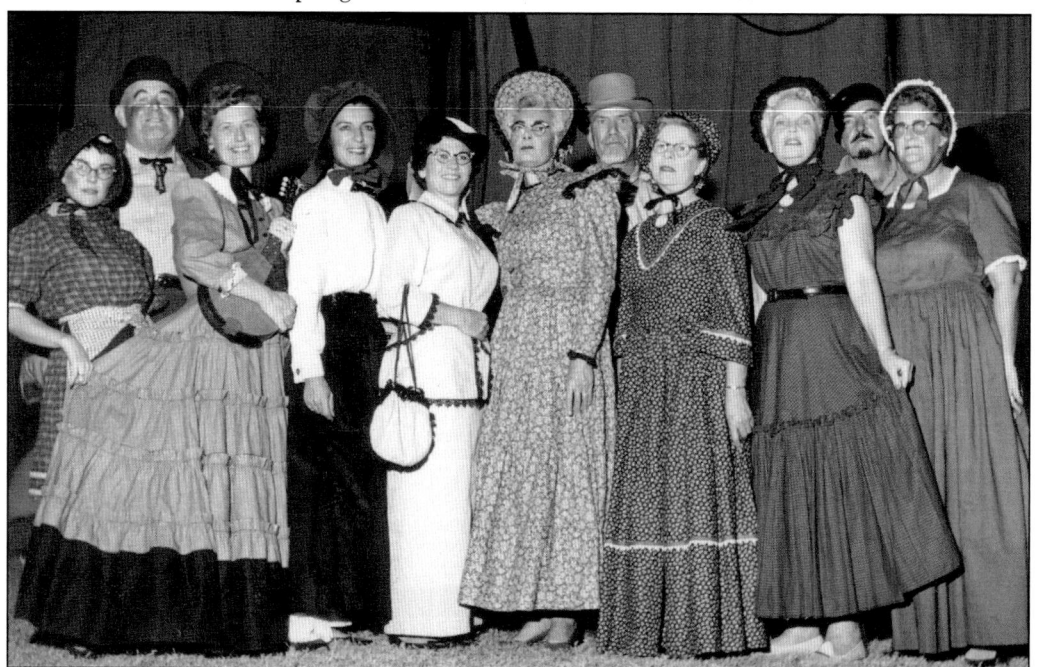

All dressed up for the 50th anniversary are, from left to right, Charlene Hulen, Clat Robertson, L. G. Roberts, Helen Ford, Helen McPherson, Norma Robertson, John King, Miner King, Arbert Fontenat, Johnny Roberts, and Margaret Day. Many of the townspeople participated in the celebration, which included numerous events honoring the pioneers of Andrews County.

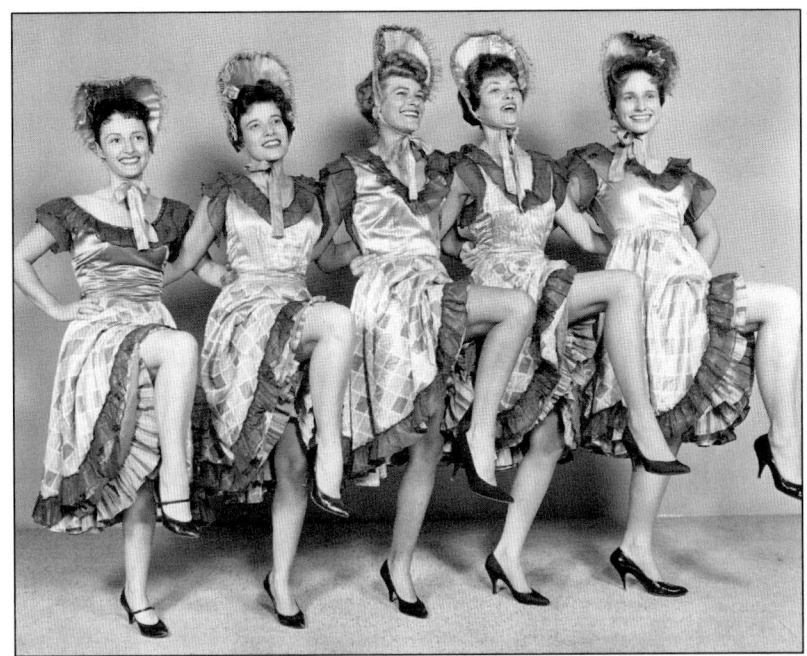

Beta Sigma Phi First Chapter representatives, from left to right, are Nadine Black, Carolyn Green, Jo Green, Sandra Parker, and Ethel Porcher. They formed a chorus line during the jubilee that honored the 50th anniversary of Andrews County. Residents enjoyed dressing up in costumes from different eras since the county's organization in 1910.

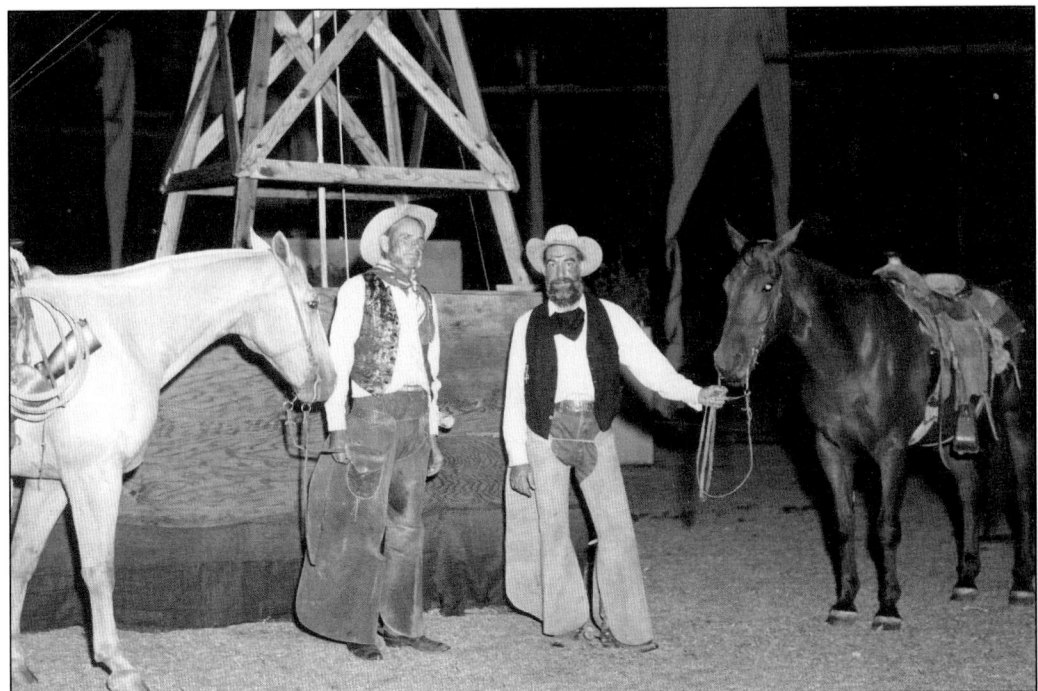

Oron Price, left, and Frank Stickney pose for a photograph near the Oil Patch Museum on West Broadway Avenue during the celebration in 1960. The two depicted the early Andrews County ranch types that helped settle the area. Ranching was the county's main economical means near the turn of the century.

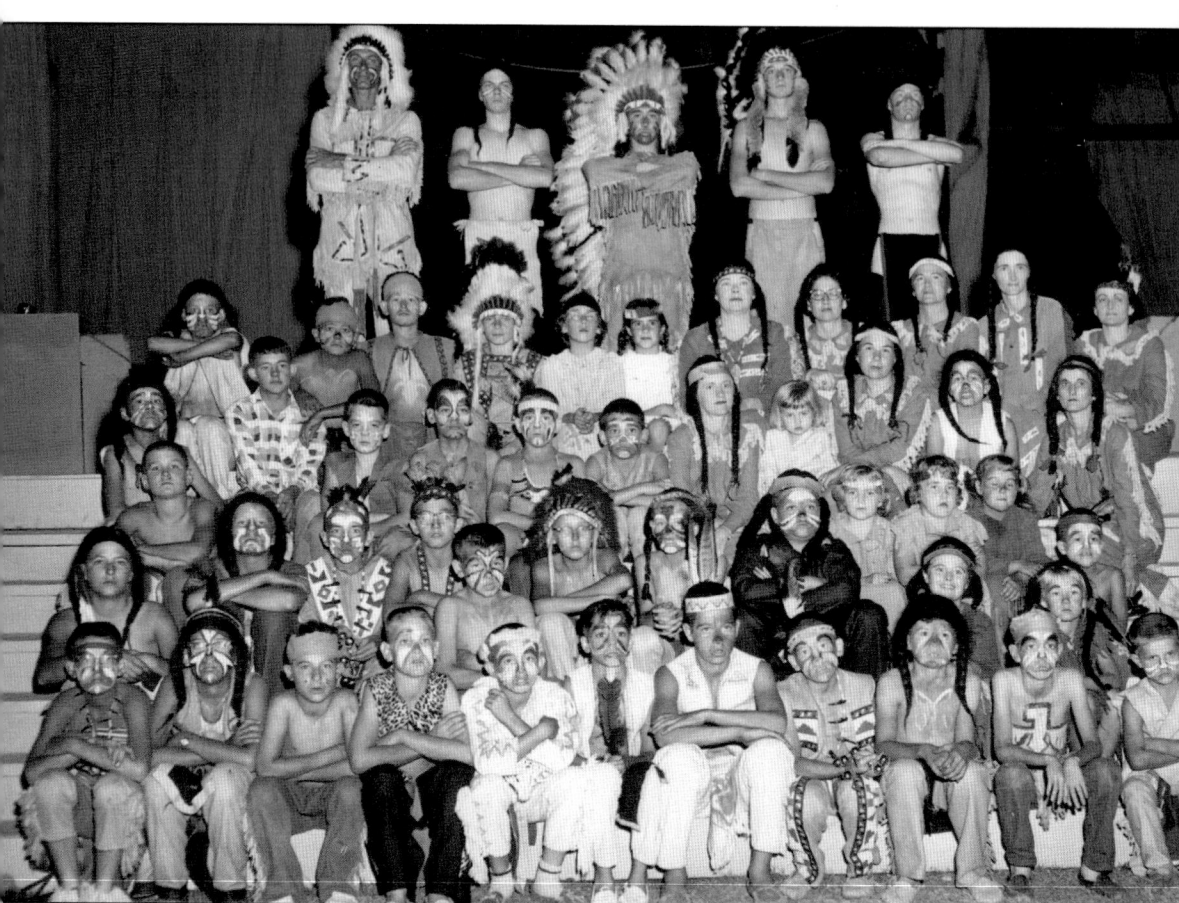

Among the participants in the 1960 jubilee were residents dressed as Native Americans, the predecessors to settlers in Andrews County. Those in the photograph included Dan Wester, Pat Fariss, Lanny Brown, Ricky Echols, Tommy Hughes, Archie Dennis, Tom Robertson, Chuck Wester, David Hendrick, Randy Smith, Martin Barrow, David Whitsett, Snuffy Tom, Gayle Slack, Lewis Allen, Steve Taylor, James Wright, Bobby Hulen, Mike Thrasher, James Baucom, George Clark, Mike Crawford, Leslie Burns, Allen McFall, Joe Allbright, John Burgess, Leroy Denny, Dickie Chapman, Eddie Solomon, Roy Parker, James Willis and Tommy Hood. Others were Mrs. W. C. Burson, Nell Brown, Maggie Allen, Ola Crawford, Mrs. Alfred Posey, Von Baucom, Floy Robertson, and Mrs. F. T. Whitsett. Also Gene Allen, Lex Crawford, Tom Brown, Dennis Crawford, Janis Payne, Susan Burcham, Bonnie Robertson, Kay Allan, Debbie Posey, Nancy Crawford, Beverly Murphree, Vannie Grissom, Katie Kulbeth, Lisa Tidrow, Susan Brown, John Underwood, Dixen Neas, Cherri Conners, Tommy Whitsett, and Harold Wilson.

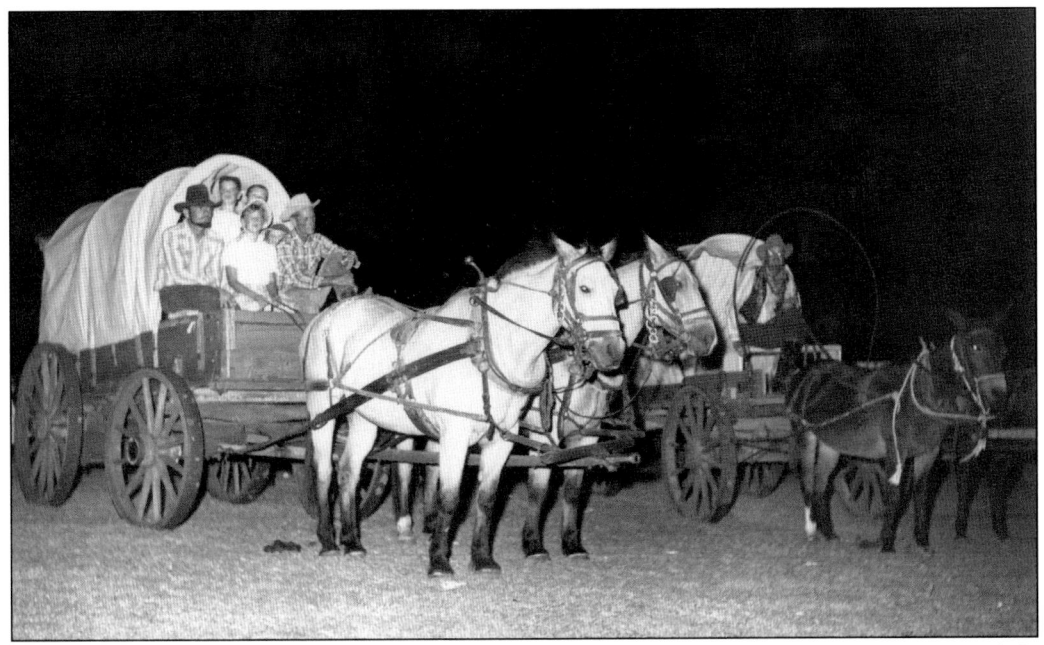

Appearing as if they are headed to Andrews County to settle a homestead are Bill Price, left, Cecil Waggner, and children. The golden jubilee celebration in 1960 included several covered wagons. The county was officially organized in May of 1910. Andrews County celebrated its centennial in July 2010.

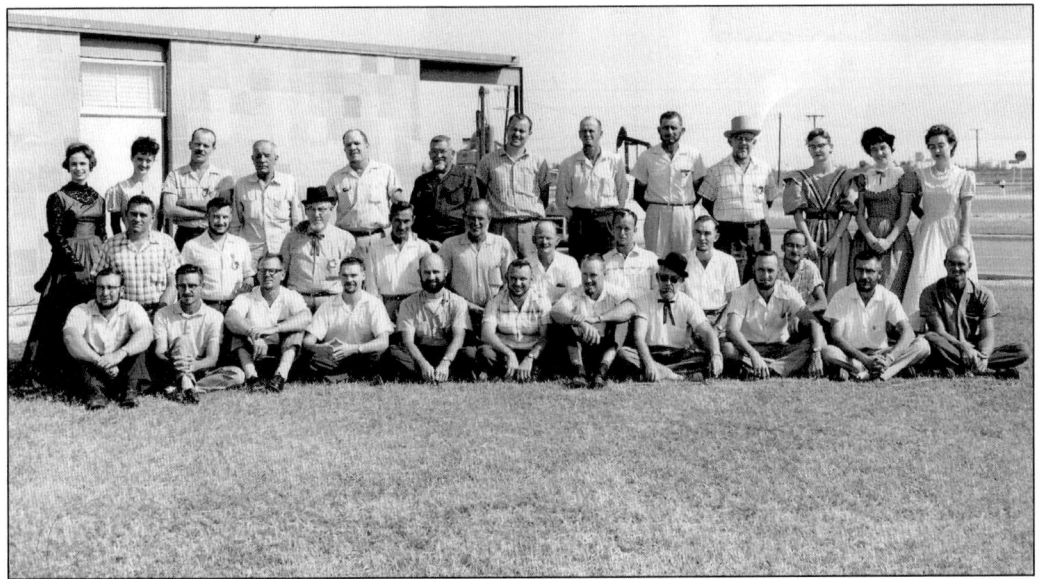

Humble Oil employees in 1960 included, from left to right, (first row) George Burrell, Wesley Shelton, Gerald Kempe, Nick Green, Cliff Sherrod, B. W. Haskins, Dan North, W. W. Petty, Jim Toles, Joe Worsching, and unidentified; (second row) Harry Tipton, Jim Bagley, George Ford, Barton Guyton, J. B. McNeil, Red Hoosier, M. M. Florence, Wayne Baker, and Roy Smith; (third row) Ethel Porchet, Jan Wheeler, Bob Berry, Bill Credicott, Elmo Walling, Blackie Ham, John Young, Odie Gibson, Walter Gayle, district superintendent Jack Shepherd, Carolyn Lloyd, Mona Spurlock, and Dorothy McElreath.

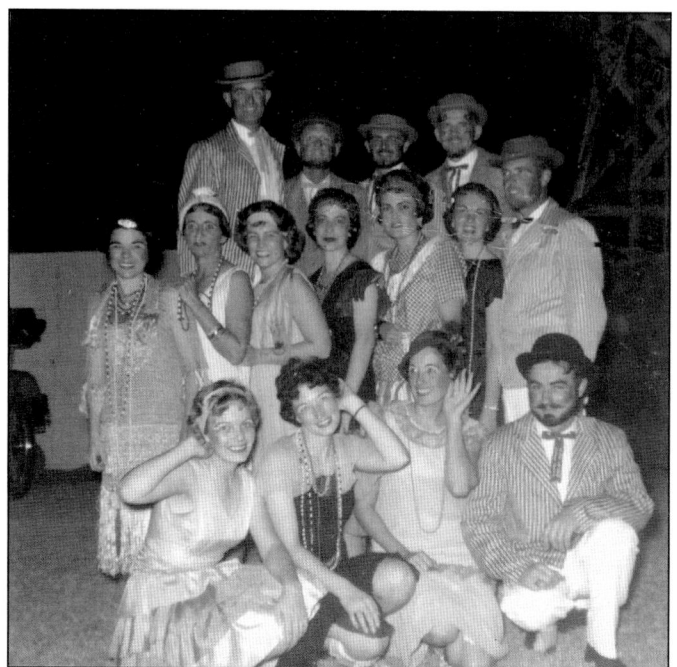

Entertaining the nightly crowd during the jubilee were the Charleston Dancers, who performed at Hamilton Field. Among those in the picture are Billy and Nell Cox, Cliff and Joann Blackwelder, Bill and Mary Hart, Bill and Jane Sanders, Jake and Jean Donaldson, Bobbie Cox, Gertrude Averyt, Elmer Hurley, Ann Smart, and Ann Thomas.

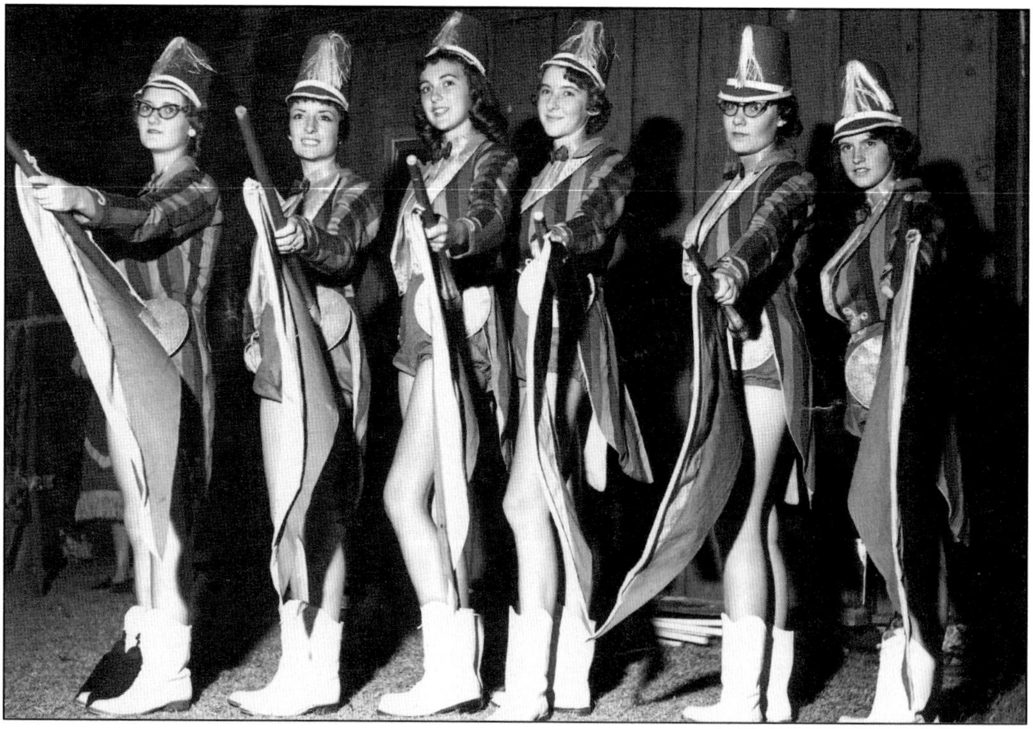

Official trumpeters for the 1960 jubilee were busy during the weeklong celebration for the community, which consisted of a nightly pageant at Hamilton Field. The trumpeters included, from left to right, Lou North, Betty Oden, Shelia Villines, Elsie Fisher, Willie May Eades, and Janice Williams. The community celebrated its 50th anniversary with a multitude of events honoring its past and celebrating its future.

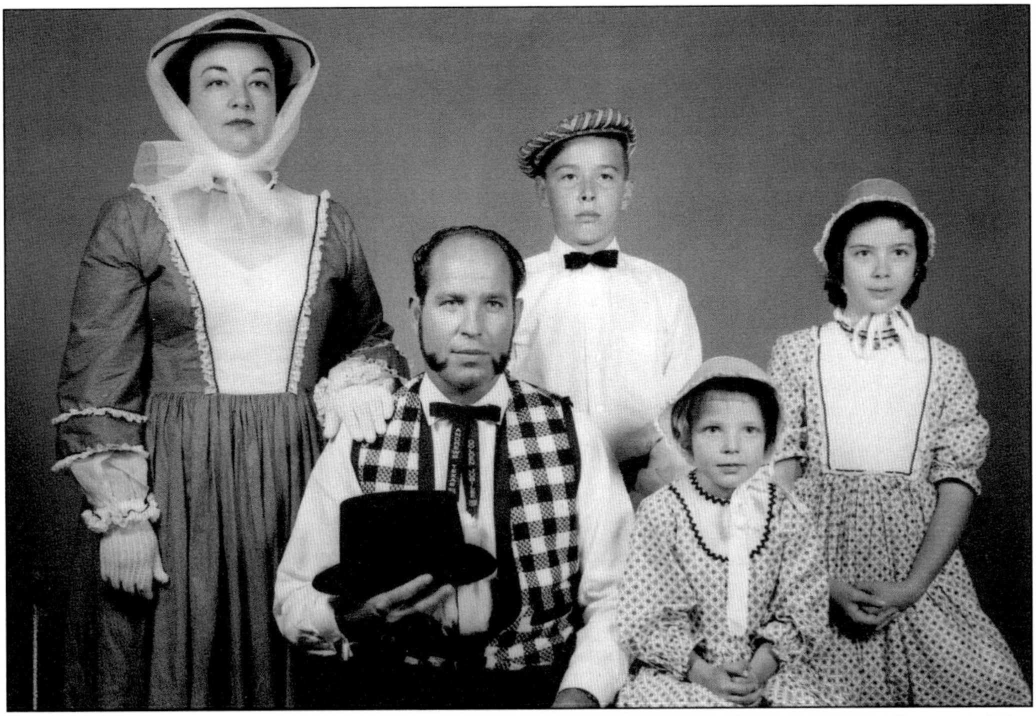

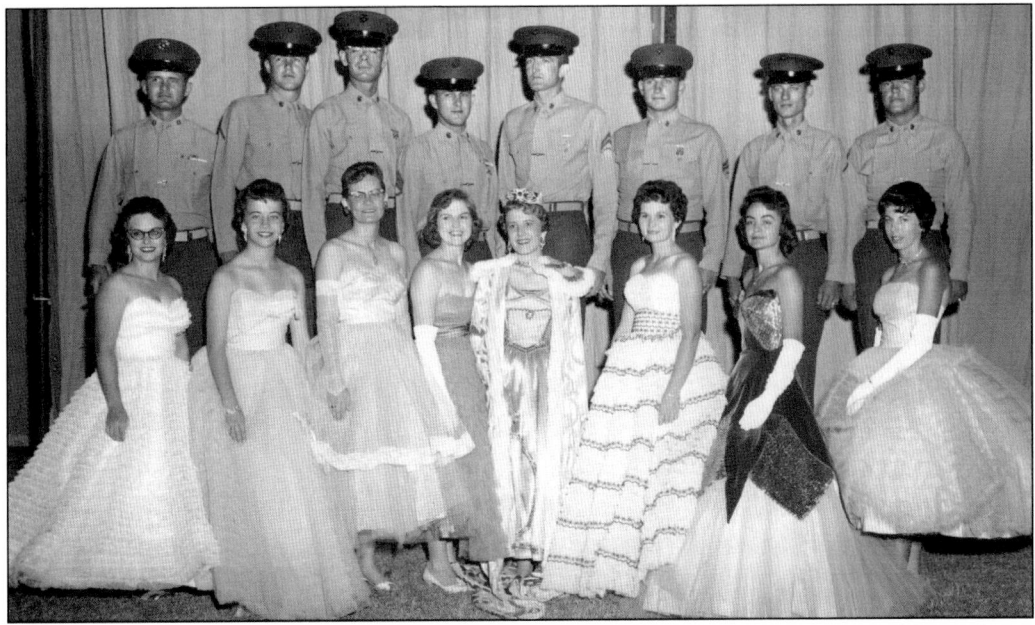

Dressing for the occasion, the Jack Morris family looked as if they had stepped right out of the early 20th century. The family included, from left to right, Aileen, Jack, Greg, Debbie, and Suzan Morris. Residents celebrated each night for a week in September 1960.

Pictured is the Andrews County Golden Jubilee Queen and her court, escorted by military servicemen during the extravaganza, including, from left to right, Delsie Echols, Mariglen Frazier, Carolyn Morris Lloyd, Charlena Blackburn, queen Jerry Sue Smith, Sue Johnson, Jan Ellis, and Dru Dunn. The fanfare lasted for a week and included skits and other entertainment.

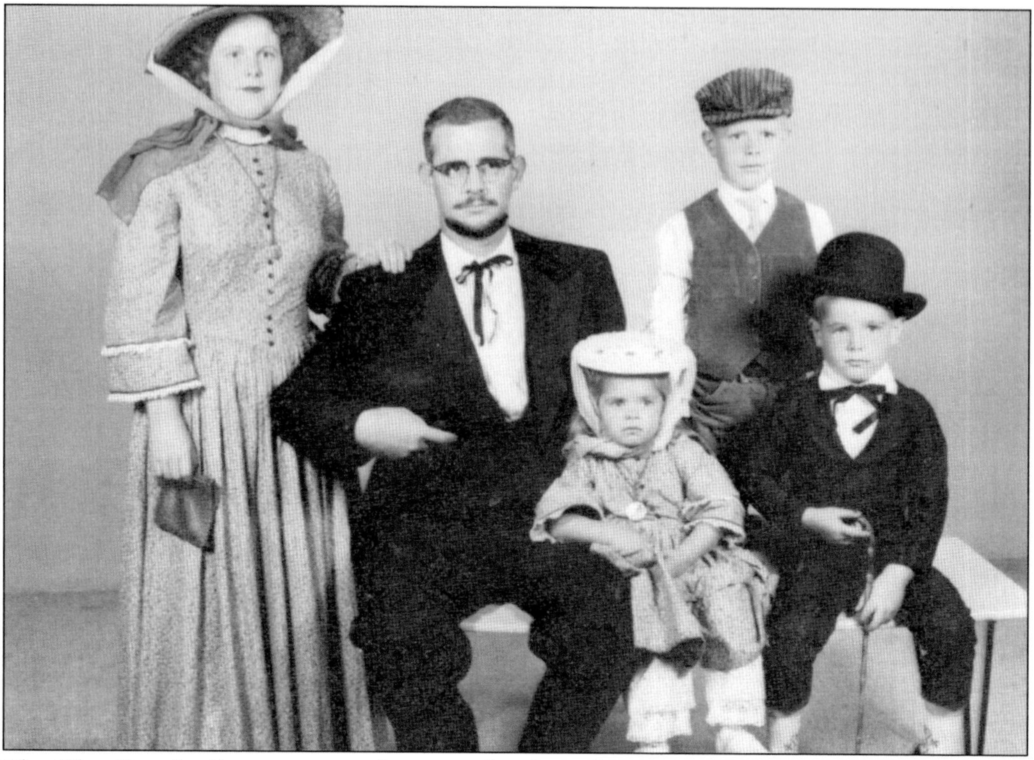

The Glen Rex family was among the many families who participated in the celebration. The family, posing in yesteryear attire, consisted of, from left to right, Lou Ann, Glen, Susan, Rusty, and Jimmy.

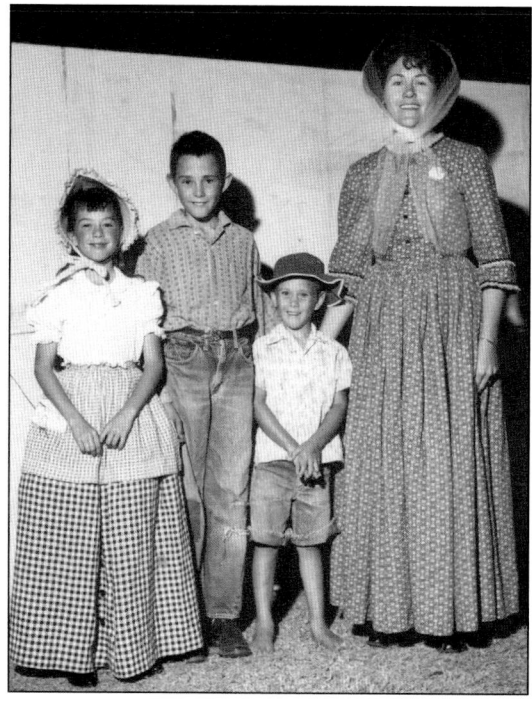

The Jones family was among the many families and individuals who joined the 50th birthday of the community in 1960. They included, from left to right, Maxine Jones and children Barbara, Mike, and Glen. The jubilee involved a variety of events, contests, and pageants.

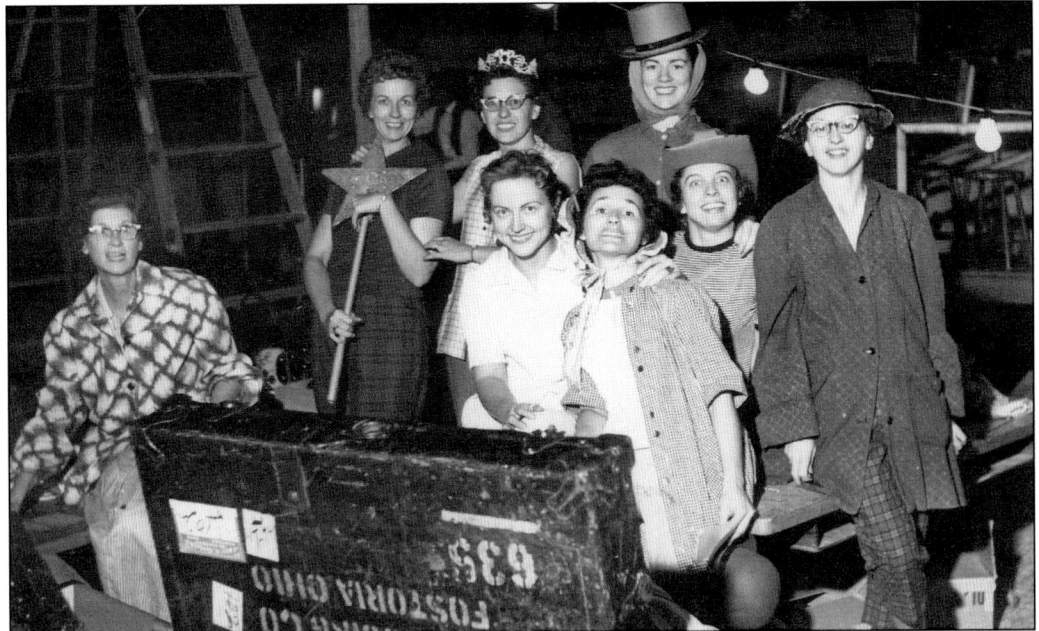

Helping behind the scenes were the stagehands, who included those pictured here: Thelma Barnes, Jane Clay, Betty Barry, Jan Ball, Mary Beth Taylor, Lois Wallace, Rochelle Smith, and Joyce Brenholtz. The stage attendees helped keep everything running smoothly during the weeklong series of events and entertainment at Hamilton Field.

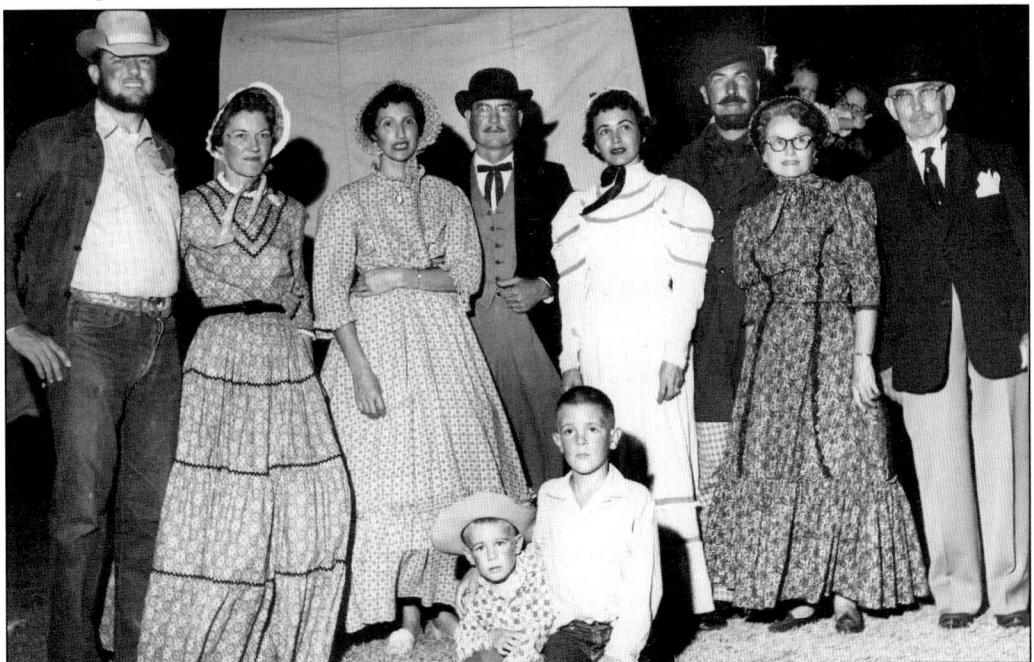

Enjoying the pageantry associated with being involved in the 1960 golden jubilee were, from left to right, Ted Alls, Ruby Alls, Evalene Queen, Lloyd Queen, Jerry Rehders, Tome L. Rehders, Rachel Messecar, and mayor L. F. Craft. The two youngsters in front include one of the Alls boys, left, and Donald Leatherwood.

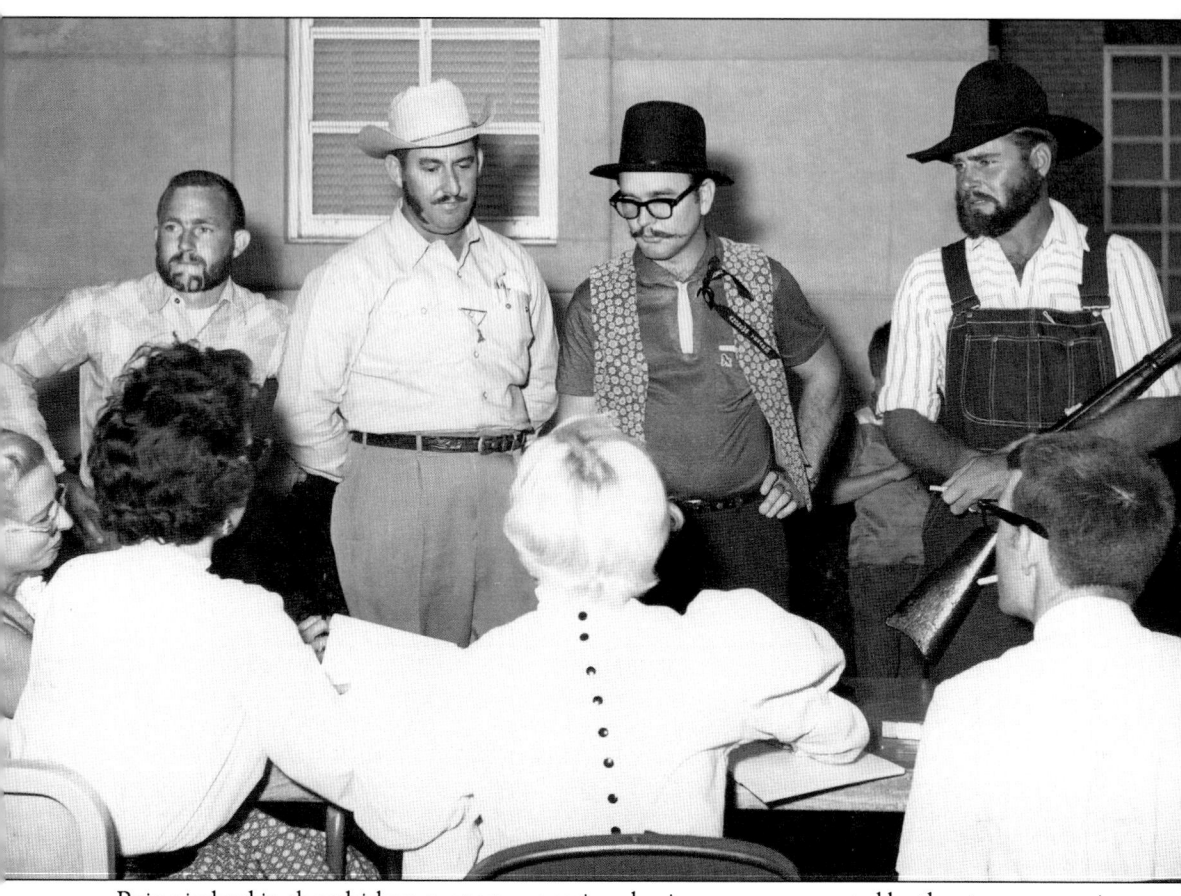
Being judged in the whiskers contest was serious business, as represented by the stern expressions on the faces of the men being evaluated at the Andrews County Courthouse square. Pictured are, from left to right, Conrad Phillips, T. T. Carter, Ed Phillips, and Buddy Lindsey.

Four

OUR COMMUNITY

Perhaps no other individual had as major an impact on Andrews as James Roberts, son of Charles Sr. and Lena Roberts who founded the *Andrews County News* in 1934. Roberts promoted diversification to avoid oil's "booms and busts." He touted using the county's liabilities—low population and little water—for luring nuclear-related industries to Andrews. Today, Waste Control Specialists (WCS) and Louisiana Energy Service (LES) are major employers and hint of more on the horizon.

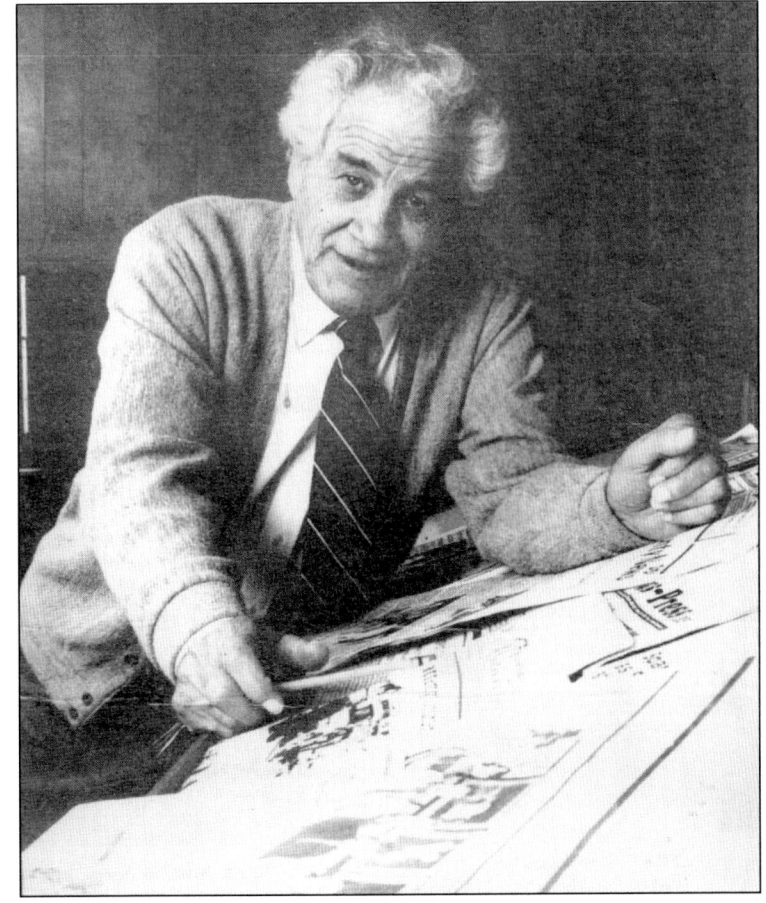

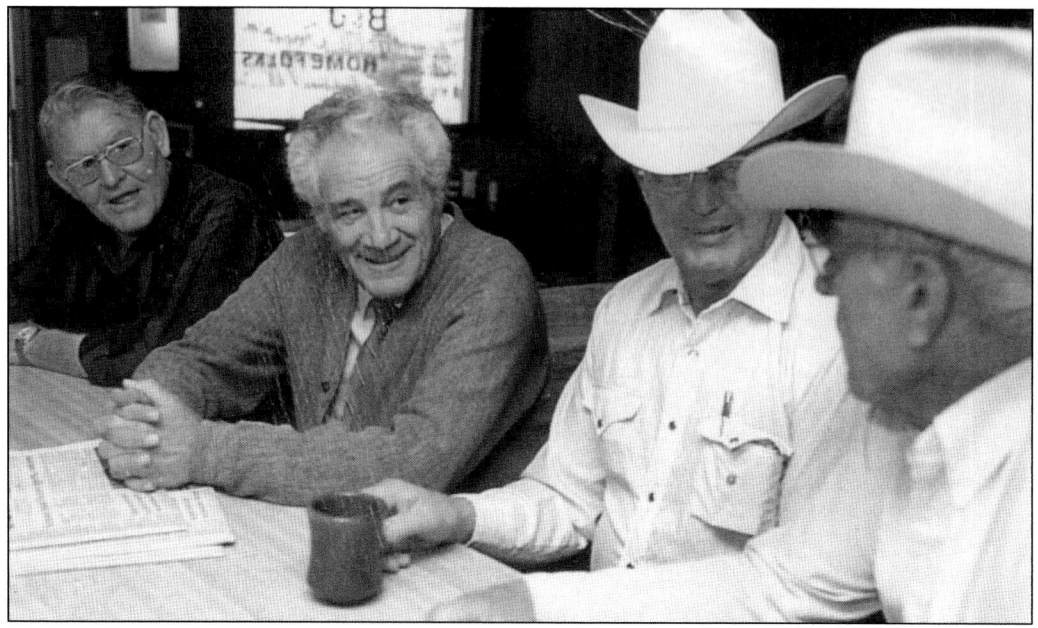

Taking time out for a cup of coffee at the popular B&J Restaurant during the early 1990s are, from left to right, Les Emfinger, farmer; James Roberts, publisher of the *Andrews County News*; Duane Ratliff and Gordon Cox, both longtime ranchers. Cooperation among governmental entities resulted in a lack of duplication of services and forward steady progress, while community-minded planners looked for ways to broaden the economy.

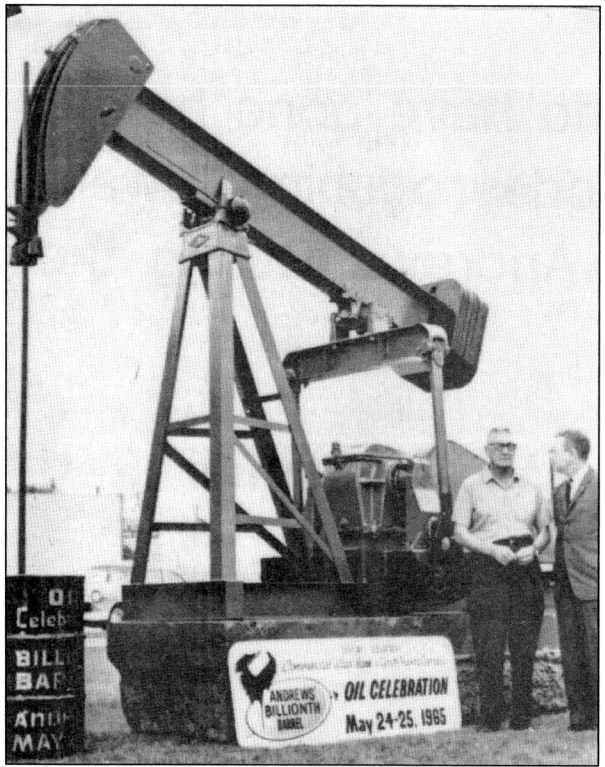

Among the town's community-oriented businessmen who helped promote and steer Andrews in the right direction were longtime oilman Charlie Carruth, left, and banker Gerald McCaskill pictured during the Billionth Barrel Celebration in 1965. Other leaders included L. Z. Brown, Johnny Smith, Dr. Z. W. Hutcheson Jr., John R. Parish, Darrel Jackson, Len Wilson, and many more who provided support and guidance and a progressive and rewarding path.

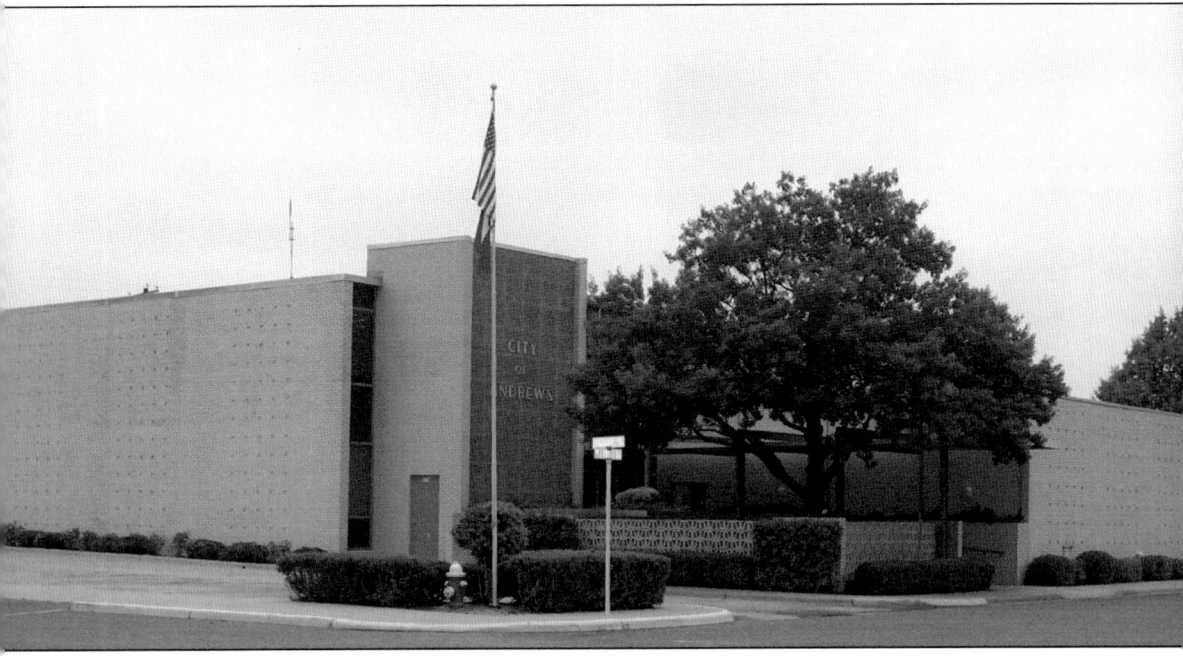

Andrews City Hall was constructed in 1960 on Logsdon Avenue and holds various city departments, including the city manager's office, utilities department, and the Andrews Economic Development Corporation. City manager Glen Hackler was instrumental in numerous community projects, some including the assistance of the county, as with the construction of the Andrews Business and Technology Center or community college. The city also purchased new water rights for future growth and proposed a city-wide reverse osmosis project for all residences on the municipal water supply. Other projects completed recently include the downtown beautification and streetscape project, dilapidated structure removal, the Andrews Birding Center, and the new Wetlands Park in northeast Andrews, which tied into the county's new ballparks fields in the southeast part of town. The city spearheaded a truck reliever route around the community to relieve streets of truck traffic and snarled intersections. The city and county have actively supported diversification, including nuclear-related industries. The city's strong financial base was largely the brainchild of city manager Len Wilson, who was Hackler's predecessor.

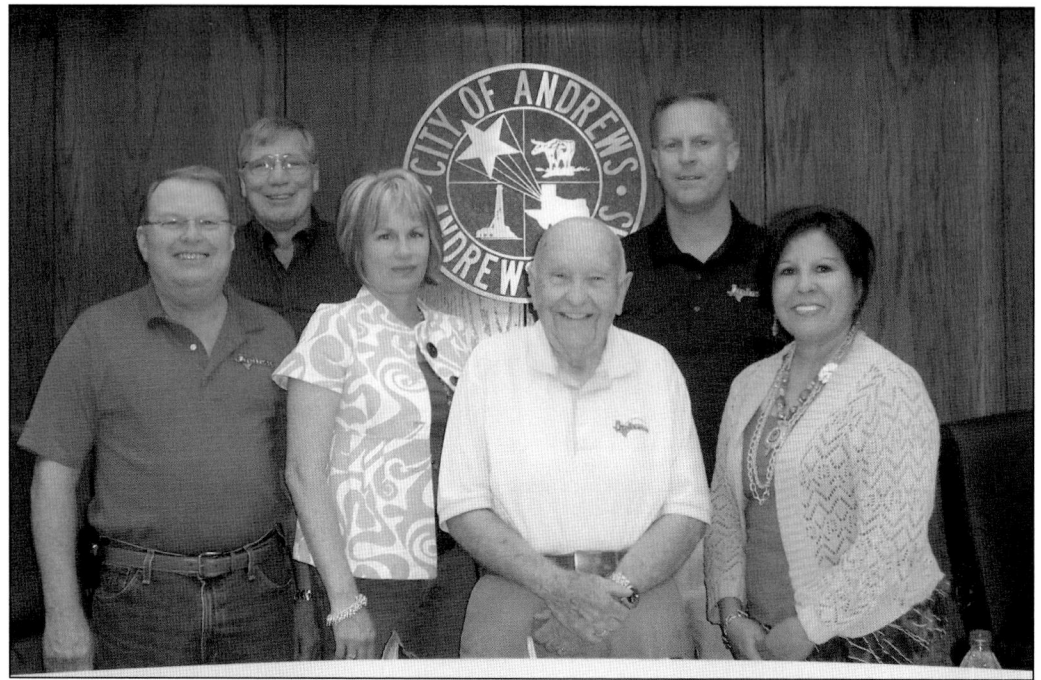

The 2010 Andrews City Council was a diverse group but was also as steadfast as those in the past about being fiscally conservative and progressive in nature. The city council pursued downtown beautification, construction of the Andrews Business and Technology Center, and the Andrews Public Safety Building. Those on the council included, from left to right, Ron McCormick, Charles Vogt, Pam Brownlee, mayor Bob Zap, Lynn Fisher, and Flora Braly.

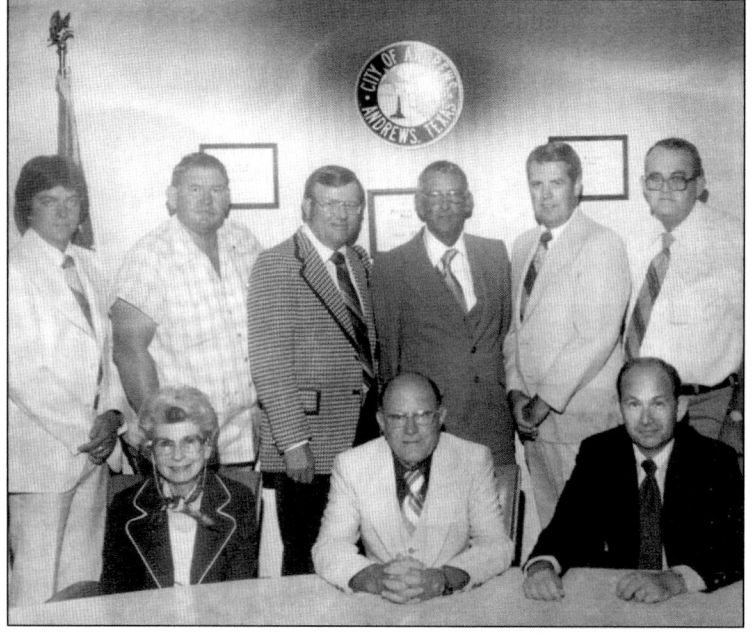

Andrews City Councils going back to the late 1960s led the way in the community with a pay-as-you-go philosophy. Council members in this 1985 photograph included (first row) city secretary Marcella Cure, Mayor Maurice Simmons, and city manager Len Wilson; (second row) Steve Smith, Les Emfinger, Bubba Hoermann, Duane Fitts, Jake Donaldson, and city attorney Bob Barber.

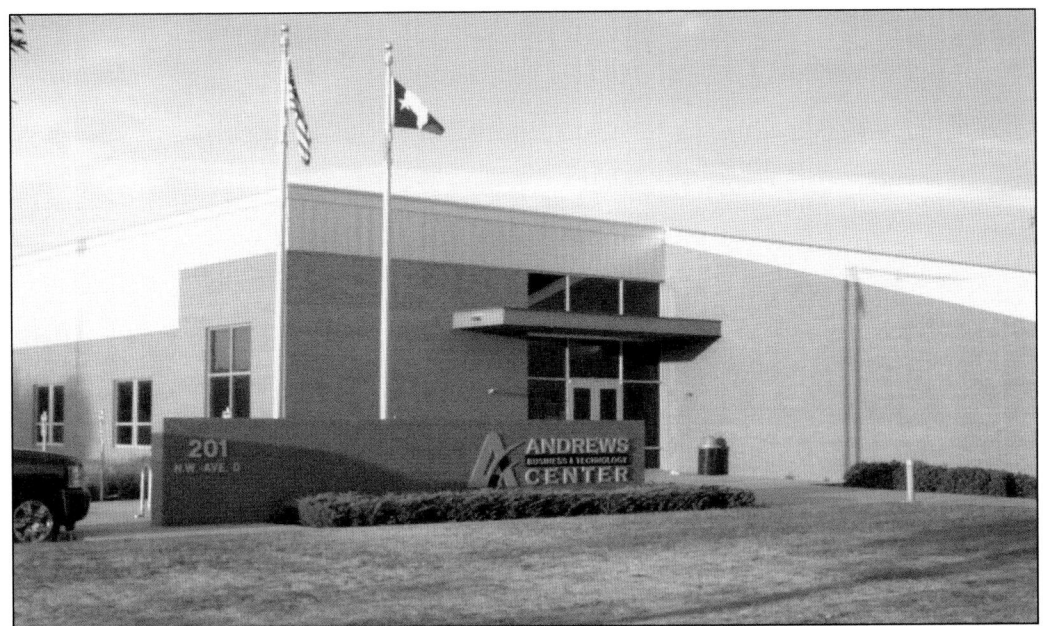

A major achievement was the construction of the Andrews Business and Technology Center. The community college was constructed through monies from the city and county as well as a state grant. Assisting considerably was Odessa College and the University of Texas of the Permian Basin with curriculum and instructors. The technology center was built on the site of the former Glorieta Elementary School, and scholarships are available for eligible candidates.

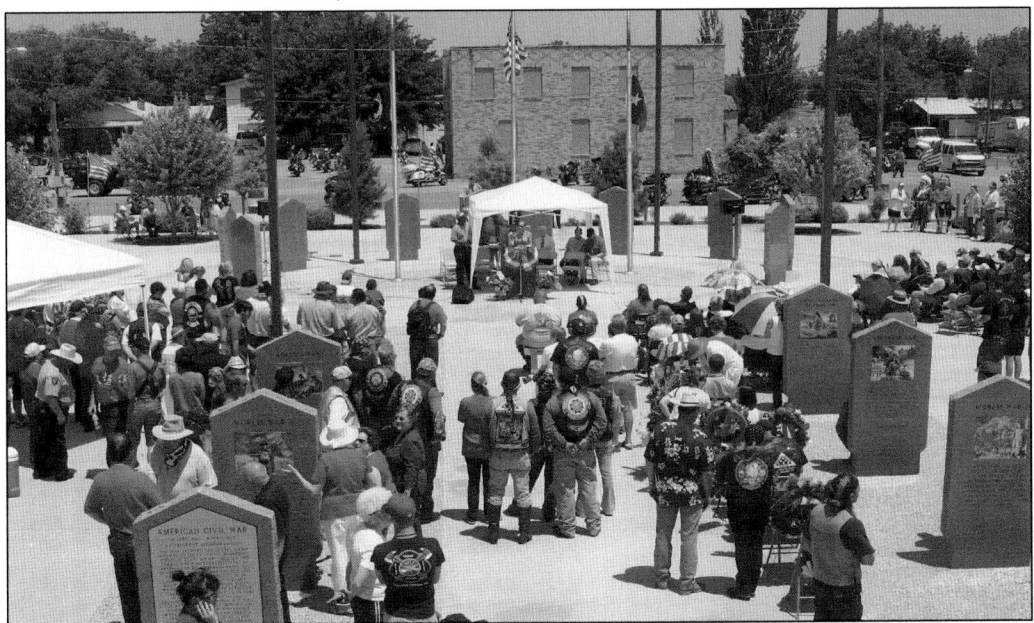

The completion of the Andrews Veterans Memorial was a major undertaking in 2006 and completed with donations by local entities, companies, and individuals in a little more than two years. The veterans memorial is located on West Broadway Avenue next to the Andrews Chamber of Commerce and includes military veterans from all branches associated with Andrews. It is the site each year on Memorial Day for recognition of the country's veterans.

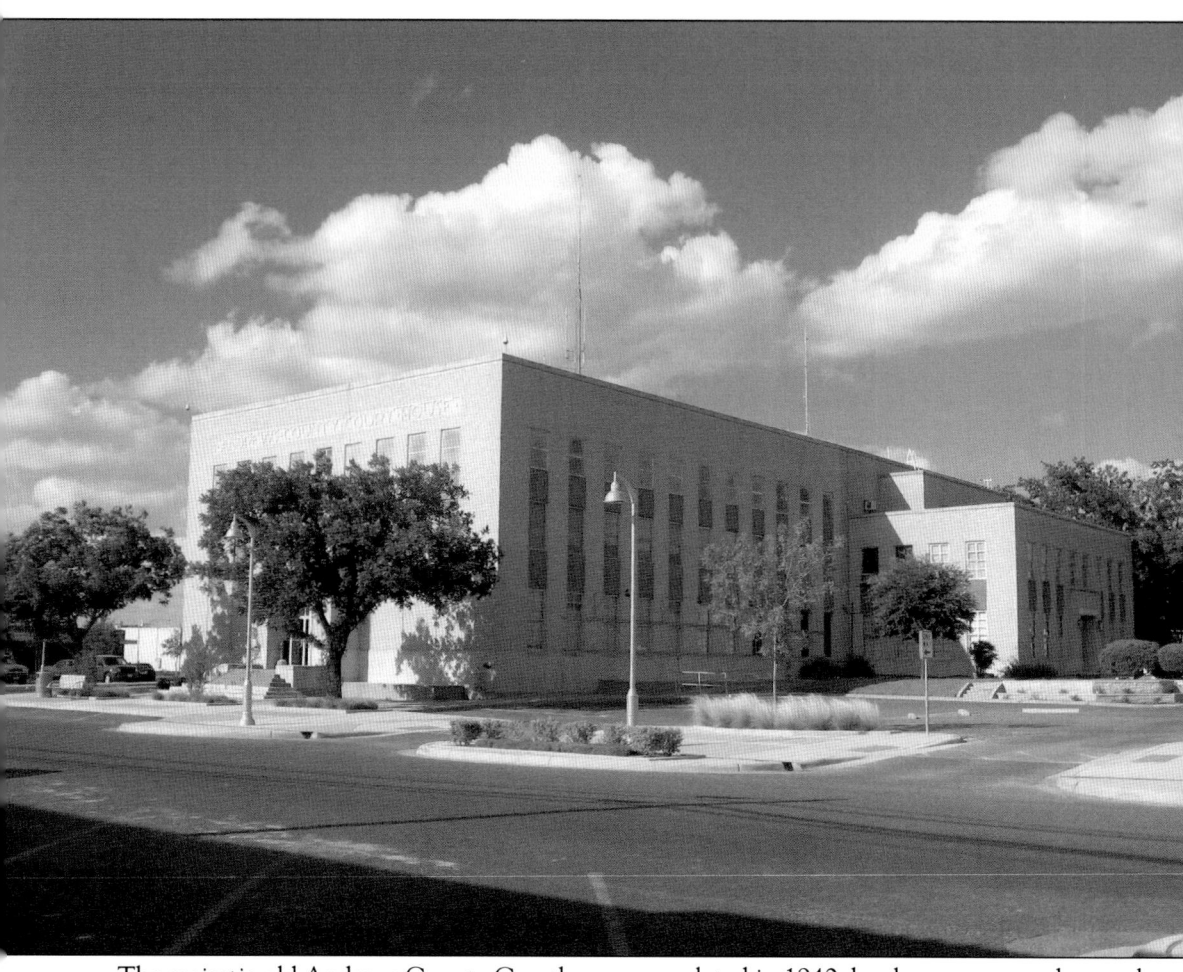

The majestic old Andrews County Courthouse, completed in 1940, has been renovated several times to keep the building current and accommodate periods of growth. Within the facility are the judge's office, commissioners' courtroom, county courtroom, 109th district court, district clerk, county auditor, and tax assessor-collector's office. Nearby offices on the courthouse square hold the county attorney's office, probation department, and county clerk's office. The main courthouse also houses the Andrews County Sheriff's Office and jail, which is scheduled to get its own facility in the near future. The county and city participated in a major downtown beautification project in 2008 that modernized the appearance around the courthouse, adding more improvements, landscaping, and handicap parking. The courthouse is the scene each November for local, state, and national election returns, an occasional street dance, and the site of the Centennial Clock, donated by the Andrews Rotary, on the southeast corner of the square.

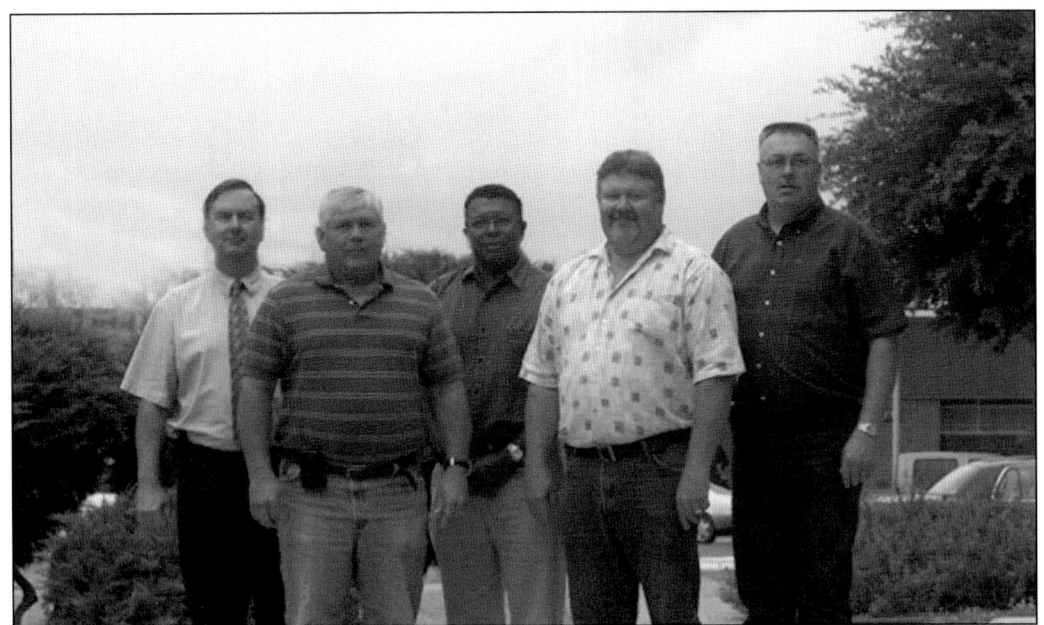

Andrews County is led by its county officials, who oversee the operations of the county. Shown in this photograph are, from left to right, Richard Dolgener, county judge; Brad Young, commissioner, precinct No. 2; Hiram Hubert, commissioner, precinct No. 3; Randy Rowe, commissioner, precinct No. 1; and Jim Waldrop, commissioner, precinct No. 4. Not pictured is Rodney Noble, county auditor. Recent projects completed by the county included the ACE Arena, downtown beautification, and eight new lighted ballparks.

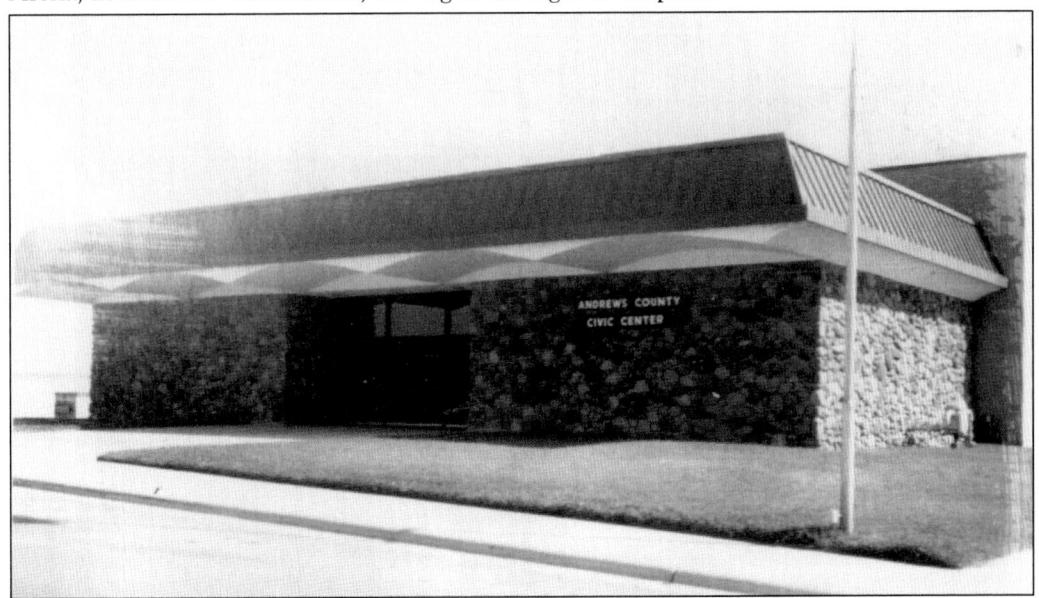

The James Roberts Civic Center was constructed in 1975 and named after a community activist. Roberts, publisher of the *Andrews County News*, died suddenly in 1998, but his visionary and prolific promotion of the community is still vividly remembered today. Roberts served on numerous boards and committees over the years and helped organize the Andrews Industrial Foundation to seek other industry and diversification.

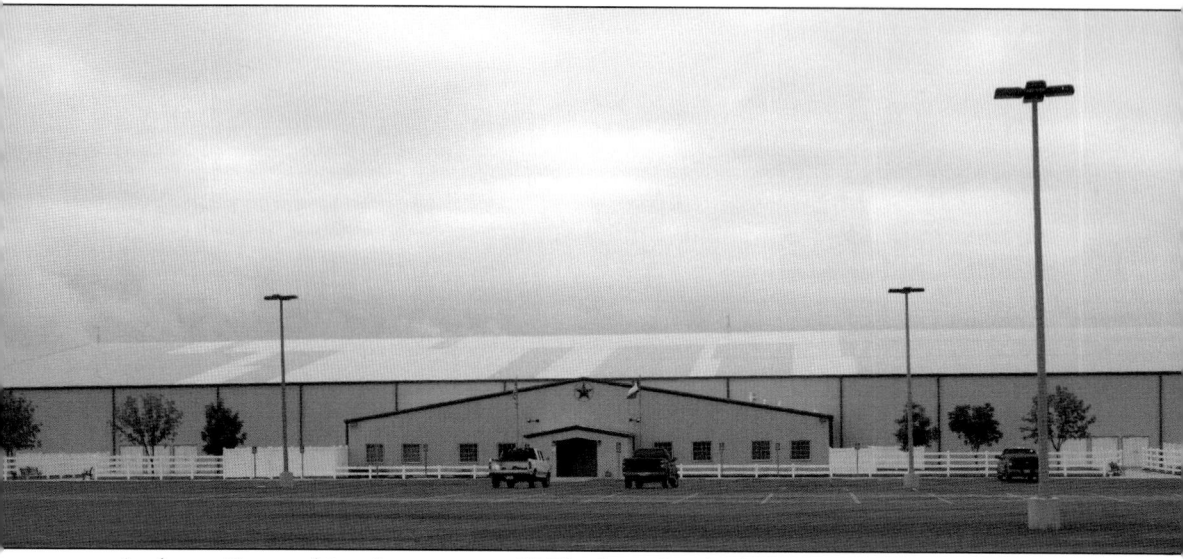

Andrews County hit a homerun in 2007 when the Andrews County Exposition Arena was constructed just east of the city for attracting rodeos and other activities to Andrews. The ACE Arena has turned out to be popular among local and regional cowboys and cowgirls for roping events, bull riding, barrel racing, and other competitive events and is booked almost every weekend. The size of the arena is also competitive with larger cities nearby such as Midland and Odessa. The facility draws hundreds of out-of-town performers who help stimulate the local economy by renting hotel and motel rooms, eating meals at restaurants, and purchasing fuel for their vehicles. Other events are also staged at the arena, including motorcycle races, wrestling matches, and other entertainment. In addition, the ACE Arena is used by the Andrews County 4-H Club during its junior livestock show held each spring.

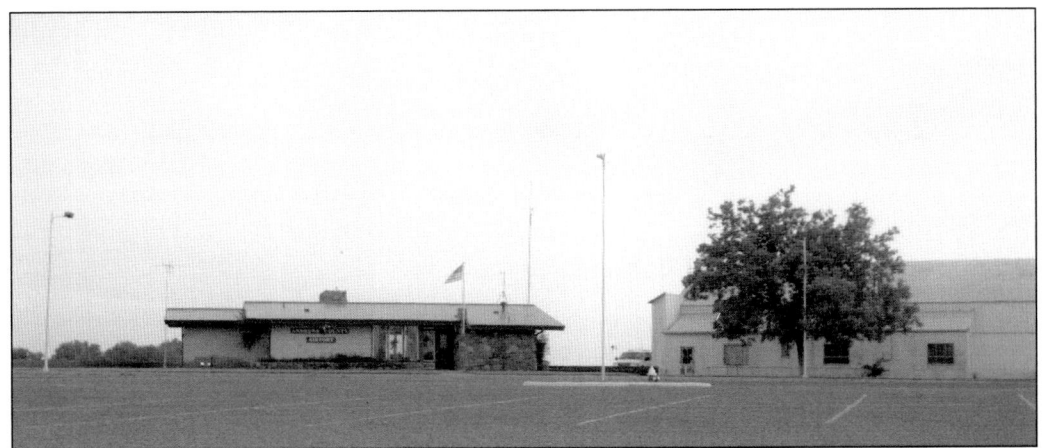

The Andrews County Airport offers the ease of convenience for local pilots and other travelers and is located just east of town. The airport was originally constructed in 1940 and includes several runways, a small lobby, and several hangars. The airport can accommodate small jets, which are sometimes used by businessmen and others.

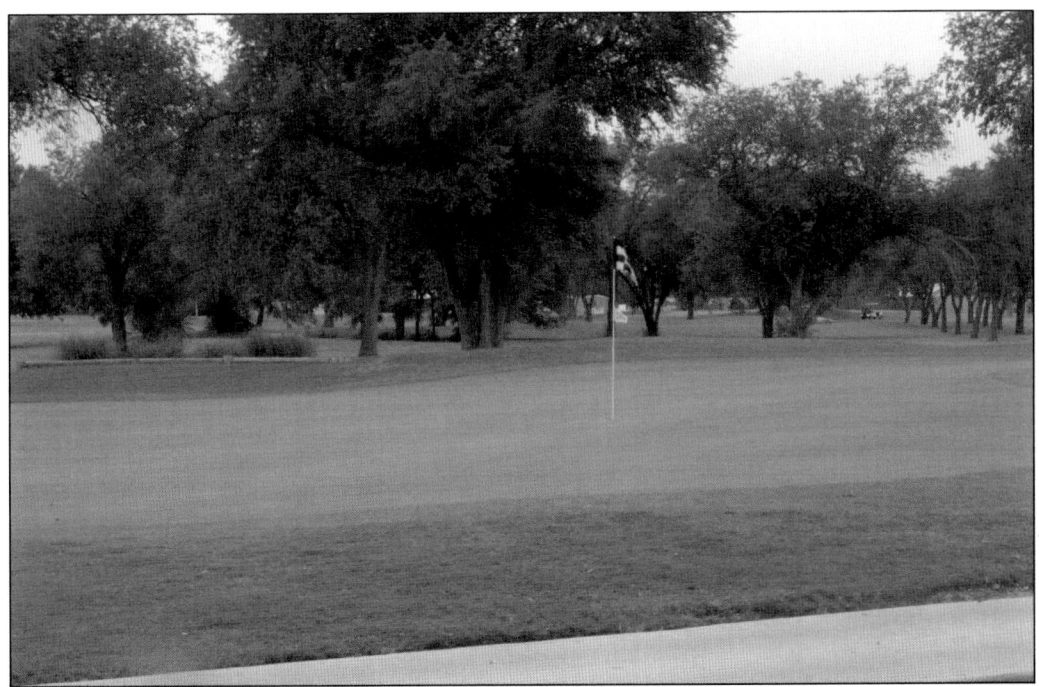

The Andrews County Golf Course is an oasis in the West Texas landscape thanks largely to an agreement years ago between the county and city to use recycled water from the water reclamation plant for irrigating the facility. Today, as in the past, the golf course is extensively used by locals and out-of-town golfers because of its condition and inexpensive fees.

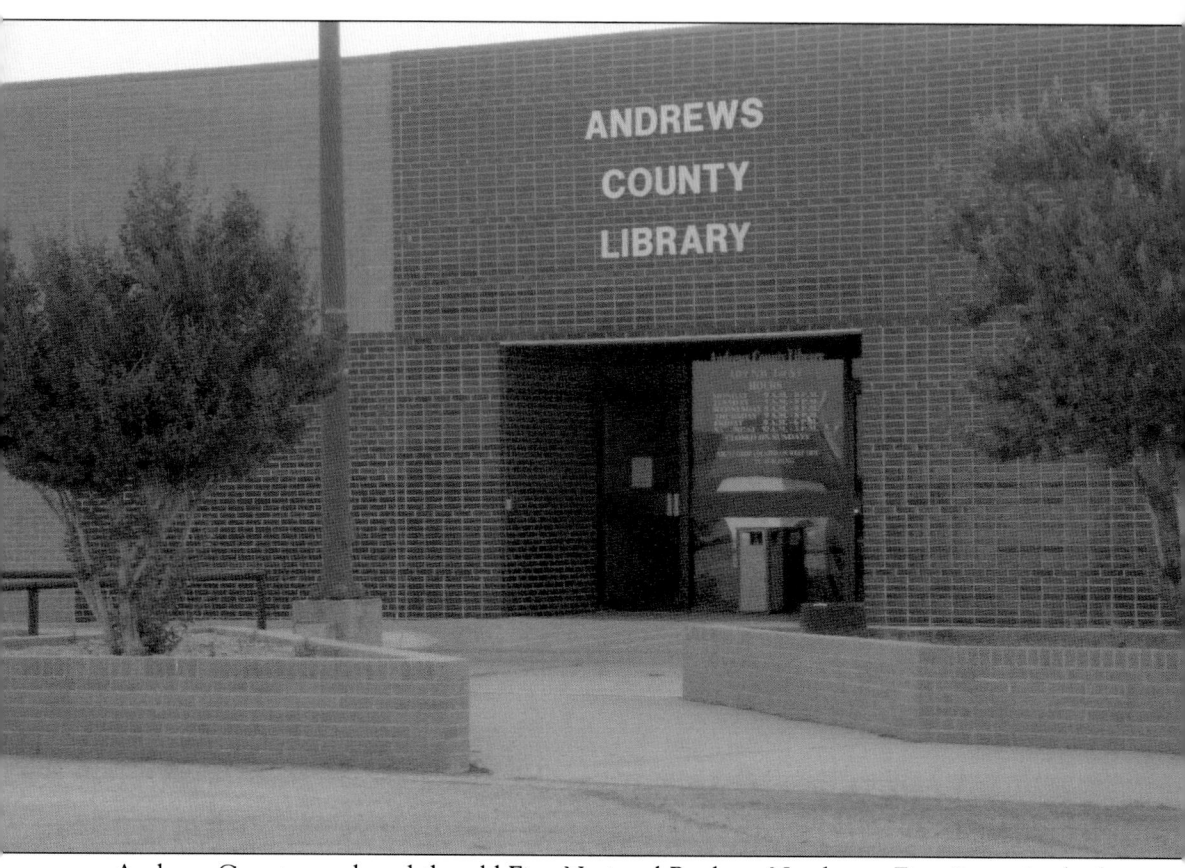

Andrews County purchased the old First National Bank on Northwest First Street in the late 1990s and spent around $1 million refurbishing the facility. The completed product in 1999 was a library at least three times larger than the older facility built in 1945. The community celebrated the project by participating in a book brigade of helpers shuffling books from the former library down an alley and across a street to the sparkling new facility. Today the library is a hubbub of activity, with patrons selecting books and using the reading rooms while clubs and organizations frequent the meeting rooms and students take advantage of the services and a quiet setting. The library has computers available for public use and sponsors summer reading programs, speakers, book signings, and other events in the user-friendly environment. Bringing much support and donations over the years has been the Friends of the Library, which helped promote the need for a new and larger library.

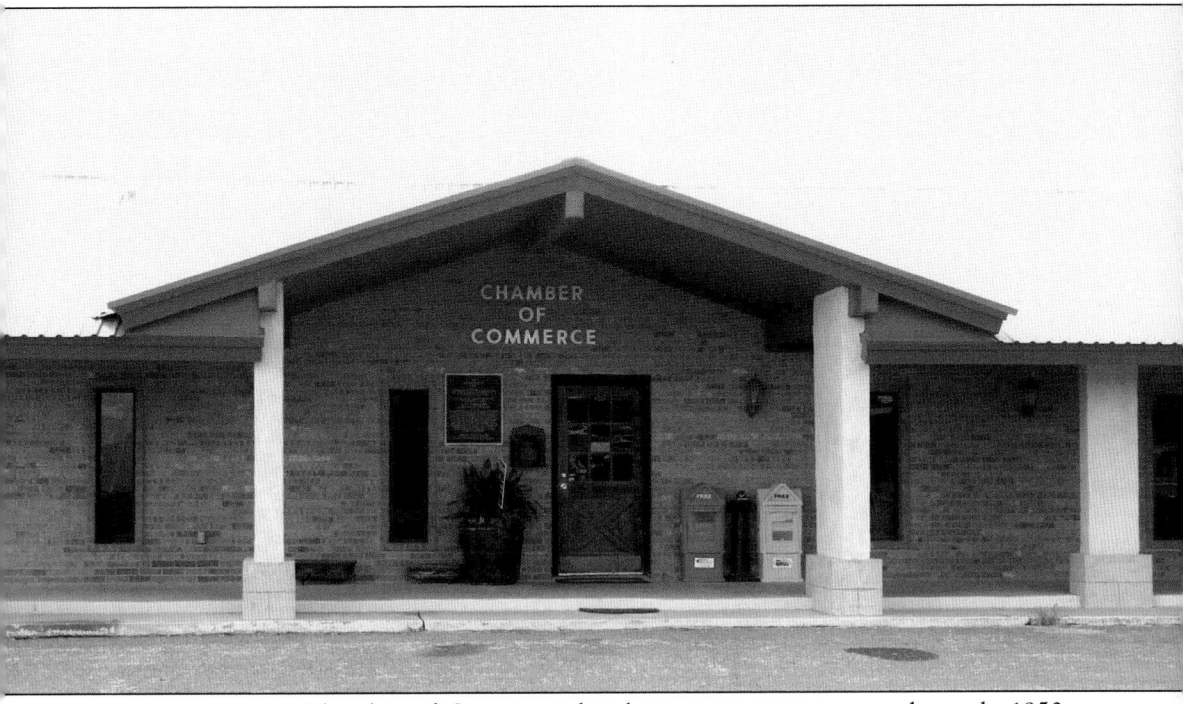

The Andrews County Chamber of Commerce has been in existence since the early 1950s and is dedicated to promoting local businesses and also aiding with economic diversification. A new chamber building was constructed in 1976 during America's bicentennial, when the community celebrated the event with lots of fanfare. Local entities, businesses, and individuals donated funding for the chamber building during the festive occasion. The Andrews Chamber is located on West Broadway Avenue, and besides holding the annual chamber banquet when the community honors a deserving resident and pioneer, it also sponsors and coordinates the Fourth of July festivities. It periodically sponsors seminars on business affairs and does surveys on the local business climate. The chamber also provides the setting for the meetings of the Andrews Industrial Foundation, which has sought to diversify Andrews for decades. Located behind the chamber are hook-ups for tourists traveling in recreational vehicles, and the service is free of charge for a few days. The chamber hands out maps of Andrews and the region as a way of promoting tourism.

Andrews High School is the pride and joy of the community, and although constructed in 1962, the sleek, modern design continues to impress and draw rave reviews from newcomers and guests alike. The high school is home to the Andrews Mustangs and is noted for its academia and sports successes. Upgrades and remodeling have occurred over the years, including after

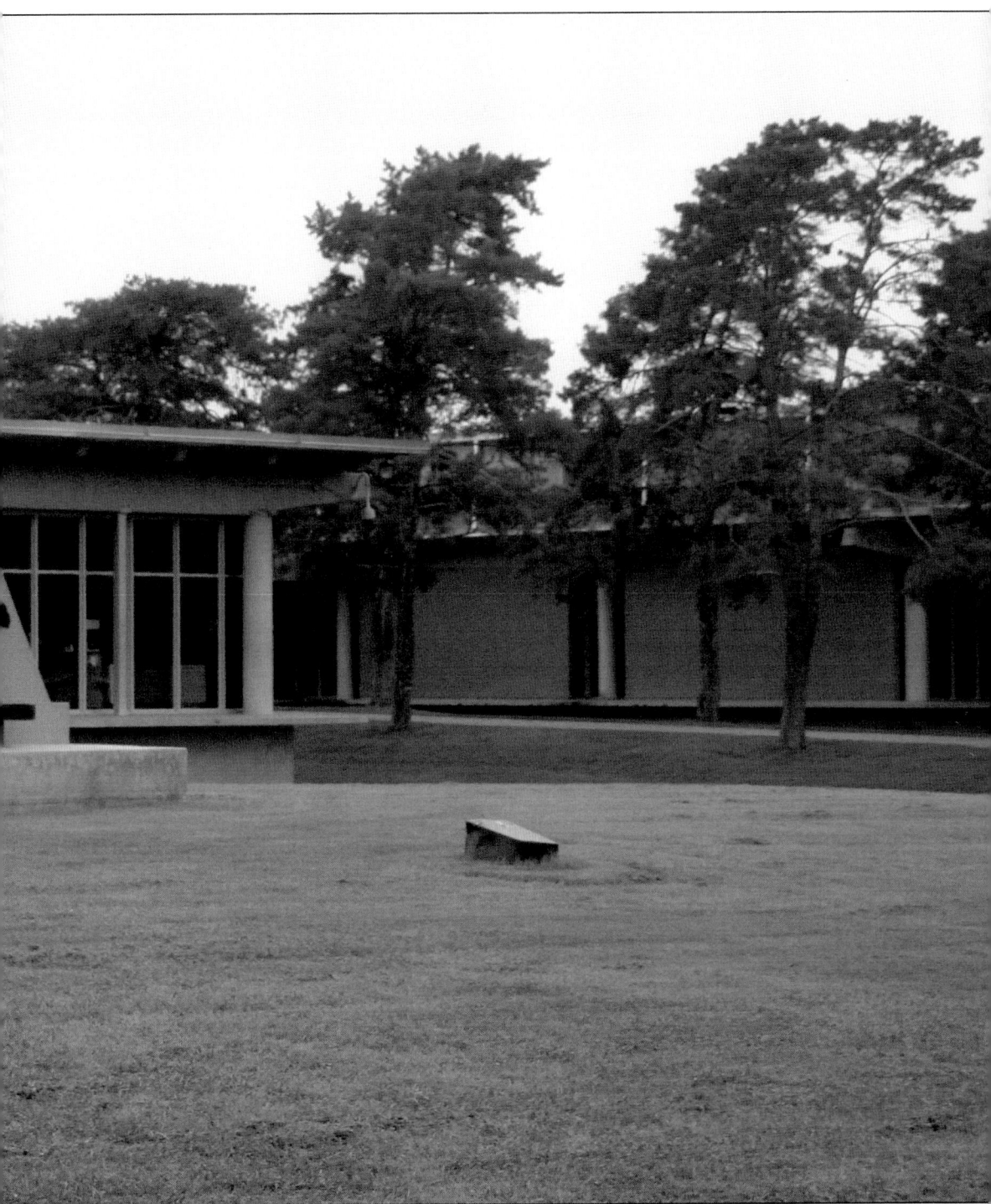

voters approved a $31 million bond in 2000 to add more classrooms, replace old fixtures and infrastructure with more energy efficient equipment, and revamp wiring for new computers for the school's classrooms. A new performance center was also built behind the high school near Mustang Stadium, which houses athletic accommodations for students and fans.

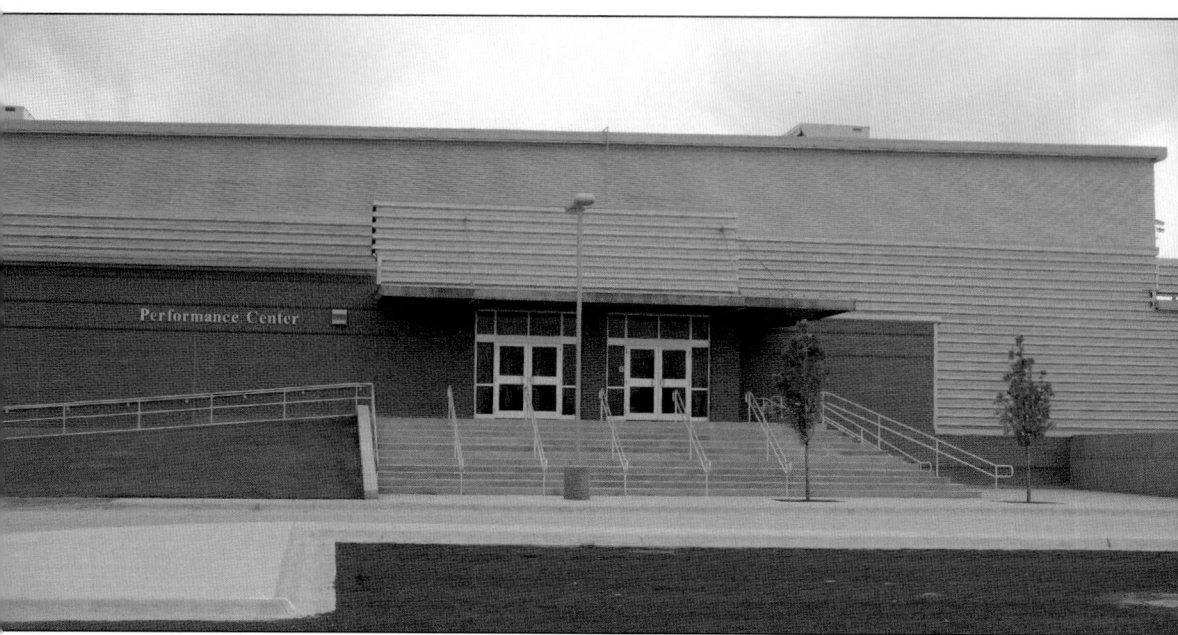

Following a second successful bond election in 2006, the Andrews Independent School District built two new elementary schools, added on classrooms to the Andrews Middle School, and constructed a state-of-the-art Andrews High School Performance Center housing a 3,000-seat basketball arena, competition swimming pool, two diving pools, locker rooms for male and female athletes, community room, coaches offices, weight room, and concert hall. The concert hall was used in 2009 for the chamber banquet's featured entertainment, cowboy singer Michael Martin Murphey, and in 2010 for religious author and speaker Max Lucado, an Andrews High graduate. The multistoried performance center is located behind the high school just north of the football field, encompassing where a former one-way street and old field house was originally located. The school district also built a new baseball field and softball field while adding synthetic turf and new lighting to the track and football field.

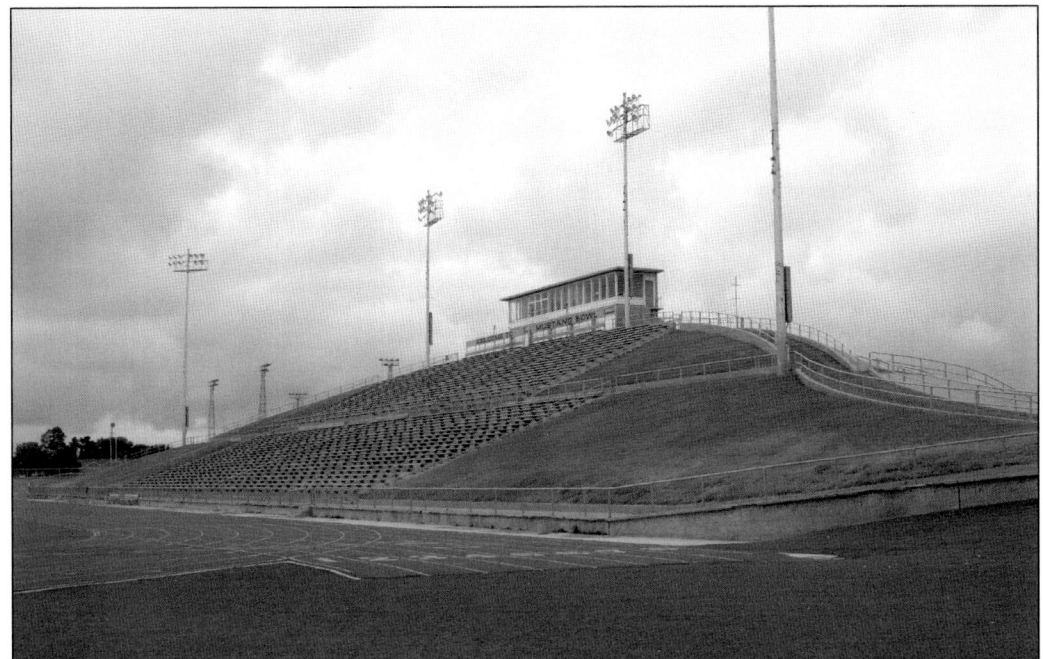

The Mustang Bowl was constructed in 1959 prior to the construction of the high school. The stadium was given a makeover in 2006 using bond monies to refurbish lighting, seating, and the press box. The stadium was also outfitted with synthetic turf to cut down on maintenance and water. New locker rooms were added with the completion of the performance center, which is located at the north end of the field.

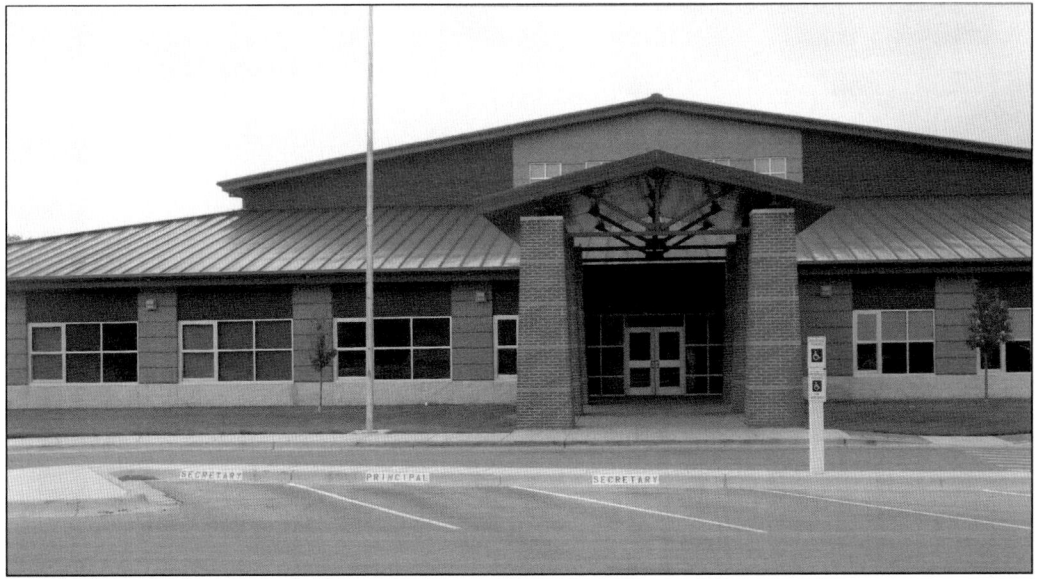

The new Devonian Elementary School opened in 2009 after the older Devonian Elementary on Northwest Avenue K was demolished to make way for the larger, more modern school. Bond monies paid for two new elementary schools, including Devonian and Underwood. Refurbishing was also completed on Clearfork Elementary School on Northeast Avenue K. All of the elementary schools were named after oil-producing formations.

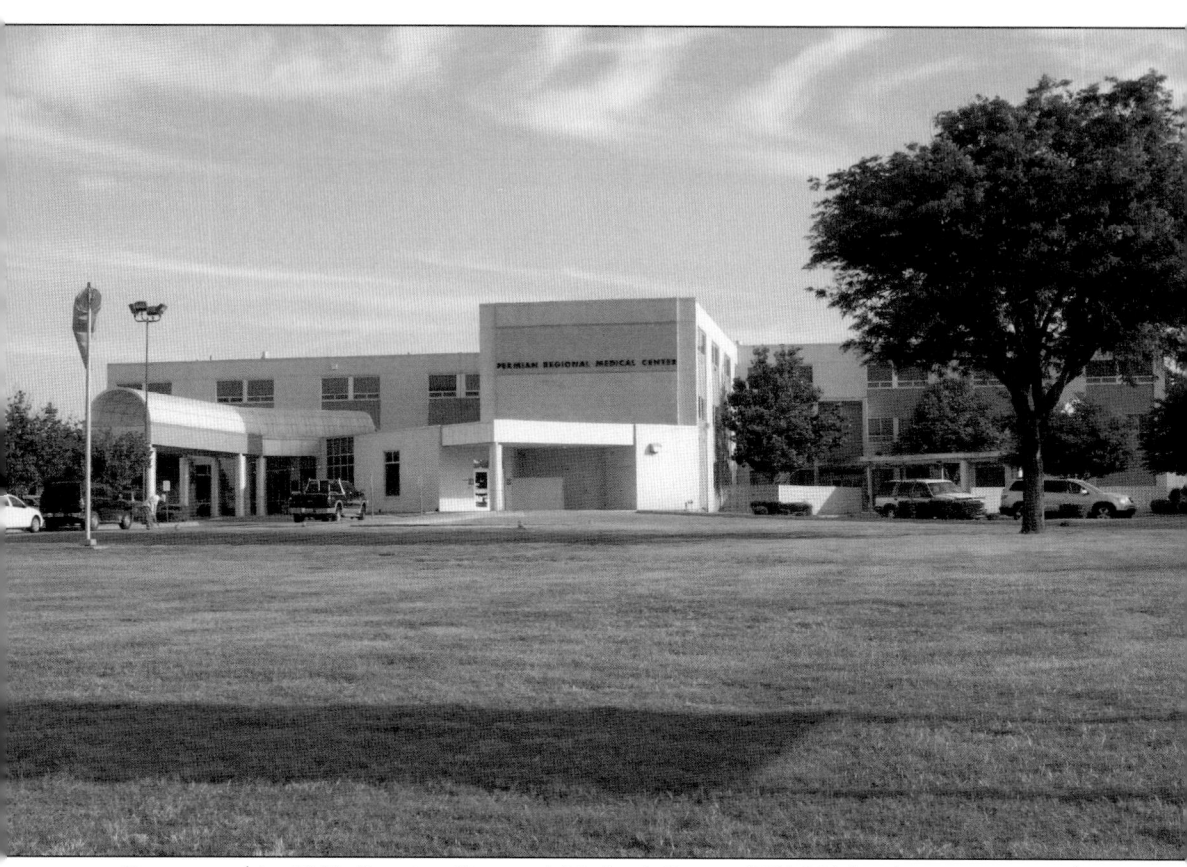

Constructed in 1962, Permian Regional Medical Center (PRMC) has been maintained quite well due to periodic improvements and renovations, like a new emergency room in the late 1990s, redesigned patient rooms, and computerized charts for physicians and staff. Additionally, the Dr. Brian and Sue Gordon Imaging Center was built in 2008 to house MRIs for diagnosing patients and a new nursing home with Permian Residential Care Center opened in 2006. The hospital's clinic area accommodates approximately 20 doctors and recently acquired a mobile medical unit to be used in outlying communities or in case of a local emergency. Also the hospital district recently opened a new senior living campus across from PRMC giving senior residents in Andrews the opportunity to downsize from their residences into smaller duplexes.

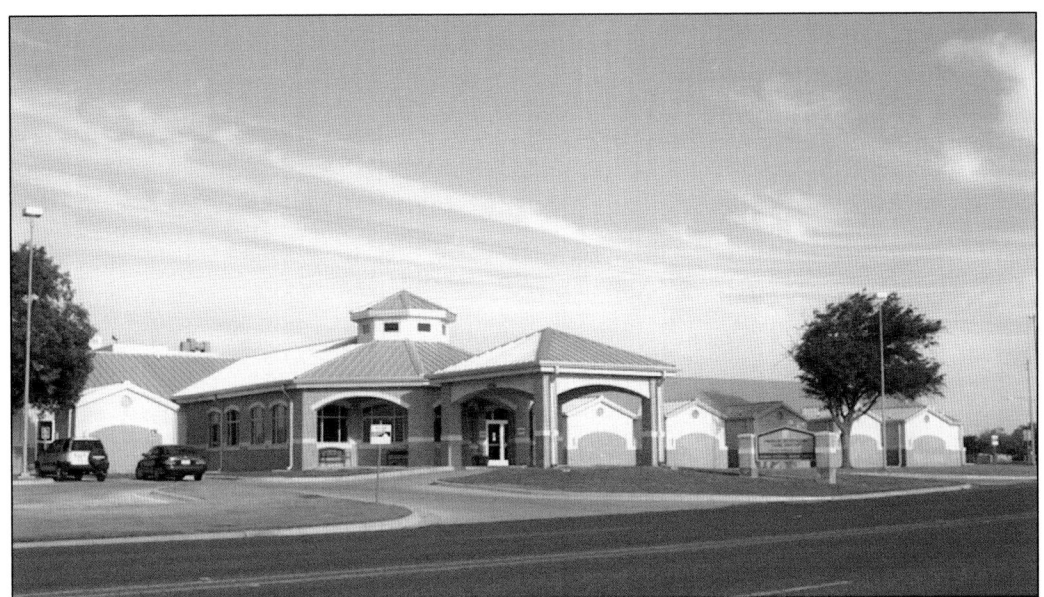

Permian Residential Care Center was constructed in 2006 and has the capacity for 90 residents. The hospital district built the facility when the previous nursing home in Andrews filed for bankruptcy and families were faced with decisions about where to put their loved ones. PRCC is attached to the hospital for easier care of elderly residents. The facility is known for its good service.

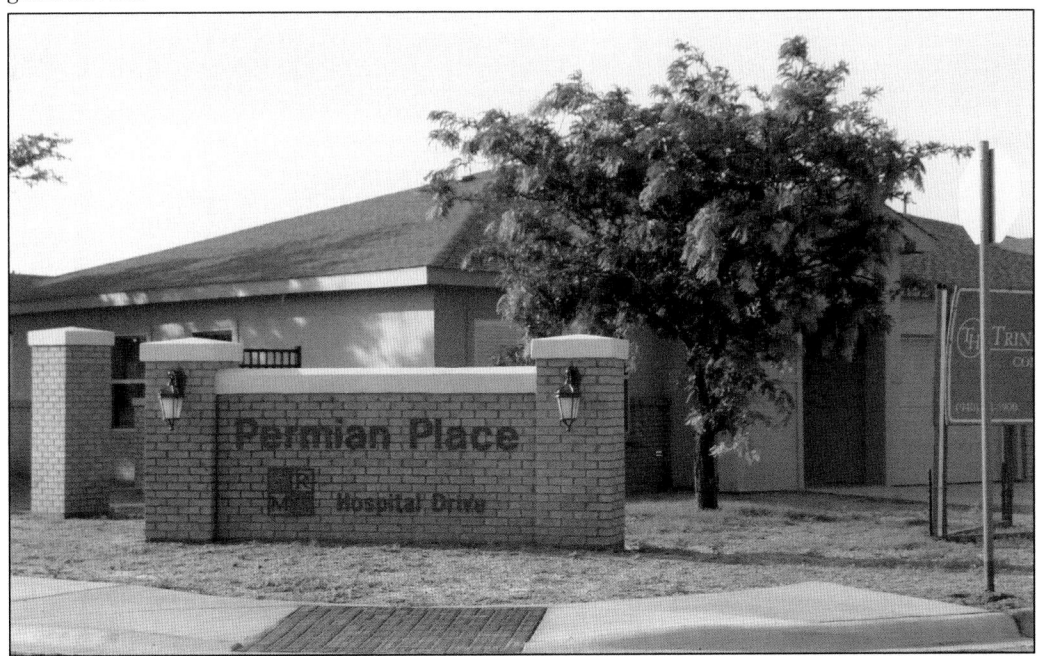

In an effort to provide for a segment of local senior citizens, in 2009 the Andrews County Hospital District constructed Permian Place, a senior living campus consisting of duplexes with a full range of amenities. The campus allows senior citizens wanting to downsize into a smaller living arrangement the convenience of being among their peers and near the hospital for any medical needs.

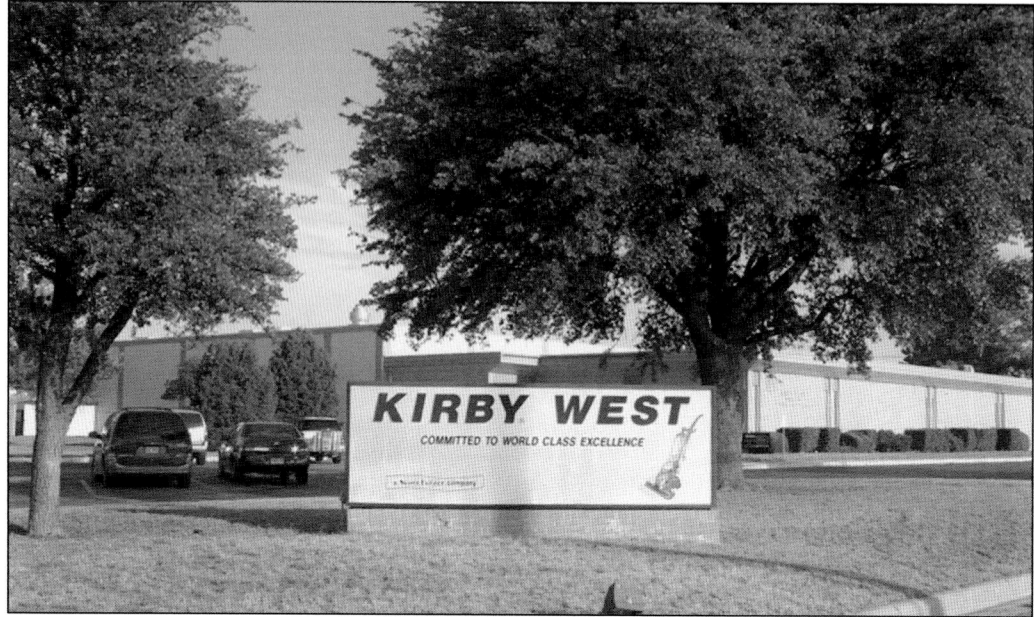

Andrews was fortunate to have Kirby West begin operations in 1972 at the industrial park just north of the city. Scott and Fetzer Vacuum Cleaner Manufacturing moved into a vacant building and since then has continued to turn out the latest in Kirby vacuum cleaner designs. Kirby West has been a major employer in Andrews for more than three decades, employing several hundred workers and helping diversify the local economy.

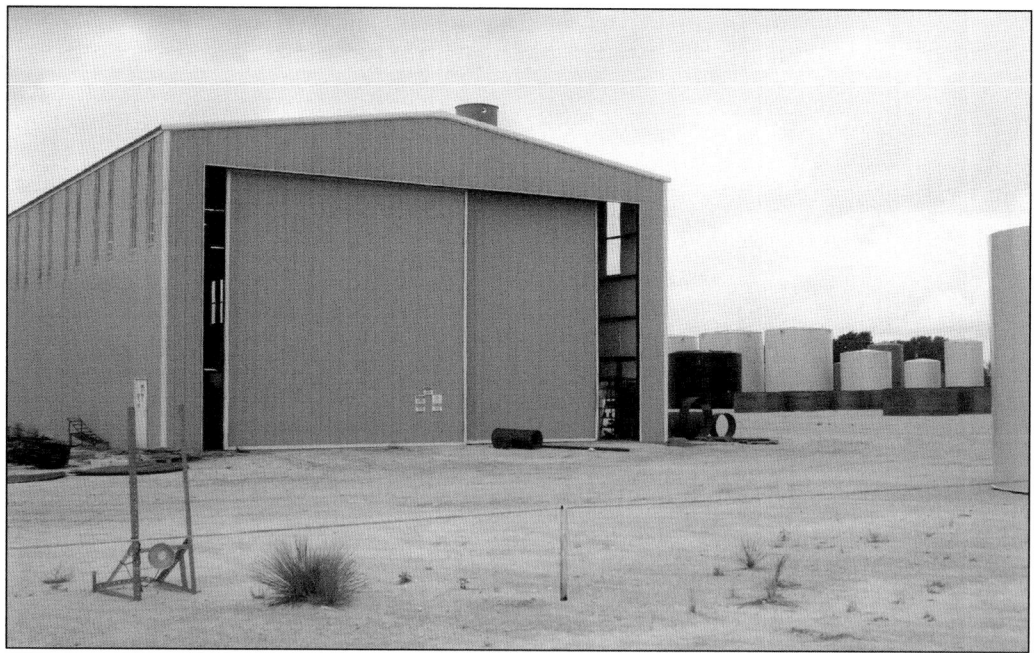

Palmer Tank Manufacturing is another industry in the north industrial park. It manufactures fiberglass and steel tanks for the oil and gas industry as well as for other uses. The company employs more than 100 workers and sends their tank products all over the country. The company recently added the capacity to build steel tanks in conjunction with their other operation.

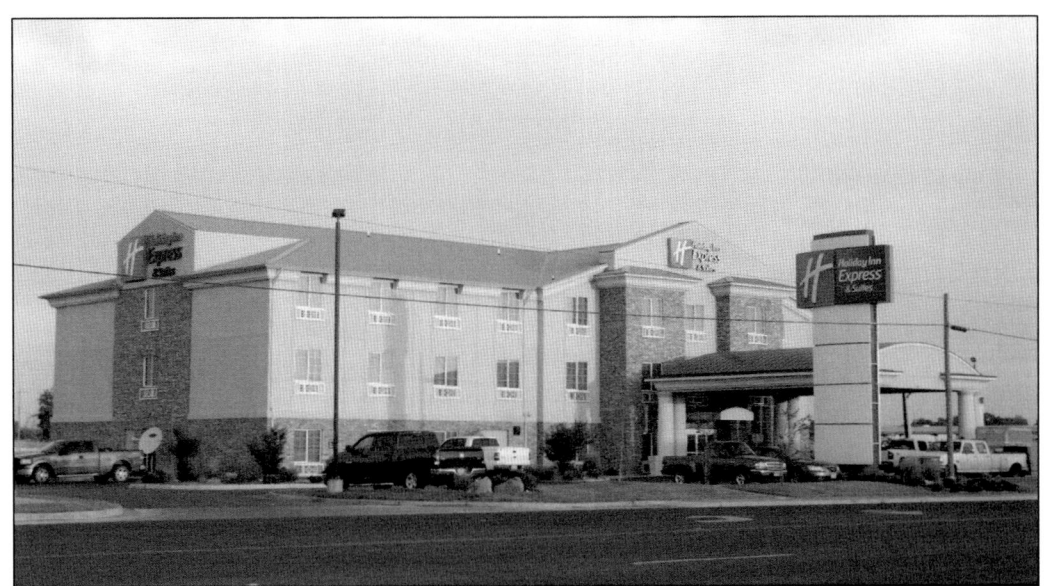

Getting a major hotel chain to open in Andrews had been a main goal of community leaders for decades. The Andrews Economic Development Corporation began pursing the goal in earnest and in 2007 finally received a commitment by an interested hotel operator. The hotel, located on South U.S. 385, was a piece of the puzzle for attracting visitors, tourists, and sports fans and athletes participating in local sporting venues.

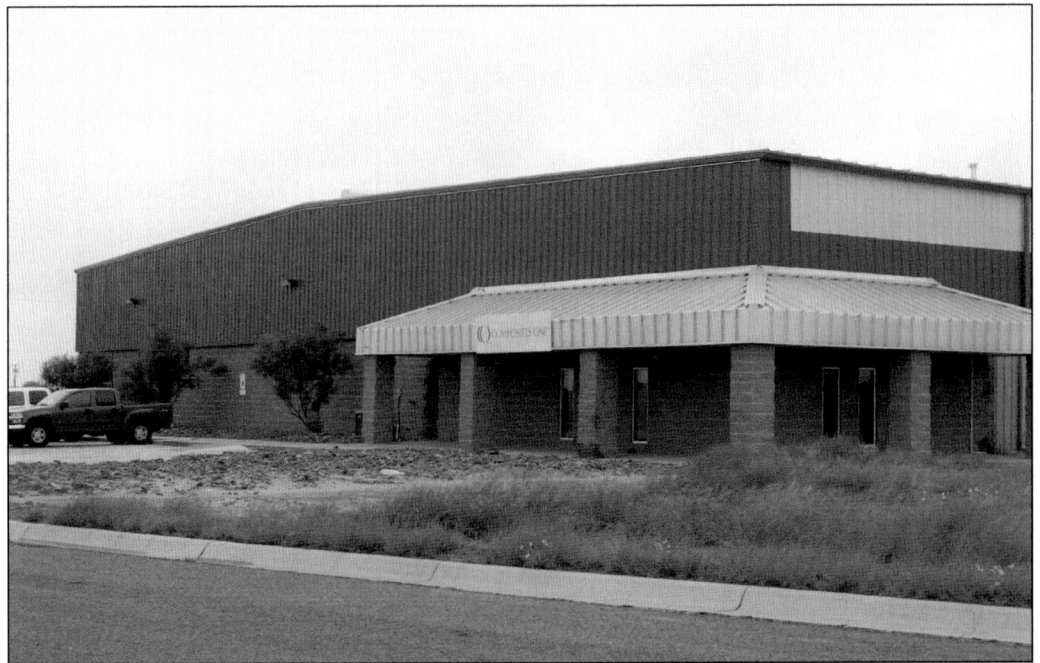

Composites One was the first business landed for the new Business Park South, an industrial area located on South U.S. 385. The business is linked to the construction of fiberglass tanks and other equipment used in oilfields. The new business showed that the community was serious about diversifying, and voters in 2005 approved a fraction of a tax addition to the sales tax for funding an economic development corporation.

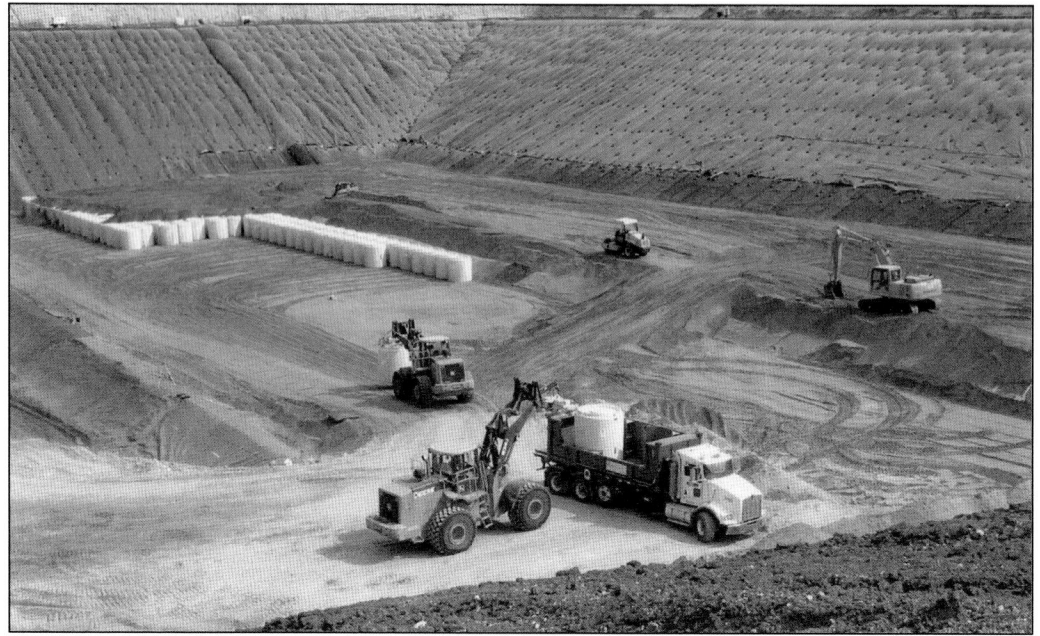

A major milestone was achieved in the late 1990s when Waste Control Specialists began operating in far western Andrews County. The move was the first big success in years for diversifying the local economy and has led to much activity in regard to both employment and related company growth. Presently WCS employs more than 100 people.

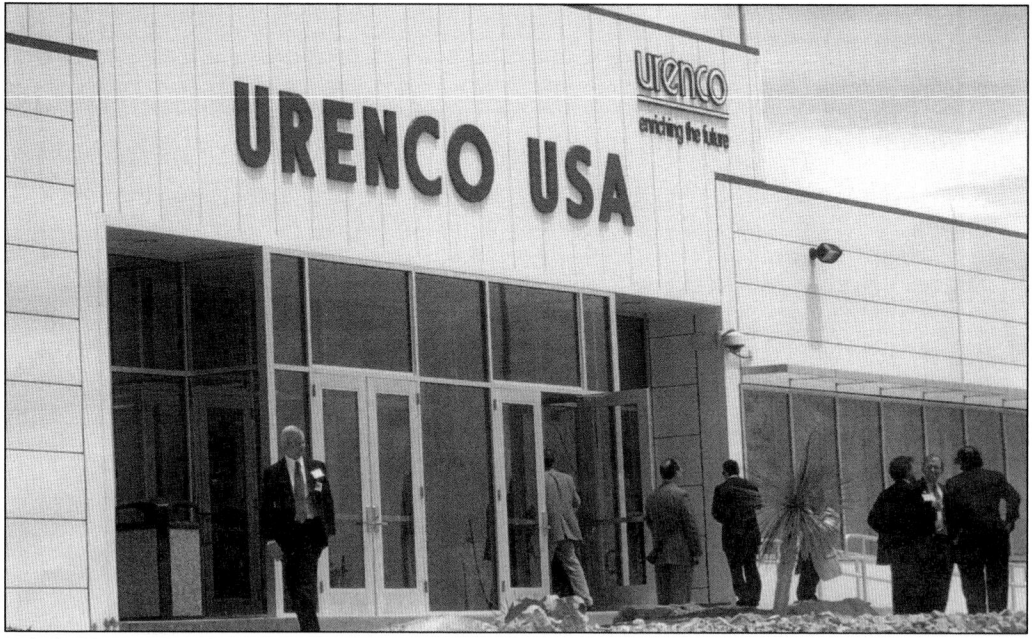

While Urenco USA's Louisiana Energy Service project was not built in Andrews County, but in nearby Lea County, New Mexico, the $2 billion price tag for the uranium-enrichment facility resulted in jobs and new residents moving to Andrews. Both Andrews and nearby Eunice and Hobbs, New Mexico, have benefited from the operation, which brought more than 1,000 construction jobs for several years. More than 300 people work full time at LES.

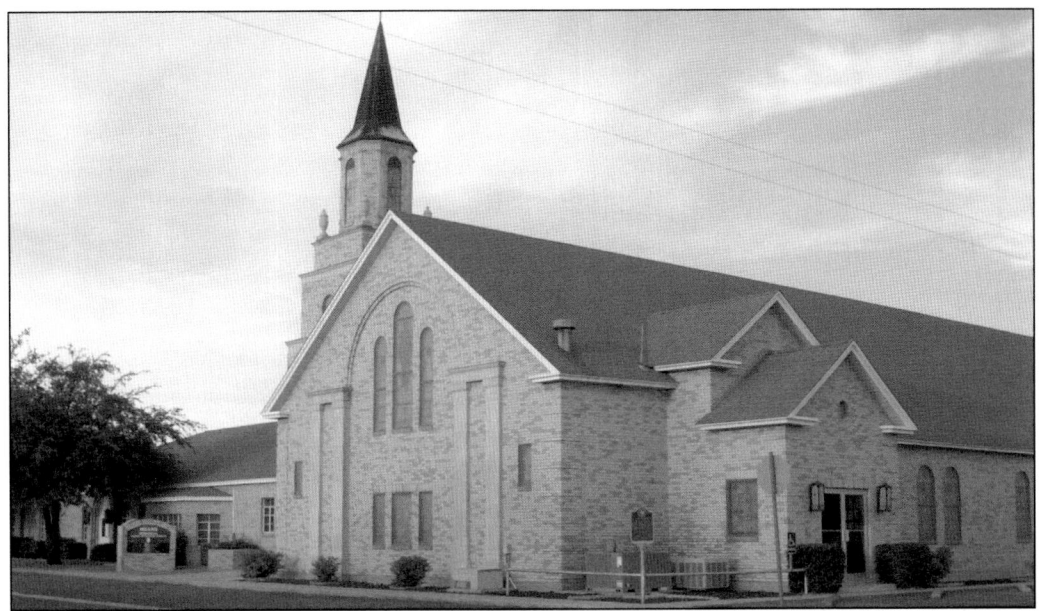

The Methodist church in Andrews was organized in 1907 and was the first organized denomination in the city. The original church was constructed on South Main Street, but following a fire in 1943, a new church was constructed on the current site in 1946. The church was dedicated as the Means Memorial United Methodist Church, honoring the Means family for their many contributions to Andrews.

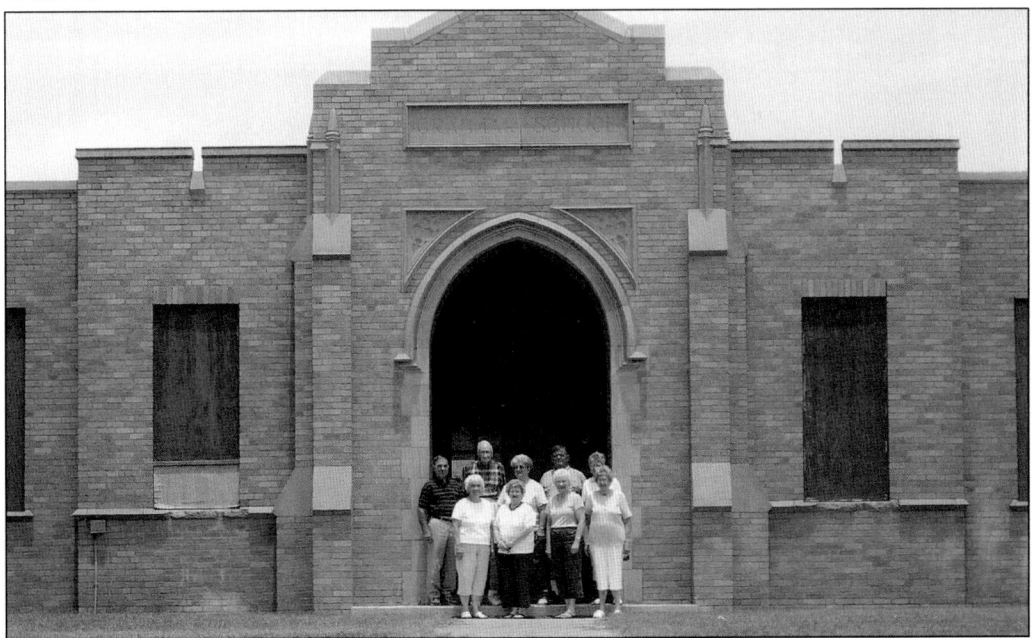

The Andrews centennial in 2010 resulted in residents working to reestablish a museum in the old Andrews Primary School at North Main Street and Northwest Avenue D. Above, members of the historical group gather in front of the primary school. Shown in the photograph are, from left to right, Joe Weatherby, Carolyn Weatherby, Forrest Scott, Barbara Puckett, Judy Scarbrough, Joyce Hamilton, Bob Price, Louise Turner, and Cleta Garms.

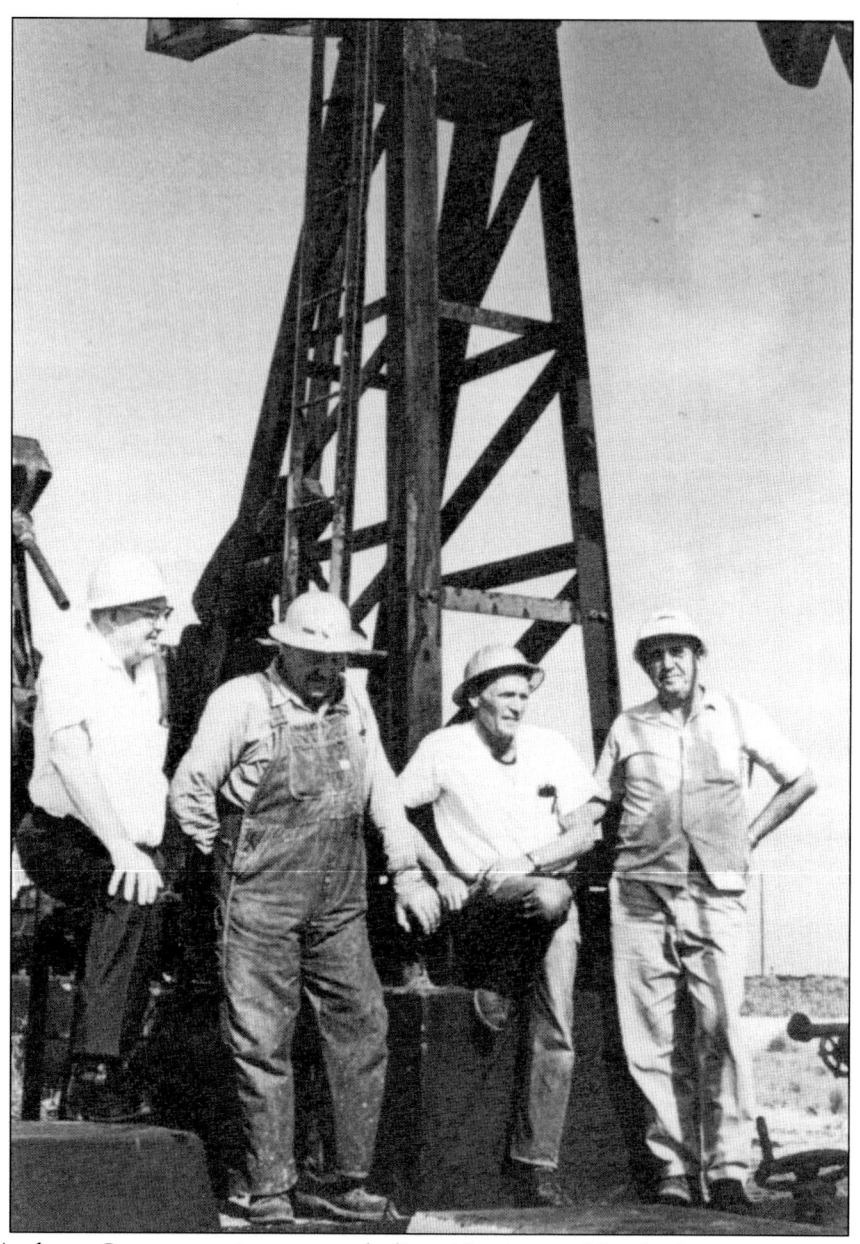

While Andrews County continues to seek diversification and has had some successes, the oil and gas industry continues today to be the mainstay of the local economy as it has for more than 80 years, employing countless workers in various oil and gas companies. Numerous other businesses employ workers in related oilfield service companies. Oil revenues from ad valorem taxes pay 90 percent of the ad valorem taxes in Andrews County, contributing significantly to the budgets of Andrews County, Andrews Independent School District, and Andrews County Hospital District. Most residents realize the importance of oil and the impact it has on their lives. While the community may look toward growth with diversification, it will forever remain indebted to the role that oil has played in Andrews County. Shown above in a picture taken for the Billionth Barrel Celebration in 1965 are former oilfield workers, from left to right, J. W. "Ham" Pinnell, B. F. Seay, J. B. McNeil, and C. A. Farmer. (Courtesy Martha Page.)

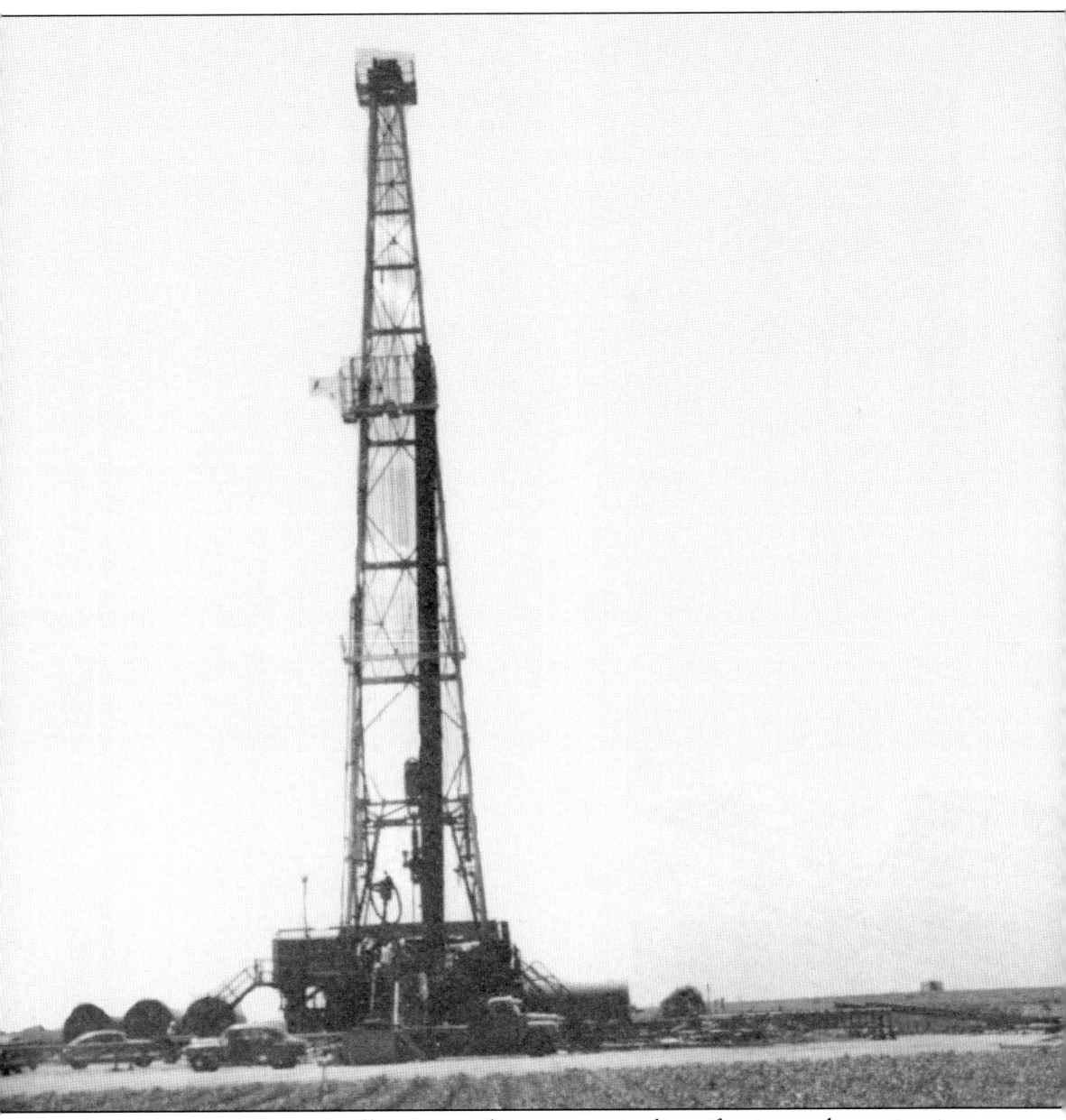

As Andrews enters the new millennium seeking economic diversification and experiencing growth from several avenues, including newly found nuclear-related companies, residents still understand and appreciate the untold blessings and opportunities that befell the community because of the discovery of black gold in their county. It was a blessing but was achieved through good luck tempered with hard work and sweat from the brows of many men and women who helped Andrews while helping themselves. Andrews may encounter new beginnings and new types of entrepreneurship in its future, but its heritage was forged from the dedication of settlers who arrived long ago seeking better times. They came, they worked, and they prospered but never forgot their past or took their successes for granted. Today they still strive even harder for a better tomorrow. Andrews is and always will be a little rough around the edges but is true to its roots of an honest day's pay for an honest day's work. Andrews is pure West Texas.

www.arcadiapublishing.com

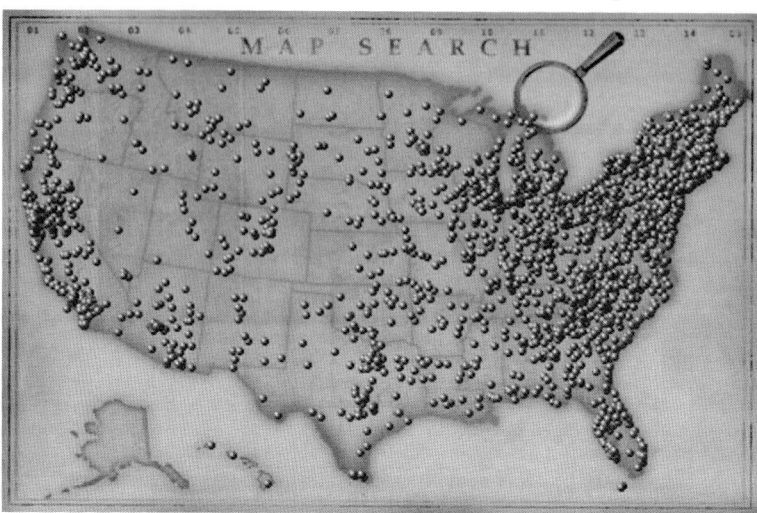

Discover books about the town where you grew up, the cities where your friends and families live, the town where your parents met, or even that retirement spot you've been dreaming about. Our Web site provides history lovers with exclusive deals, advanced notification about new titles, e-mail alerts of author events, and much more.

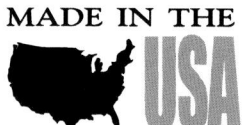

MADE IN THE USA

Arcadia Publishing, the leading local history publisher in the United States, is committed to making history accessible and meaningful through publishing books that celebrate and preserve the heritage of America's people and places. Consistent with our mission to preserve history on a local level, this book was printed in South Carolina on American-made paper and manufactured entirely in the United States.

This book carries the accredited Forest Stewardship Council (FSC) label and is printed on 100 percent FSC-certified paper. Products carrying the FSC label are independently certified to assure consumers that they come from forests that are managed to meet the social, economic, and ecological needs of present and future generations.

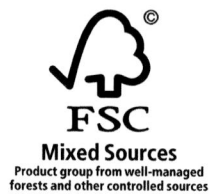

FSC
Mixed Sources
Product group from well-managed forests and other controlled sources
Cert no. SW-COC-001530
www.fsc.org
© 1996 Forest Stewardship Council

Find Your Place in History.